Terracotta Warriors

GUARDIANS *of* IMMORTALITY

秦始皇兵马俑

永恒的守卫

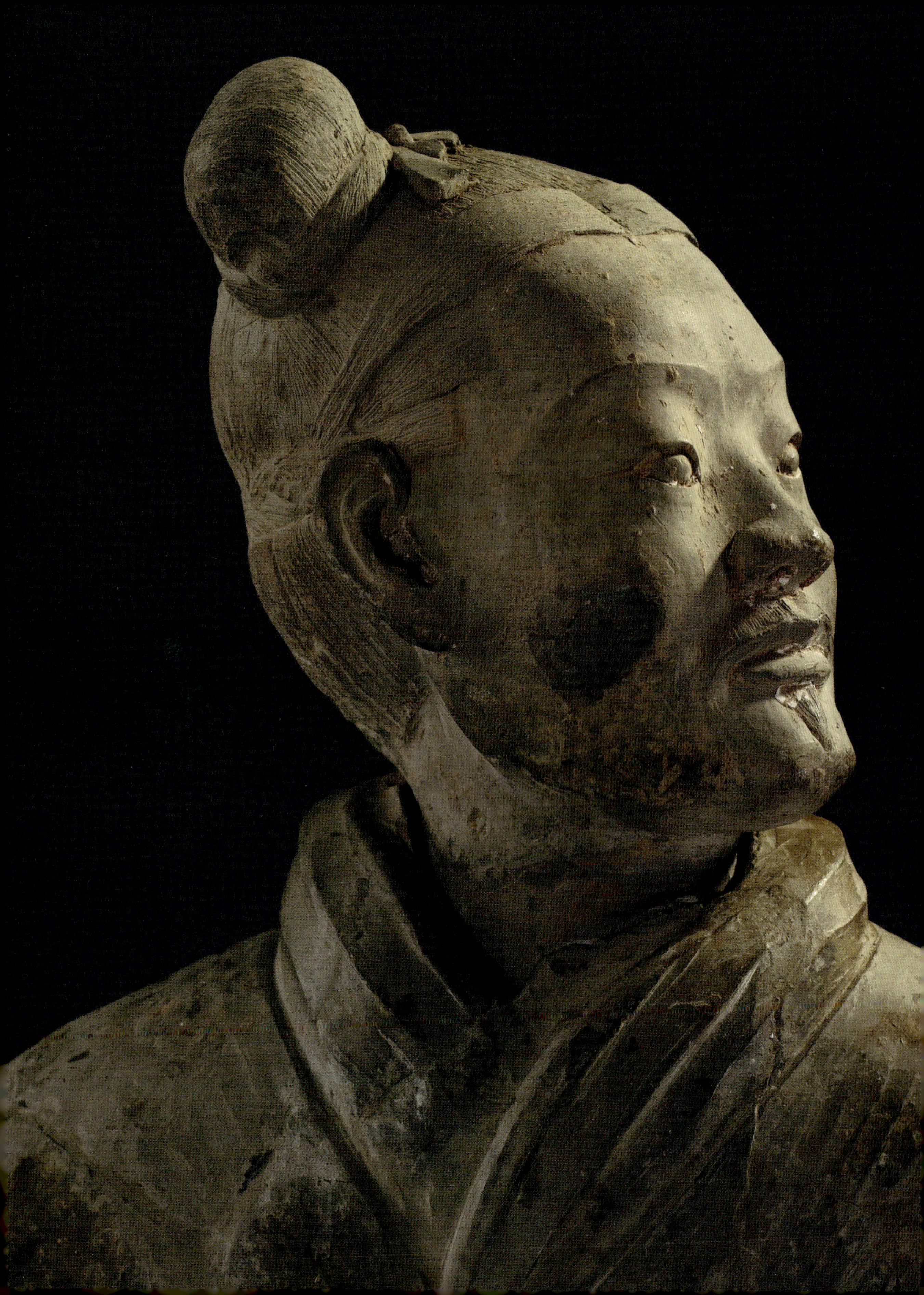

Terracotta Warriors

秦始皇兵马俑
永恒的守卫

GUARDIANS *of* IMMORTALITY

Edited by
REBECCA RICE

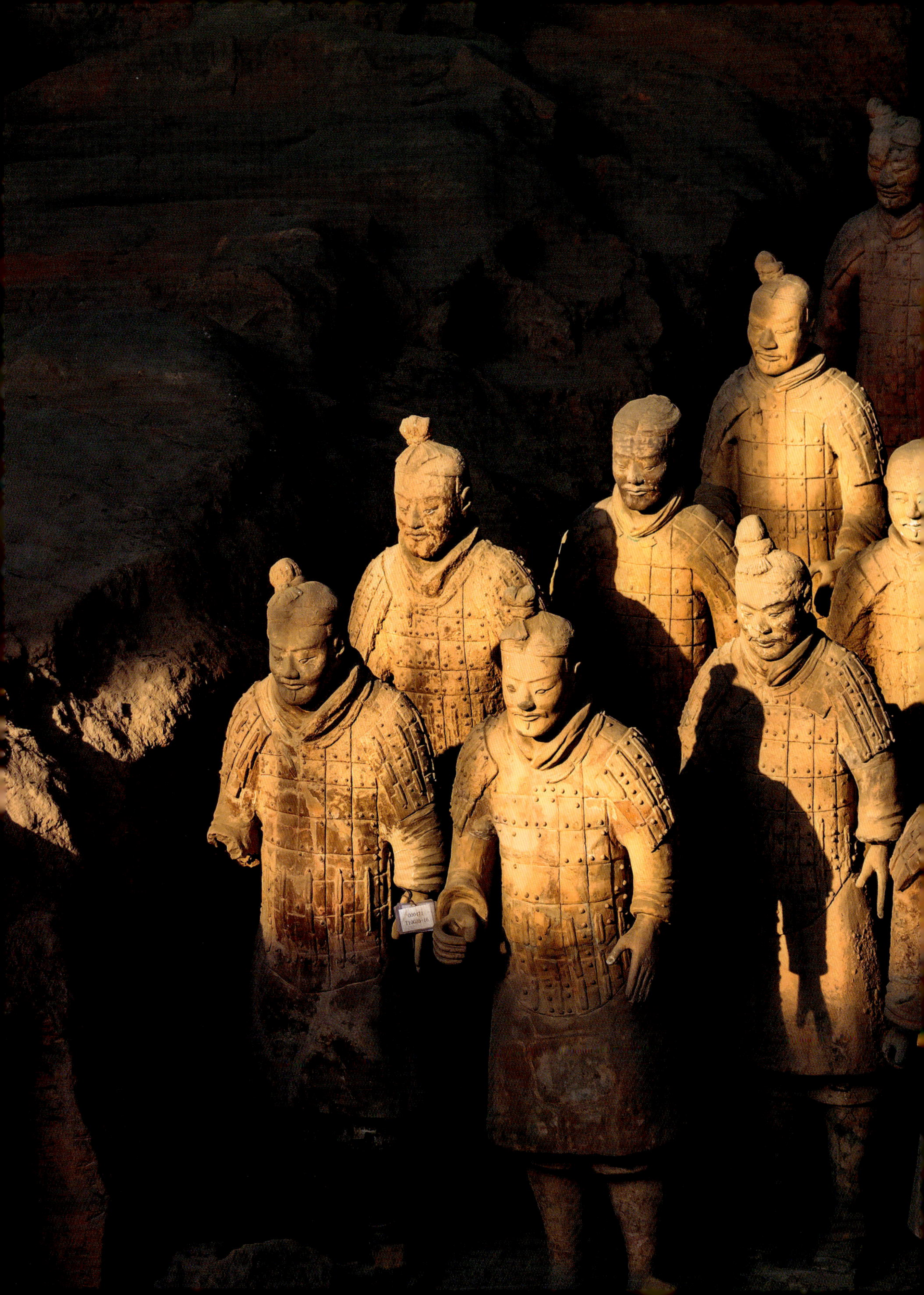
000471
T10G05-16

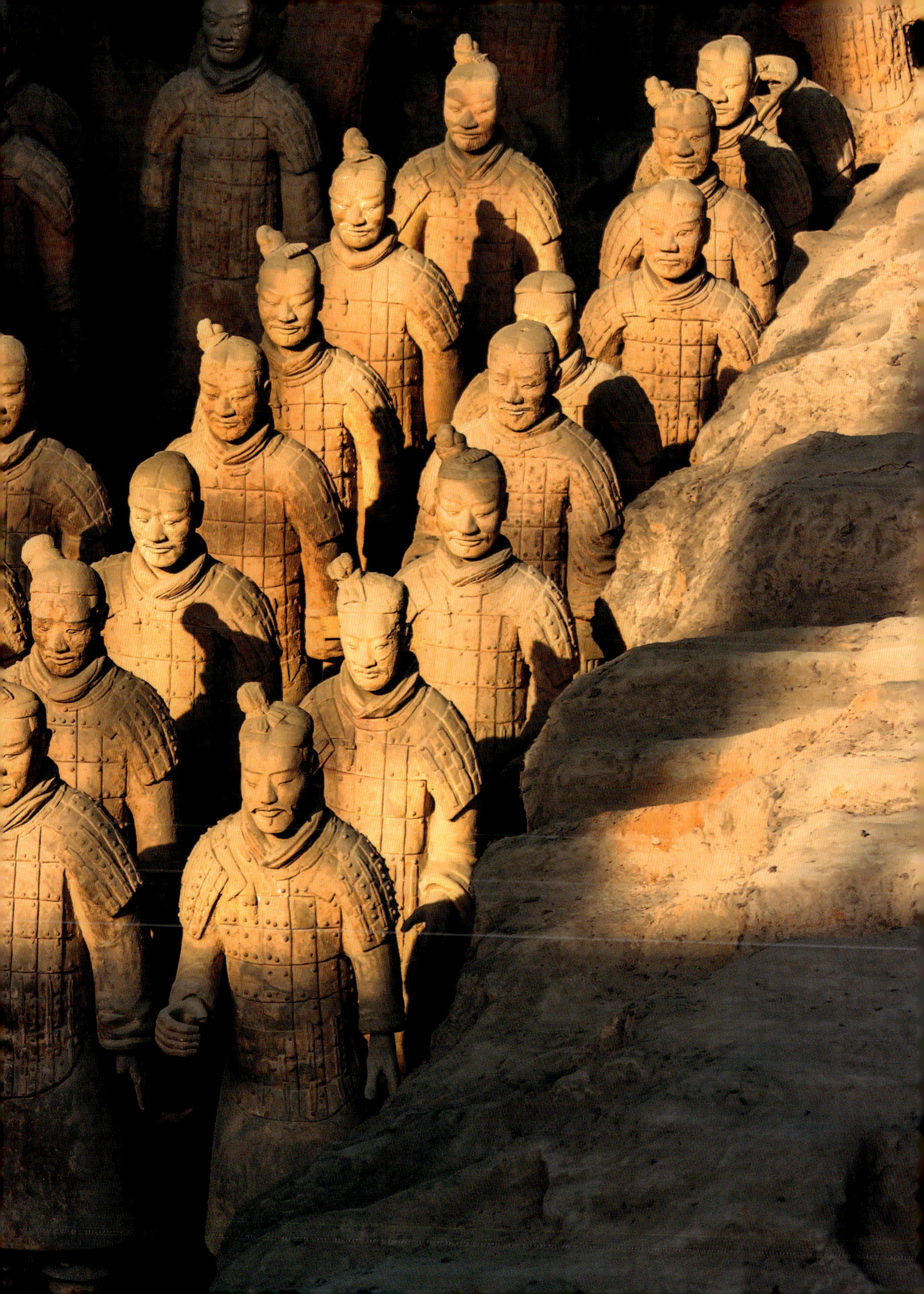

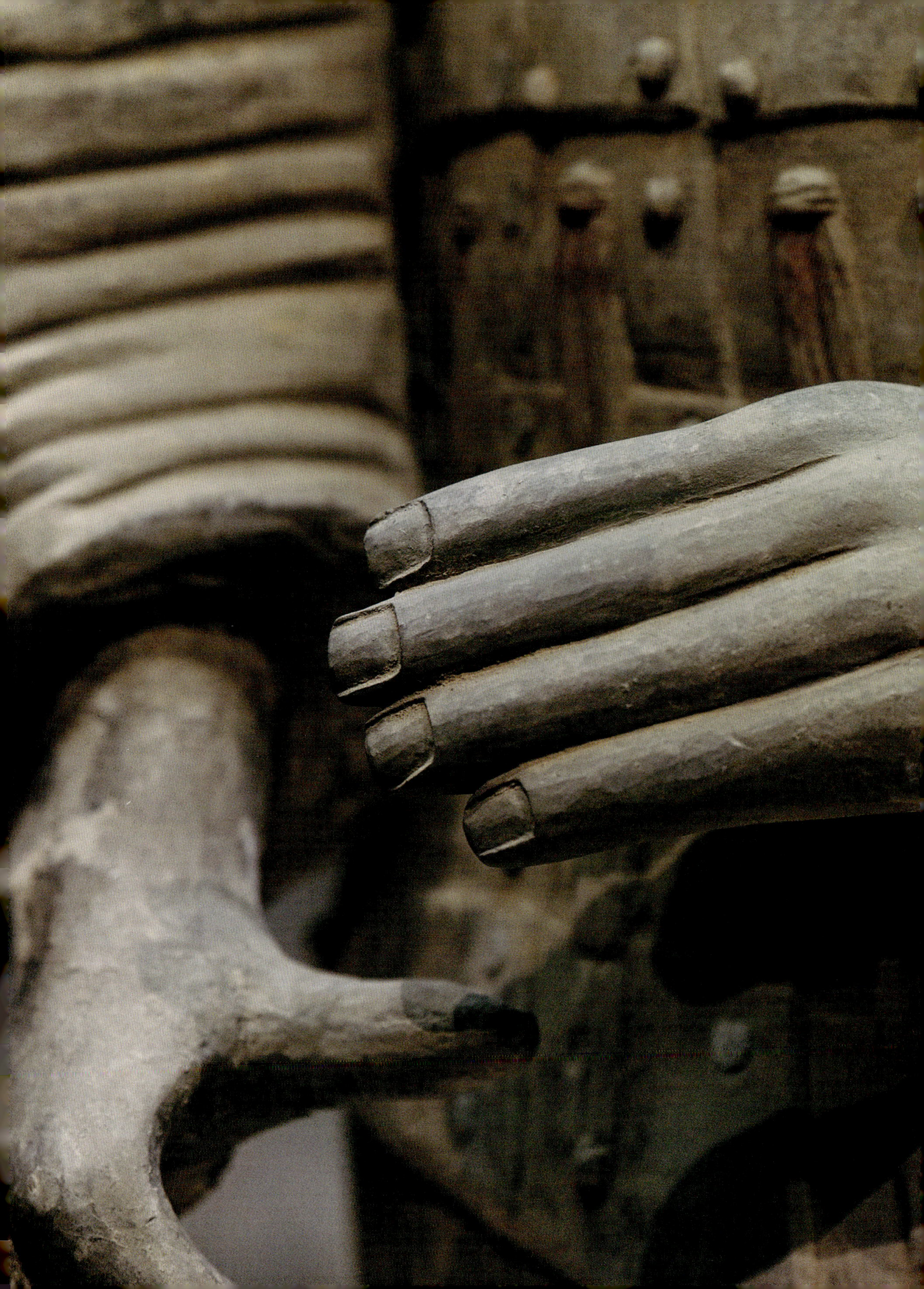

CONTENTS

Forewords

In 1986, the Rt Hon David Lange, Labour Prime Minister of New Zealand, wrote the foreword for the exhibition catalogue heralding the first visit of the Terracotta Army to New Zealand.

Thirty years on, I am honoured to welcome treasures from the First Emperor's tomb and beyond to the Museum of New Zealand Te Papa Tongarewa.

Here in New Zealand, we are proud of our rich and enduring relationship with China. It's a relationship that has its roots in the efforts of remarkable individuals like Rewi Alley, who showed how friendship and humanity can play such an important part in developing links between people of different countries and cultures.

Diplomatic relations between New Zealand and the People's Republic of China were formally established in 1972 under another Labour Government – that of Norman Kirk – and have developed rapidly, especially in recent years.

In 2008, with Helen Clark's Fifth Labour Government, the New Zealand–China Free Trade Agreement was signed – China's first FTA with a developed country. And today, China is New Zealand's largest trading partner.

However, it arguably remains true, as David Lange observed all those years ago, that many New Zealanders are still not fully aware of China's rich culture, past and present.

That's why it's fantastic to have these taonga from another civilisation on our shores. *Terracotta Warriors: Guardians of Immortality* showcases the artistic and cultural developments of the Qin and Han dynasties, which established the social underpinnings of China as we know it today.

I'm thrilled to see this exhibition at Te Papa, and I wish it the greatest success. I hope you enjoy this fascinating window into China's past.

Rt Hon Jacinda Ardern
Prime Minister of New Zealand
Minister for Arts, Culture and Heritage

On behalf of the Embassy of the People's Republic of China in New Zealand, I would like to extend my warmest congratulations on the occasion of the exhibition of the *Terracotta Warriors: Guardians of Immortality* at the Museum of New Zealand Te Papa Tongarewa.

The discovery of the First Emperor of Qin's Terracotta Warriors and Horses was one of the greatest archaeological events of the twentieth century. These artefacts represent the acme of ancient Chinese artistic endeavour and have been hailed as the 'Eighth Wonder of the World'. In 1987, they were included in UNESCO's World Heritage List. I believe that this exhibition will further enhance the understanding of Chinese history and culture on the part of the New Zealand people and will play an active role in further promoting cultural exchange and cooperation between our two countries.

Over the years, cultural exchanges and cooperation have always been an important part of the China–New Zealand relation and have made a positive contribution to the development of this relationship. This exhibition is not only a grand event in the context of such exchanges and cooperation between our two countries, but serves also as a prelude to the '2019 China–New Zealand Year of Tourism'. I believe that with the joint efforts of China and New Zealand, through this exhibition and a series of activities such as the 2019 China–New Zealand Year of Tourism, the cultural exchanges and cooperation between the two countries will surely achieve bounteous harvests and further enhance the friendship that exists between our two peoples, serving to deepen and enhance the relations between our two countries and thus ensuring new and ever-greater achievements in our relationship.

I wish the exhibition of the *Terracotta Warriors: Guardians of Immortality* all the greatest success.

HE Ambassador Ms Wu Xi
Ambassador Extraordinary and Plenipotentiary of the People's Republic of China to New Zealand, the Cook Islands and Niue

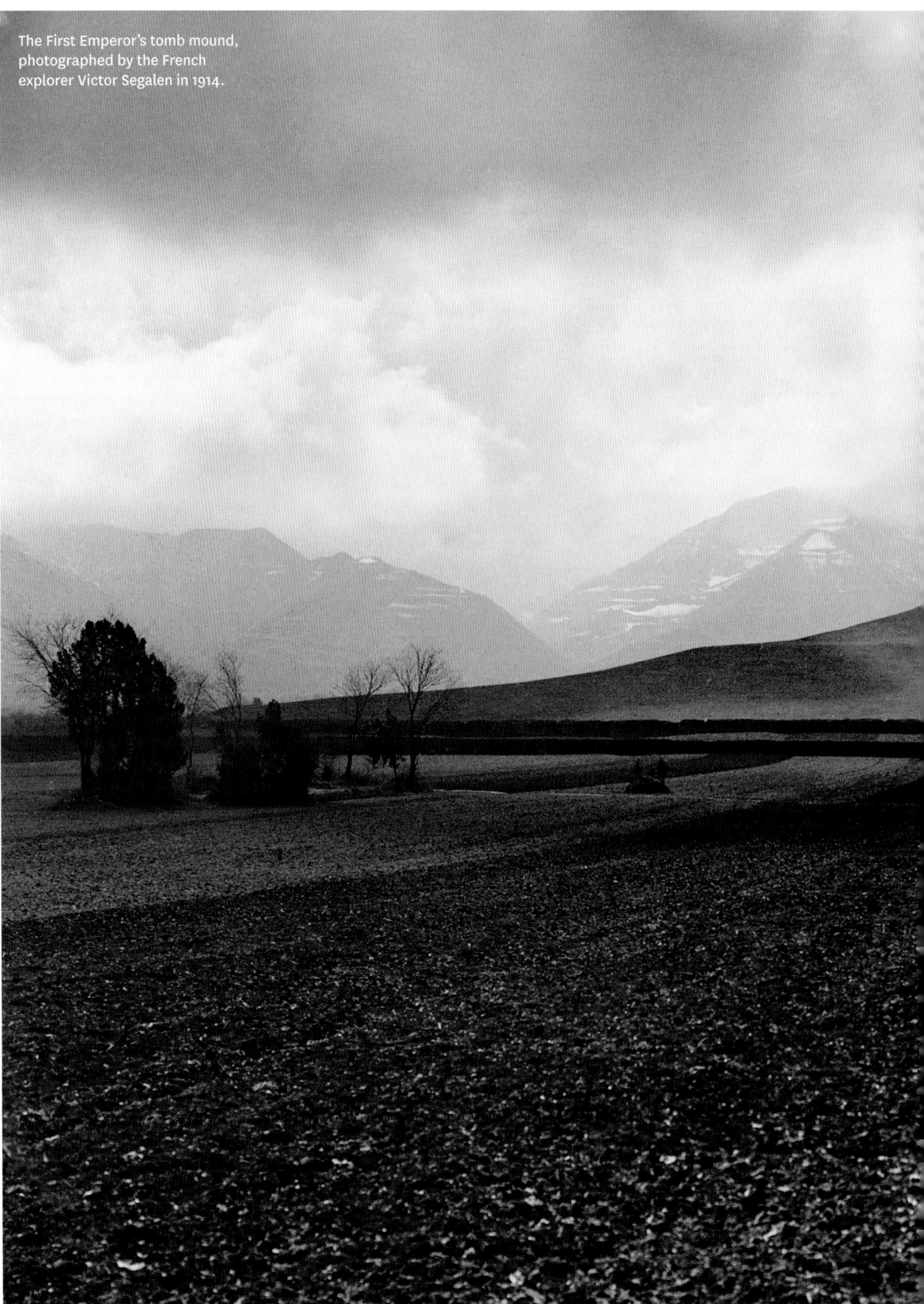

The First Emperor's tomb mound, photographed by the French explorer Victor Segalen in 1914.

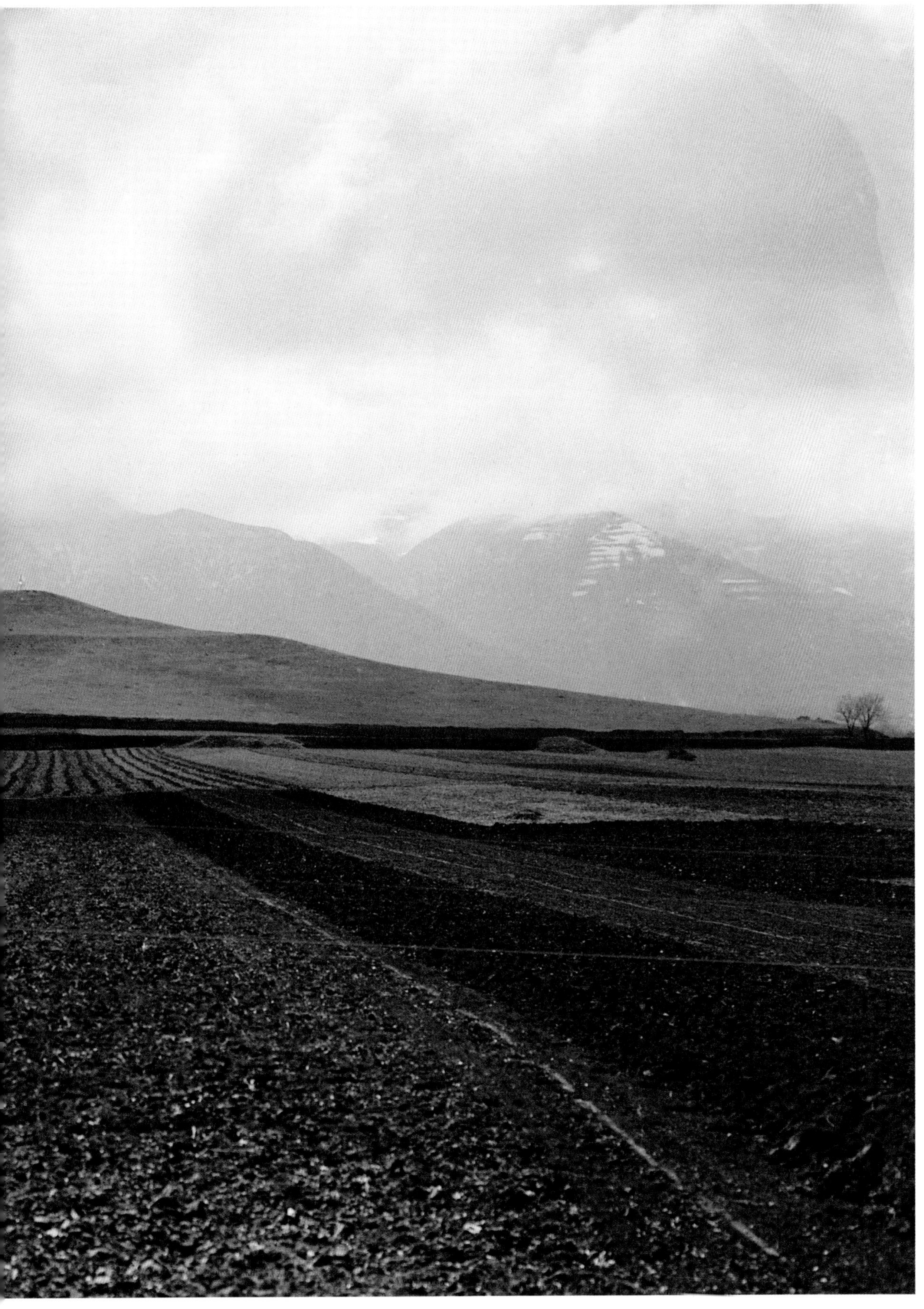

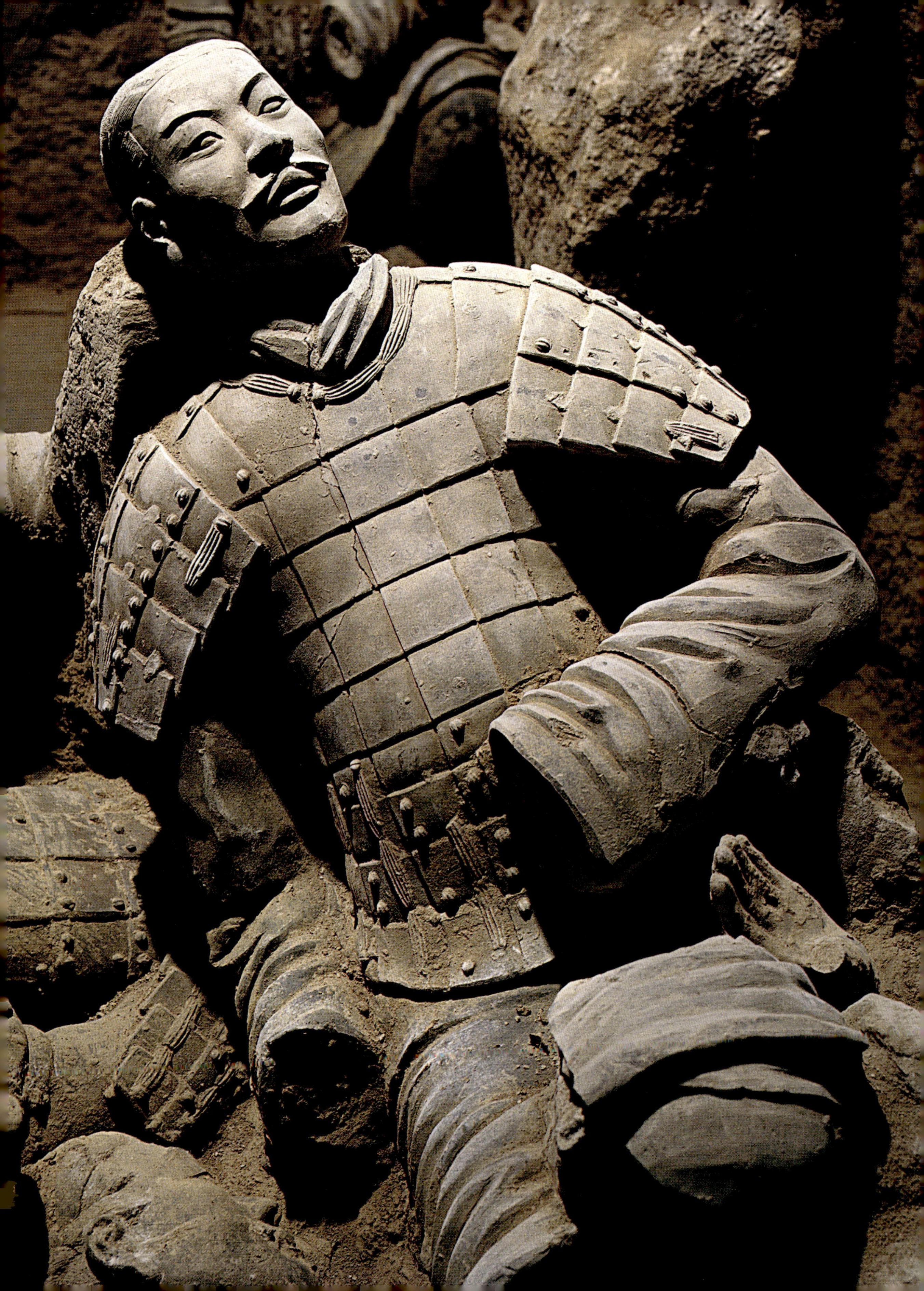

The Terracotta Army and the Mausoleum of the First Emperor of Qin

ZHANG WEIXING 張衛星
TRANSLATED BY DUNCAN M CAMPBELL

In the spring of 1974, the Terracotta Army was discovered quite by chance. In March that year, the people of Xiyang Village sank a large well on a slope in the northern foothills of Mount Li in order to irrigate their fields. While doing so, having excavated through layer after layer of jumbled earth mixed with stones and sand, they came across shards of baked red clay. Although the shards were hard, the villagers dug on, hoping to go deeper. Once they were past the baked red clay, however, rather than finding a layer of pure loess soil as they had expected, they encountered piece after piece of what they thought were the remains of a tutelary god, the Lord of the Earthenware Pitcher (*Waguanye* 瓦罐爺).

What they had actually uncovered were pieces of the Terracotta Army. At a depth of some 5 metres, they found a number of bronze objects along with pieces of pottery, piled up on a surface of Qin-era bricks. The villagers had lived in this area for many generations, but as the site was a good 2 kilometres away from the large and sealed earthworks of the First Emperor's Mausoleum 秦始皇陵, they had no way of knowing that the objects they had stumbled on were important artefacts associated with that mausoleum. The pieces of the terracotta soldiers were then reassembled by the late Mr Zhao Kangmin 趙康民, an expert with the Lintong Museum, and the news was later conveyed to the top leadership in Beijing by the reporter Lin Anwen 藺安穩.

As early as 1960, when the state authorities had determined that the First Emperor's Mausoleum would be included in the first list of Major Historical and Cultural Sites to be Protected at the National Level, the Committee of the Bureau for the Management of Cultural Artefacts of Shaanxi Province had organised a team of experts to undertake the first scientific archaeological work conducted on the mausoleum. Although this work was not particularly productive a number of important sites were uncovered, and a plan of the sites of the core area of the mausoleum drawn up.

previous spread **Partially excavated kneeling archer from Pit 2 of Qin Shihuang's tomb complex.**

opposite page **Portrait impression of the First Emperor of China from the eighteenth-century album *Lidai diwang xiang*.**

With the discovery of the Terracotta Army, the archaeological work on the First Emperor's Mausoleum began to be accorded the attention it deserved. As they were undertaking the excavation of the Terracotta Army, the archaeological teams began to find many important artefacts in the area surrounding the sealed earthworks of the mausoleum itself, these discoveries serving to establish the framework for understanding the First Emperor's tomb complex.

From a scholarly perspective, the discovery of the Terracotta Warriors and Horses Pit exposed the tip of the proverbial hidden iceberg of the massive scale of what is buried in the First Emperor's Mausoleum. As the First Emperor's Mausoleum began offering up bronze chariots, stone armour, terracotta acrobats, bronze aquatic animals and other important 'marvellous vessels of all kinds, things both precious and rare' – as Sima Qian 司馬遷 (*c*.135–86 BCE) described the secret mausoleum in his *Records of the Grand Historian* (*Shi ji* 史記) – excitement grew in anticipation of what was yet to be found. Many years of systematic archaeological work have now made it possible for us to have a far better understanding and appreciation of what is hidden in the mausoleum, providing us also with a basis for further investigation.

The importance of the mausoleum is due to the fact that it belonged to Ying Zheng 嬴政, the man who brought to an end the wars between the Seven States, who unified the empire, and who named himself First Emperor (Qin Shihuang 秦始皇). The dynasty that he established, the great Qin empire, was to influence the political structure that underpinned the development of Chinese civilisation for the following two thousand years. For several decades now, along with exhibiting the archaeological finds of the First Emperor's Mausoleum and deepening the research in the field, the ontological value of the mausoleum itself, and its extended value, are now being more widely recognised, and have become an important component of the spiritual storehouse of the Chinese people.

The First Emperor's Mausoleum is a product of the combination of contemporary funerary concepts, a specific moment in time, the contemporary social background, and the forces of production available. It was the site of the emperor's funeral, and it remains as a lingering trace of that transitioning process, in material terms. The funeral ceremony was not just a ritualistic recognition of the end of the emperor's life and of the reality of his death; it was in essence even more the inauguration of the existence of the First Emperor in another form. This type of existence was the fruit of the historical developments of the Warring States: the development of the forces of production, the accumulation of social capital, and the concentration of centralised political power.

Understood in a narrow sense, the First Emperor's Mausoleum refers to the entire complex of funerary remains that are related to the burial of the First Emperor. This includes both the content of those remnants, and what is embodied by them – the contemporary space and environment. From a broader perspective, the mausoleum can be said to refer to the northern foothills of Mount Li, as well as to the Qin dynasty artefacts and the First Emperor's burial site. The core of this area is marked by the double city wall that demarcates the cemetery, and that stretches southwards to where a ridge of Mount Li divides the flow of the river – to the

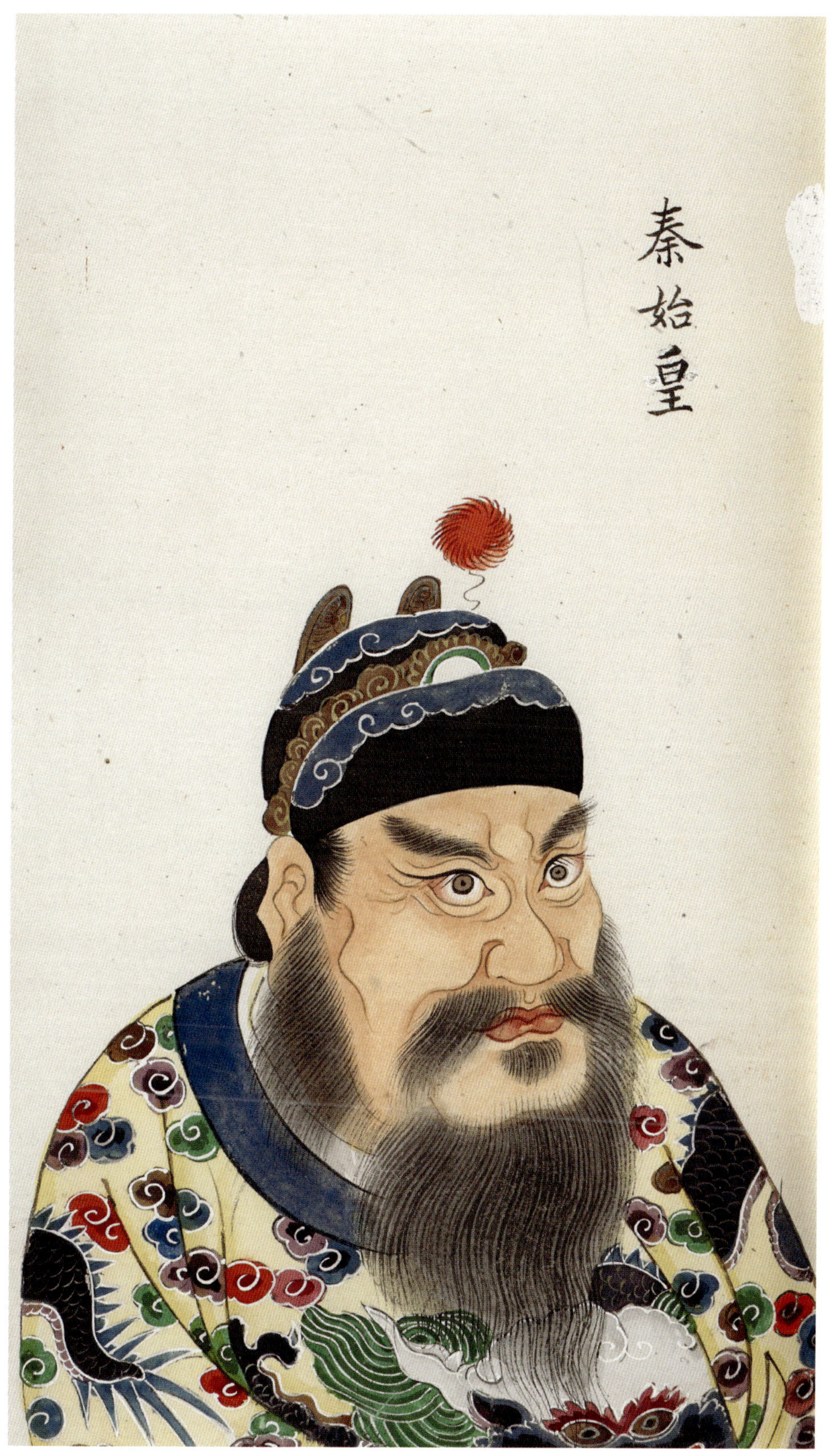
秦始皇

THE TOMB COMPLEX OF THE FIRST EMPEROR

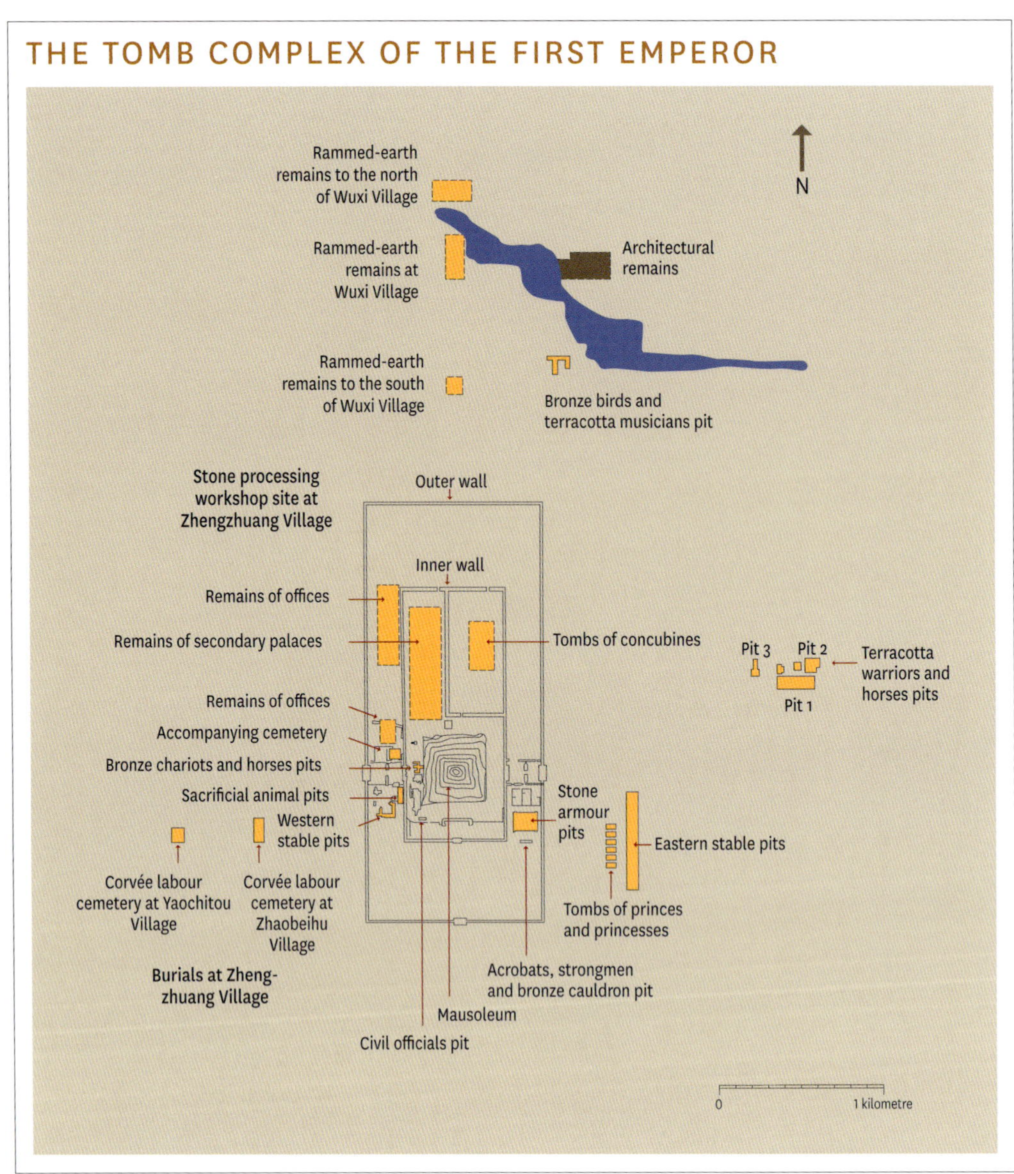

north to the Wei River, to the west to Zhiling, and to the east, perhaps, to the Xi River.

According to reports of the explorations of this area, we now know that the most important remains of the tomb complex include the cemetery's architectural structures, tomb tunnels, tomb burial chambers, the gate watchtowers, walls, roads and coffins, as well as accompanying tombs, pits and mausoleum villages. The mausoleum is also the product of supreme engineering and architectural efforts, including the construction of massive dykes and channels to prevent flooding, underground sluice walls, drainage channels, man-made lakes and ponds, and so on. There are also a large number of facilities that are protective of, and associated with, these mausoleum structures, such as the remains of factories and workplaces, kilns and the tombs of those working on the mausoleum. There would also be fording places, wharfs and the like.

So the mausoleum has its own inherent spatiality and temporality; it has an inherent mechanical structure, too. Nine aspects of the remains incorporate the mausoleum's funerary status: the structures above the tomb; the tomb roads and chambers and the burial chamber; the accompanying burials; the human sacrifices; the sacrifices of food and drink; the encircling walls; the gate observation posts; the roads; and the tomb villages. In terms of their ritualistic function, we can view these as constituting nine sub-systems, each of which has its corresponding design, structure, content and function. Each sub-system has its own particular external connections and synchronicity with the entire structure; and together they form the ritualistic significance of the Mount Li tomb.

At present, our work continues along two lines. The first is the excavation of important sites, including the Terracotta Warriors and Horses Pit, the Bronze Chariots and Horses Pit, and a number of other such sites; the second is the systematic archaeological exploration and investigation of the 100-square-kilometre area of the northern foothills of Mount Li.

As incrementally we are getting more complete archaeological material, a number of vital questions to do with the archaeology of the First Emperor's Mausoleum are gradually being resolved. One example is the design, structure and function of the inner and outer northern gates, the roads, the sacrificial buildings, and the burial tombs and other remains.

Even more importantly, our analysis of new materials has also served to push us beyond the material evidence, and forced us to engage in deep reflection about some of the most important and core issues encountered in our archaeological investigation of the First Emperor's Mausoleum, and the theories, ideas, methods and systematic structures that we bring to our work. Our purview includes the environment of the mausoleum, and its space and scope; the deepening of our comprehension of the material and technical aspects of the Qin dynasty; our understanding of the ritualistic structure of the First Emperor's Mausoleum; an appreciation of developments in material technology; and the analysis of ritual at the level of concept and idea.

Tombs constitute a place of residence for the dead in another world, and are, to a certain extent, a reflection after death of the state of life before death. In life, the First Emperor took charge of All-under-Heaven, and his mausoleum sought hard to replicate in alternative form that All-under-Heaven. The internal logic of the ritualistic structure of the mausoleum reflects the order of the empire that he sought so hard to create, and in this way the mausoleum's structure is akin to the structure of the All-under-Heaven that was in his command during his earthly life. This represents the most profound level of meaning to be found in the structure of the First Emperor's Mausoleum. Because of this, the core ideological message conveyed by the First Emperor's Mausoleum is the All-under-Heaven that the First Emperor himself knew. ■

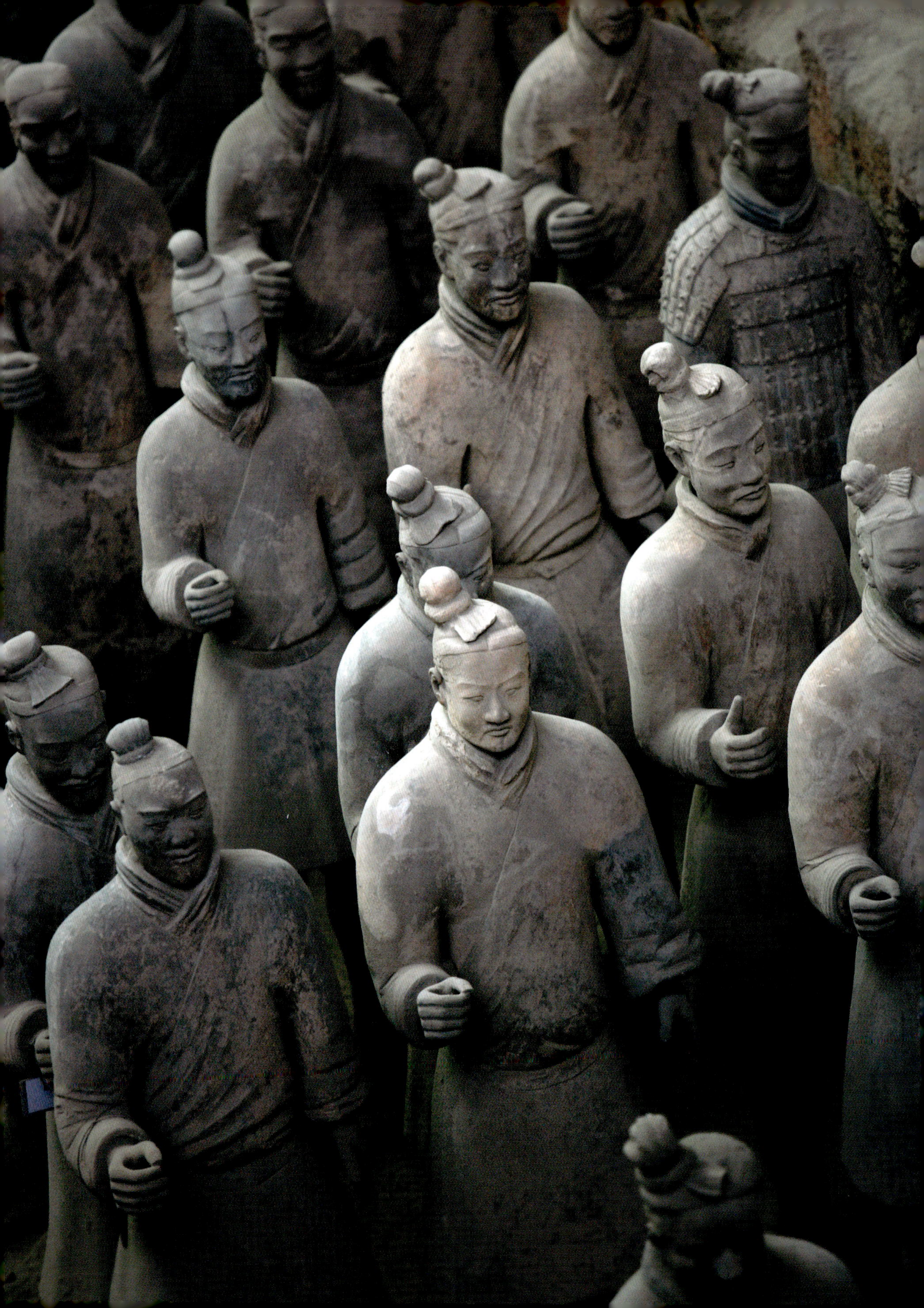

All-under-Heaven

THE ESTABLISHMENT OF EMPIRE

DUNCAN M CAMPBELL

The 450-year-long Qin–Han reign across the territory that we now know as China is a story of continuities and discontinuities, both with what had come before and with what was to follow. In different ways, these two dynasties were largely responsible for a China – understood as both a political entity and a zone of broadly shared cultural practices – that has now lasted continuously for some two millennia in terms of political and administrative culture, if not always of imperial sway.

The Qin dynasty (221–206 BCE) itself proved to be the shortest-lived of all China's major dynasties. Nonetheless, in an unprecedented manner it unified empire by destroying the various *Zhongguo* 中國 or Central Kingdoms spread across this vast geographical territory, and thus brought to an end the enduringly creative but politically catastrophic Warring States period (475–221 BCE). In its place, it established the foundations of a centralised state encompassing an estimated 20 million people, to be managed by officials selected on merit rather than the happenstance of birth. Its empire, however, should also be understood to represent the outcome of political, administrative and military reform processes that had been under way for at least the century before the watershed moment of unification in 221 BCE.

The Han dynasty (206 BCE–220 CE), one of China's longest-ruling dynasties, consolidated and expanded the Qin empire, and, after a brief experimentation with more traditional alternatives, re-established the centralised bureaucracy put in place under the Qin. However much the Han explicitly distanced itself from the Qin and its 'harsh' legal code, the law that prevailed throughout its empire was nonetheless largely one that had been inherited from the Qin.

In the past, historians have tended to over-simplify this process as representing the triumph (seemingly for all time) of a state-sponsored Han Confucian orthodoxy over an unforgiving Qin Legalism, but both of these labels are now

previous spread **Unarmoured soldiers from Pit 1 of Qin Shihuang's tomb complex.**

understood to be anachronistic misnomers. Instead, it is more historically accurate to understand the shift as representing a renewed emphasis on ritual (*li* 禮) rather than law (*fa* 法) as the foundation of political and social order. Rather than contesting the legitimacy of the Qin dynasty, the Han simply offered moral and cosmological justifications for having replaced it. Both traditionally minded, the two dynasties, alike, were committed to a belief in hereditary kingship, strictly observed and gendered social hierarchies, and meritocratic processes of governance; to Order (*zhi* 治), in Chinese terms, in the face of the ever-lurking danger of Chaos (*luan* 亂).

If the first dynasty lent China the name that the outside world has referred to it by ever since, the second of them was soon adopted by the Chinese people themselves ('People of the Han' or Hanren 漢人) as an accommodating ethnic marker of their identity. Together, then, the two dynasties served to define the racial, geographical, cultural and political contours of what was to become Chinese civilisation, and, whatever the actual waxing and waning of political or military fortunes, established the idea of China as a single and integral political entity, centrally administered, and peopled by a unique race united by common bonds of language and culture.

That is not to say that this particular outcome was inevitable. There are moments when events might have led in different directions, with very different outcomes. After all, the First Emperor himself, for instance, while still King of Qin (his own name was Ying Zheng), only narrowly survived a number of well-known assassination attempts, and during the brief interregnum between the Qin and the Han, one of the contenders for the Mandate of Heaven, Xiang Yu 項羽 (232–202 BCE), had sought to re-establish the pluralistic political order that had preceded unification. The hold of the Han over empire, too, was briefly interrupted at around its midpoint by the establishment of the 'New' or Xin 新 dynasty of Wang Mang 王莽 (*c.*45 BCE–23 CE), representing another path not taken in terms of government policies, and dividing the dynasty into the Western (or Former) Han and the Eastern (or Later) Han, so named in keeping with the eastward shift of its capital from Chang'an 長安 to Luoyang 洛陽.

All empires also have enormous costs. In the case of the Qin, it is these costs – particularly in terms of the conscripted labour devoted to building such projects as the canals and roads to connect the empire, the walls that demarcated its northernmost limits, the First Emperor's Mausoleum, the Terracotta Army associated with the tomb – that help explain its rapid collapse after a short fifteen years. 'Yet once the Qin had become master of the whole empire and established itself within the fastness of the Pass, a single commoner rose in opposition to it and its ancestral temples toppled, its ruler died at the hands of men, and the dynasty became a laughing stock of All-under-Heaven', wrote the brilliant young Jia Yi 賈誼 (201–169 BCE) in his essay 'Faulting the Qin' ('Guo Qin lun' 過秦論), written only decades after the Qin's collapse. 'Why was this? Because it did not rule with humanity and righteousness and because the power to occupy and the power to retain what one has thereby won are not at all the same.'

Later, Lu Jia 陸賈 (*c.*228–140 BCE) was to offer Liu Bang 劉邦 (256–195 BCE) similar advice shortly after he had become Gaozu 高祖 (*c.*202–195 BCE), the first emperor of the Han:

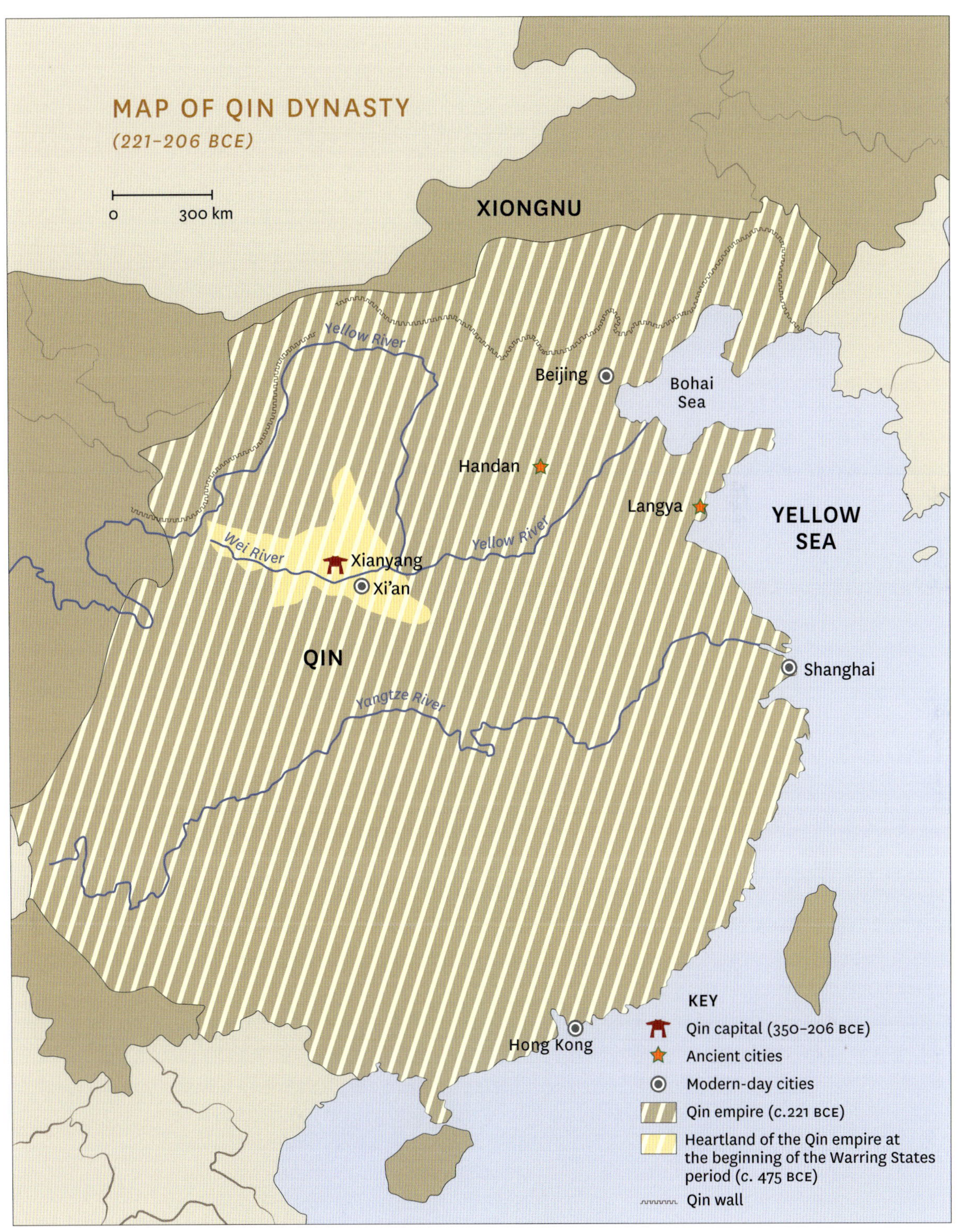
MAP OF QIN DYNASTY
(221–206 BCE)
0
300 km
XIONGNU
Yellow River
Beijing
Bohai
Sea
Handan
Langya
YELLOW
SEA
Wei River
Xianyang
Yellow River
Xi'an
QIN
Shanghai
Yangtze River
Hong Kong
KEY
Qin capital (350–206 BCE)
Ancient cities
Modern-day cities
Qin empire (c.221 BCE)
Heartland of the Qin empire at the beginning of the Warring States period (c. 475 BCE)
Qin wall

opposite page **The Great Wall at Badaling, 1957–59, by New Zealand photographer Brian Brake.**

'Yes, you may well have obtained empire on horseback, but can you bring order to it from horseback (居馬上得之寧可以馬上治之乎)?' And yet, after some 400 years of power, the Han dynasty, too, was forced to reckon with the challenges that had faced the Qin, as have all subsequent dynasties, some more successfully than others: young or inadequate rulers, disputed successions, corruption at the centre (often blamed on palace women or the eunuchs who cared for them), overly ambitious ministers or generals, centrifugal regions, onerous levels of taxation (paid in kind throughout this period either in grain or in textiles), aggressive (usually northern) neighbouring peoples, and natural disasters.

The reputations enjoyed by these two dynasties have been a study in contrast. Whereas all subsequent ages have sought to disavow the Qin (as representative of human suffering and imperial tyranny), the Han has long been actively embraced (as representative of power and authority, and of grand imperial stretch).

This present exhibition of some 170 objects, dating from this and earlier periods of Chinese history, affords us the timely opportunity to celebrate Chinese civilisation and its various and splendid products, both material and intangible, and also to reflect on its continuities and discontinuities, its paths taken and untaken, its legacy as represented by a unitary political entity stretched across a vast diversity of geographical features and ethnic realities that has now lasted two millennia, and which now, once again, sits at the centre of a global network of trade in things and ideas.

The objects on display also prompt us to explore one particular and critical aspect of this moment in Chinese time: the beliefs and practices that animate early Chinese conceptions of the afterlife. As is the case in Māori traditions, by metaphor the Chinese walk into the future backwards, their gaze always cast in the direction of what has been (以前) rather than what might lie ahead (以後). The past, after all, offers us our only reliable map of the future. If the shadow cast by the ancestors in the Chinese world has always been an all-encompassing and usually benevolent one, what were the early beliefs about what happens to us after death, where we go, and how we get there? What rituals embodied these beliefs? And what role did objects in the material world play in representing these beliefs, enabling the rituals, and propitiating one's ancestors?

For his part, the First Emperor seems to have been a man obsessed with immortality and transcendence, and, as was the case with his empire, it is the scale, if not the nature, of his tomb (if Sima Qian's report of it proves true, when eventually the technology is available to allow archaeologists to enter it without destroying its contents) and its terracotta guardians (about whom there had been, remarkably, no written record made) that is without precedent. And, as will become obvious when one views the Han dynasty funerary objects in this exhibition, it was on a scale never again to be attempted.

Many of the objects on show here – the animals and the birdlife, the bells, vessels, weapons, coins, tile-ends, weights and measures, and decorative pendants, cast in bronze, carved of jade, or moulded from clay – were designed, in real or in metaphorical ways, to facilitate communication across space and over time. Paradoxically, now they serve both

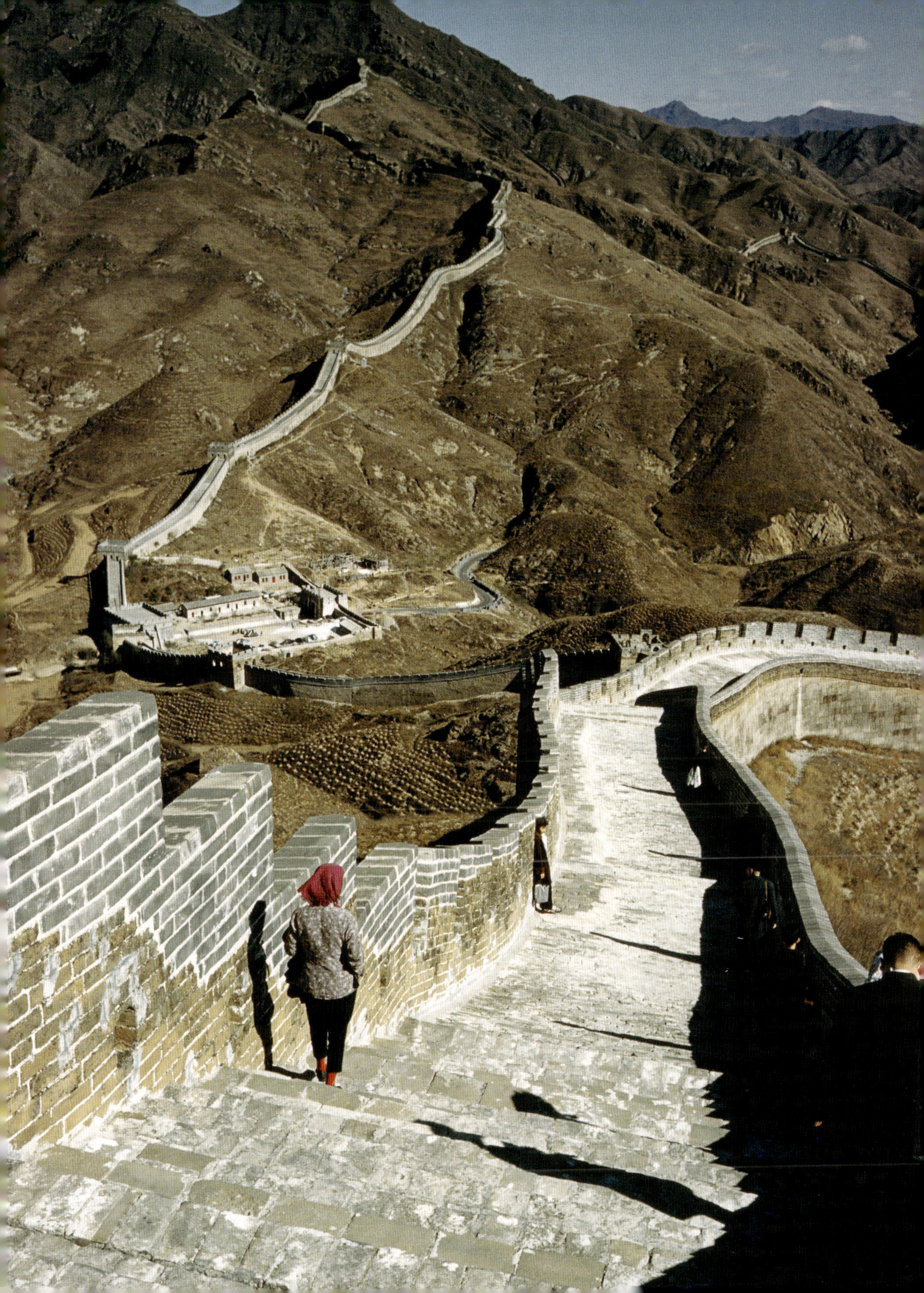

opposite page **Pair of ink rubbings of Qin Imperial inscription carved on a stele in Mount Yi, dated 219 BCE and re-carved in 933 CE, from the Art Gallery of New South Wales.**

to make us aware of the exceptionality of the brief moment of Qin time in Chinese history, and to help us understand this moment in terms of what came before and what followed. These objects continue to perform their communicative function now as they allow us access to that past.

This was a period during which China achieved a new stage of political and cultural unification and centralisation. What measures, initiated by the Qin and continued by the Han, were necessary for this development? Most critical, perhaps, in the long term, was the abolition of the various feudal states that Qin had subjugated, the removal of their now powerless aristocratic clans to the capital of Xianyang 咸陽, and the melting down of all their weapons in order to smelt ritual bells and statues. The empire was to be partitioned into thirty-six (later, forty-two) commanderies (*jun* 郡), each further subdivided into counties (*xian* 縣), and each given into the charge of centrally appointed military and civil officers, recruited from throughout the empire.

Following this came the standardisation of weights and measures, axle-lengths, coinage, the formats of official reports and the manner of ensuring their confidentiality, and the written script – this last, a process that took a considerable period, but which represents perhaps the Qin dynasty's most abiding legacy.

Huge infrastructural projects – roads, canals, irrigation works, walls, the emperor's Epang Palace (阿房宮) – were embarked upon; and detailed laws and regulations were promulgated, covering all aspects of life, and requiring of local officials that a constant stream of information be conveyed to their superiors in the capital. Each evening, as he travelled relentlessly about his empire, the First Emperor would work his way through the pile of files that had been presented to him – an estimated 30 kilograms' worth each day.

Many of these policies had been implemented in the state of Qin a century earlier by the great reformer Shang Yang 商鞅 (390–338 BCE); now, the First Emperor extended their reach throughout his new empire. In doing so, he relied on the wise counsel of his Chancellor of the Left (*Zuo chengxiang* 左丞相), Li Si 李斯 (*c.*280–208 BCE), and, earlier, the advice of the brilliant Legalist philosopher Master Han Fei 韓非子 (*c.*280–233 BCE). Both men had been students of the Confucian philosopher Master Xun 荀子 (*c.*310–*c.*235 BCE), from whom they had learned the importance of punishments in ensuring social order ('Crooked wood must be heated and bent before it becomes straight; blunt metal must be ground and whetted before it becomes sharp').

Both were to meet unpleasant ends; the latter ordered to drink poison some time before the unification of the empire, the former, after the death of the First Emperor and as an elderly man, sliced in two at the waist. Growing up, the First Emperor had relied on the guidance given him by the merchant Lü Buwei 呂不韋 (291–235 BCE), an associate of his father whose sometime concubine had become the emperor's mother; he, too, fell foul of the First Emperor and was required to commit suicide.

After a brief attempt to return to a pre-Qin form of governance, the Han dynasty ensured that the measures taken by the First Emperor were to become a permanent feature of Chinese political culture, further extending the processes of standardisation to cover, for instance, the progression of time throughout the day, and the

皇帝立國維初在昔嗣世稱王討伐亂
逆威動四極武義直方戎臣奉詔經時
不久滅六暴強廿有六年上薦高號孝
道顯明既獻泰成乃降專惠親巡遠方
登于繹山群臣從者咸思攸長追念亂
世分土建邦以開爭理功戰日作流血
於野自泰古始世無萬數陀及五帝莫
能禁止迺今皇帝壹家天下兵不復起
災害滅除黔首康定利澤長久群臣誦

略刻此樂石以著經紀皇帝曰金石刻
盡始皇帝所為也今襲號而金石刻辭
不稱始皇帝其於久遠也如後嗣為之
者不稱成功盛德丞相臣斯臣去疾御
史大夫臣德昧死言臣請具刻詔書金石
刻因明白矣臣昧死請制曰可

秦相李斯書嶧山碑跡妙時古殊為世重故散騎常侍徐公鉉酷耽玄學垂五十年時無其比晚節獲嶧
山碑摹本師其筆力自謂得思於天人之際因是已之舊跡焚擲略盡文寶受學徐門粗堅企及之
志太平興國五年春闈舉進不中東遊齊魯客登嶧山求訪秦碑邈然無覩逮於旬浹怊悵于懷
燕之下借異神蹤將墜於世今以徐所授摹本刊石長安故都國子學庶博雅君子見先儒之指歸淳
化四年八月十五日承奉郎守太常博士陝府西路計度轉運副使賜緋魚袋鄭文寶記

opposite page **A scene from an eighteenth-century album showing the First Emperor directing the burning of books and ordering Confucian scholars to be buried alive, as recounted in Sima Qian's *Records of the Grand Historian*.**

progression of the days and months throughout the year, by means of standard water clocks and an imperially prescribed calendar. The information-gathering processes of the Qin, too, were further extended and strengthened.

All of these developments required expanded levels of literacy, and it is over the course of this period of history that the role of the all-important *shi* 士, or officer of the imperial government, was transformed, becoming less that of a 'knight' than a 'man of letters'. The rhetorical use of language, both written and spoken, became itself a focus of attention (and a powerful way of achieving a form of immortality), and this period saw the production of some of the earliest examples of Chinese lexicography, most importantly Xu Shen's 許慎 (*c.*55–149 CE) *Characters Complex and Simple Analysed* (*Shuowen jiezi* 說文解字).

It is in this context that we best consider the two most abidingly notorious measures undertaken during the Qin dynasty: the 'Burning of the Books' in 213 BCE, and the execution of some 460 scholars the following year (*fenshu kengru* 焚書坑儒). Modern-day understandings of both of these events, to the extent we continue to believe them to have taken place, if still condemnatory, tend to see them in a somewhat more circumscribed light than has often been the case in the past.

With the first measure, it was the circulation of only certain types of books in private hands that was the issue (particularly, the *Book of Odes* [*Shi jing* 詩經] and the *Book of Documents* [*Shangshu* 尚書], both to later become vital parts of the Confucian canon), with practical manuals of medicine, agriculture and fortune-telling explicitly excluded from the proscription. Copies of all of the books then available were to be housed in the Imperial Library in Xianyang; tragically, when the capital was sacked upon the fall of the dynasty, the fires burnt for a full three months and the library and its contents were reduced to ashes.

The second measure, also, was more an attempt to control knowledge rather than to destroy it; to take it out of the hands of (potentially disloyal) private scholars ('Masters of Methods' [*shushi* 術士], a variety of alchemists, magicians, fortune-tellers and so on) and to institutionalise it. It was aimed at those who dared to 'Use the past to criticise the present' (*yi gu fei jin* 以古非今), not, specifically, as is often said to be the case, the Confucian scholars; a group who in any case at this time are better understood to constitute the 'Classicists' (*Ruzhe* 儒者), and who remained important at the court of the First Emperor for a variety of ritualistic purposes.

The Qin–Han period is also one that gives us the beginnings of Chinese history, understood as a narrative account of the past that seeks to investigate both the events of that past, and the causes and outcomes of those events, in the form, most remarkably, of Sima Qian's *Records of the Grand Historian* and its explicit sequel, Ban Gu's 班固 (32–92 CE) *Book of the Han* (*Hanshu* 漢書). The first of these – completed late in Sima Qian's life and under the most difficult of circumstances, as an act of filial piety to bring to conclusion a work of private historiography started by his father – sought to present a summation of the entire knowable past down to the author's own age. Ban Gu's work, also based on the earlier work of his father, and completed in 111 by Ban Gu's sister Ban Zhao 班昭 (45–*c.*116 CE) once he had

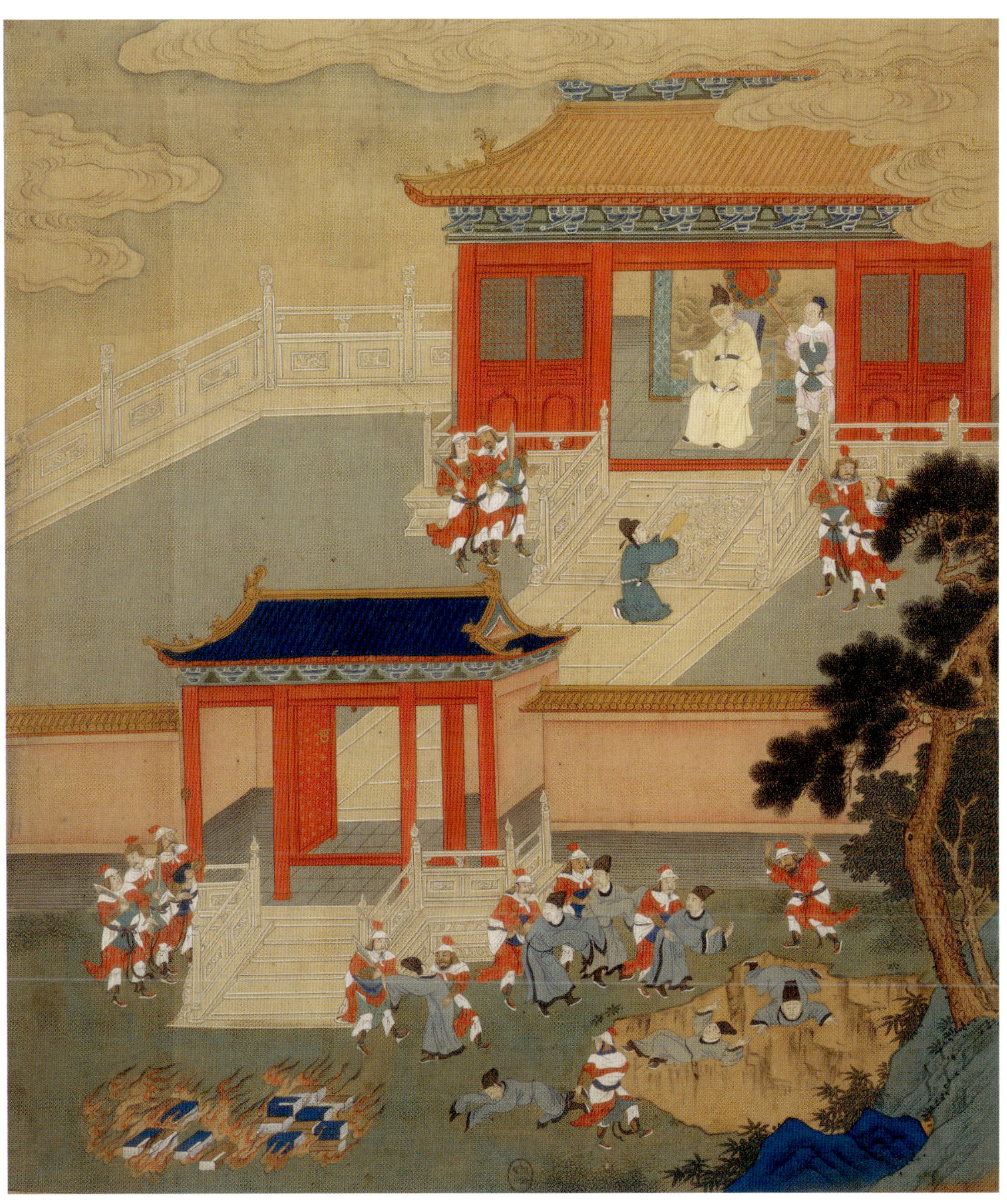

been imprisoned, covered the period from the beginning of the Han dynasty until the end of Wang Mang's 王莽 brief interregnum (9–23 CE). It was a book that established the model for all later official dynastic histories.

Almost everything that we know about the period is to be found in these two works, and again and again the rich archaeological evidence unearthed in China in subsequent ages has served to testify to the veracity of the accounts they offer, however exaggerated they occasionally seem to be. At the same time, the books also served to endorse the authoritative and orthodox Confucian view of written history as being at once the arbiter of good and evil in the affairs of humankind, and the handmaiden of all thought. 'He who does not forget the past,' Sima Qian tells us, 'is master of the present.'

Written history was but one of the many branches of learning to flourish after the cataclysm that had been (in Han dynasty reports) the Qin and the dislocation and warfare that had attended its collapse. The period saw the development of two of the major forms of Chinese poetry, for instance. The prose-poem or rhapsody (*fu* 賦) is a long and descriptive genre that takes delight in both the object described (the wind, birdlife, trees, the capital) and the language used in doing so. The ballad or folk song is traditionally understood to have been collected from the streets by a Music Bureau (*Yuefu* 樂府), established for this purpose and held to represent an expression of the *vox populi*.

Of abiding importance was the painstaking reconstruction of the texts of Confucianism, a task initially undertaken largely at the direction of the bibliographer Liu Xiang 劉向 (77–6 BCE), who was appointed Imperial Librarian in 26 BCE, and was succeeded in this post by his son Liu Xin 劉歆 (d. 23 CE). Once this set of books had been established, and equipped with an increasingly sophisticated commentarial apparatus, court positions were created in 136 CE for the interpretation of each classic, and between 175 CE and 183 CE a project under the direction of the scholar and musician Cai Yong 蔡邕 (132–192 CE) saw the text of the canon carved into stone, only fragments of which remain to us today.

This renewed commitment to classical learning and to education extended to women, too, although for circumscribed purposes; Liu Xiang also compiled an unforgiving *Biographies of Exemplary Women* (*Lie nü zhuan* 列女傳), and one of Cai Yong's daughters, Cai Yan 蔡琰, was an accomplished poet. It also gave rise to remarkable developments in a number of fields, as the following examples show. One was the field of correlative cosmological thought, with its associated proto-scientific and technological advances – Te Papa's collection contains a half-sized replica of Zhang Heng's 張衡 (78–139 CE) *Instrument for inquiring into the direction of the wind and the shaking of the Earth* [*Houfeng didong yi* 侯風地動儀], the world's earliest seismograph. Other areas were: economic policy-making (a debate later tendentiously reconstructed in the celebrated *Discourses on Salt and Iron* [*Yan tie lun* 鹽鐵論] was held at court in 81 BCE to explore the limits of state involvement in the economy); medicine; and advances in agricultural and military technology, largely connected with the increasingly sophisticated use of iron.

The religious dimensions of Chinese culture, too, underwent remarkable developments during the Qin–Han period. At the court level, as the costs associated with the proliferation

following spread **Partially excavated kneeling archer, from Pit 2 of Qin Shihuang's tomb complex.**

of ancestral rites and sacrifices to deities of one sort or another increased, officials advised degrees of rationalisation; in 31 BCE, the worship of Heaven as the most important imperial ritual was established, as had been advocated by the important Confucian philosopher Dong Zhongshu 董仲舒 (179–104 BCE) almost a century earlier. The increasing importance of the virtue of filial piety (*xiao* 孝), along with age-old ideas about the afterlife, resulted in lavish funerals and richly furnished tombs, on the part of both the emperors and the Han elites.

At a popular level, evidence, both textual and archaeological, begins to give us a better idea of beliefs among ordinary people: theirs was a world richly populated by spirits, ghosts and portents, and dominated by the figure of the Dowager Queen of the West (*Xiwangmu* 西王母) and an associated fascination with immortality. Various schools and varieties of Daoism grew in strength throughout this period, many with millenarian tendencies. It was during the Han, too, of course, that Buddhism first made its way to China, across Central Asia, quickly gaining a foothold among the unlettered sectors of urban society.

And it is also from the Han dynasty that we have the first clear evidence of a China that sits at the centre of a global trading empire, along whose arteries – over land, along the Silk Road through Central Asia; at sea, into the South China Sea, the Indian Ocean and the Persian Gulf – flowed both products (silk outwards; spices, precious gems and luxury goods of all sorts inwards) and ideas, artistic motifs, and beliefs such as Buddhism.

The end of the Han – when it finally arrived in 220 CE, and saw the empire, of now some 60 million people, descend into chaos and millenarian rebellion – was momentous; it was to be almost four centuries before China was again to be ruled by a single dynasty. The destruction and loss of life involved in the sacking of the capital of Luoyang in 190 CE by the warlord Dong Zhuo 董卓 (d. 192 CE), especially, lived on in the cultural memory, captured in the immortal lines 'How desolate now seems Luoyang,/ Its palaces and mansions all reduced to ashes./ Its walls and towers, too, have toppled over,/ And everywhere the thorns and brambles stretch up to Heaven', from a poem written by the poet Cao Zhi 曹植 (192–232 CE) in 211 CE.

In the millennium and a half since the collapse of the Qin and Han empires, however, the ideal of a unitary state, controlled from the centre by a leader working in concert with his officials, selected for their posts on the basis of their learning, as established over this 450-year-long period of Chinese history, has retained its hold on the imaginations of the Chinese people. ■

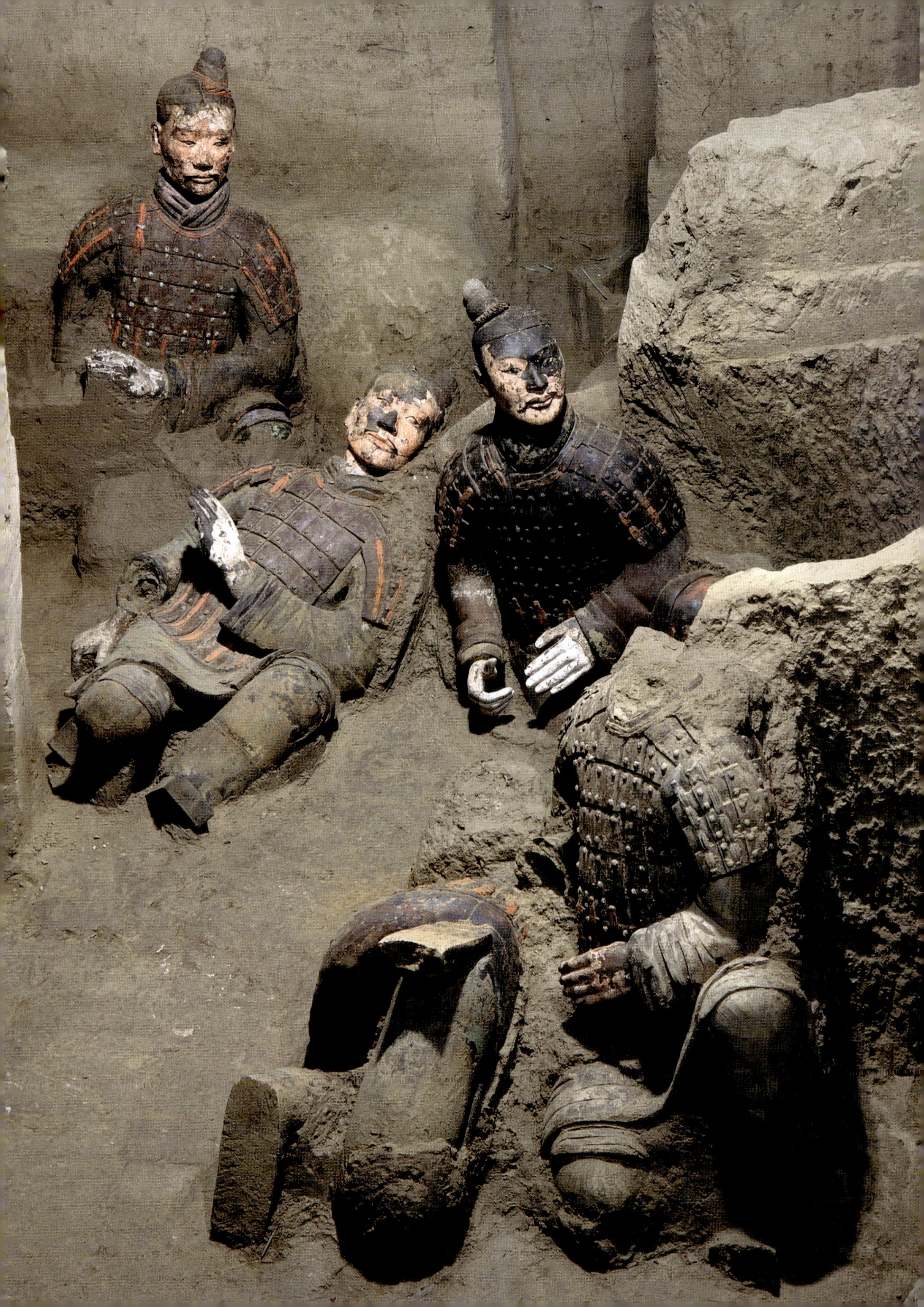

Paradise and home

TRANSITIONS TO THE AFTERLIFE

NATHAN WOOLLEY

After the formation of an empire ruled as a single bureaucratic system, the First Emperor turned to a realm he was yet to conquer. In his *Records of the Grand Historian* (*Shi ji* 史記) Sima Qian details the First Emperor's attempts to attain an elixir of immortality in the final years of his rule. As a sign of his ambitions, he proclaimed himself a 'perfected man', a divine being unharmed by fire or water and able to live as long as Heaven and Earth. He sent youths out by boat to seek a purported Isle of Immortality beyond the eastern seas, and even visited the coast himself in the hope of finding clues to the route to this land. He also sent ministers in pursuit of famed immortals to learn their secrets.

Perhaps fortunately for the people of the empire, the First Emperor's efforts would go unrewarded, for only those who forgo worldly achievement can ascend to immortality without passing through death; the two men commissioned to find the elixir came to this conclusion, and fled rather than face punishment for failure; and those sent to sea returned empty-handed. In Sima Qian's work, these attempts stand now as condemnation of the First Emperor, not only to the ultimate folly of such an endeavour, but also as a symbol of the excesses of his rule. Such misguided attempts to extend one's years were to become a reoccurring trope of imperial hubris in later Chinese history.

Yet the grandiosity of the emperor's tomb represented an alternative attempt to escape the finality of death and extend his achievements into the otherworld. In describing the emperor's tomb, Sima Qian's history tells of the construction of a microcosm under the earth, with heavenly bodies represented above and the landscape of the empire below. Representations of palaces and towers as well as officials of court were accompanied by all manner of wondrous objects. The reality of this description remains to be proven since the tomb itself remains unexcavated, but modern archaeology has revealed other subterranean treasures in the immediate vicinity, as is now well known: an army of warriors as well as numerous officials

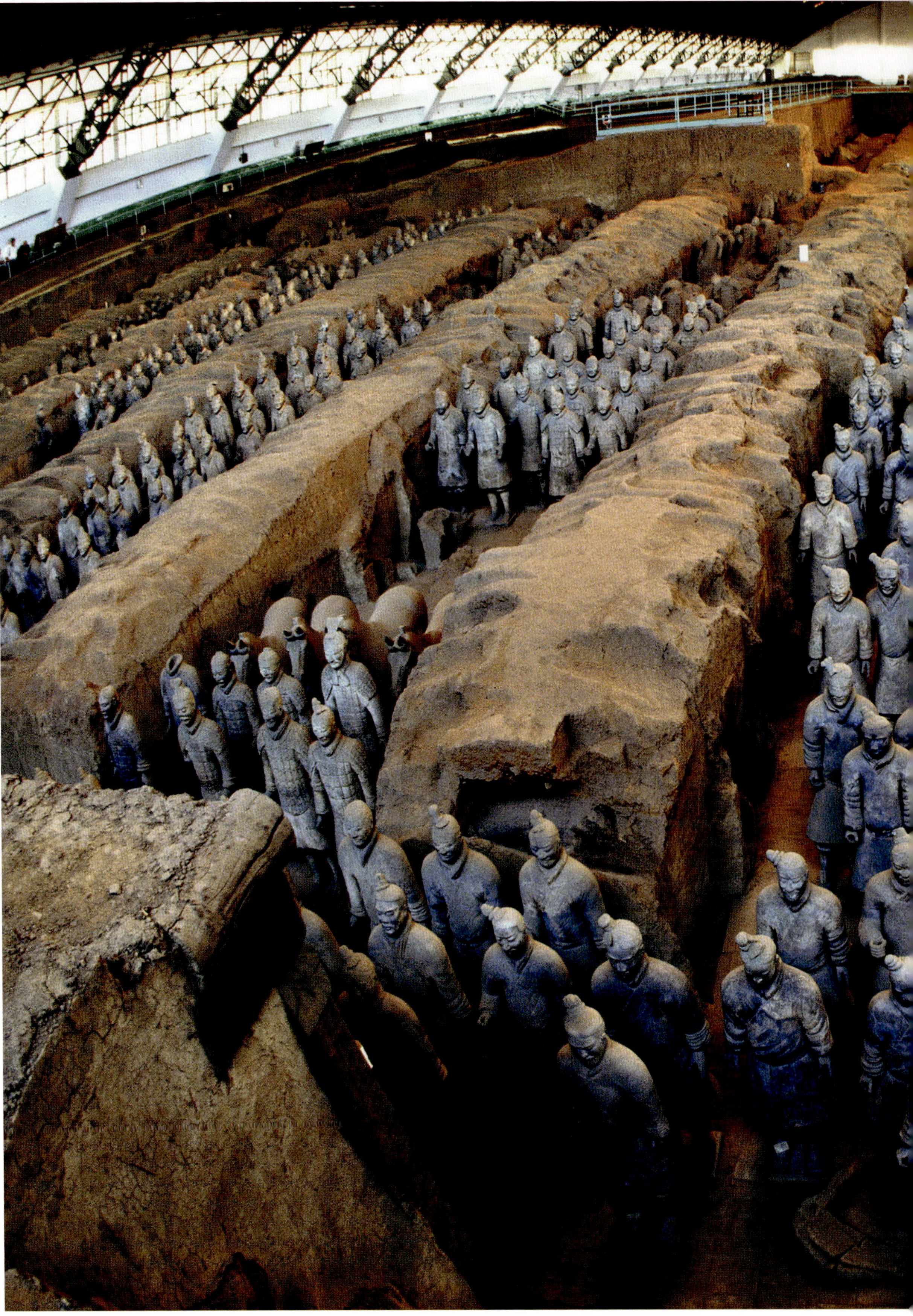

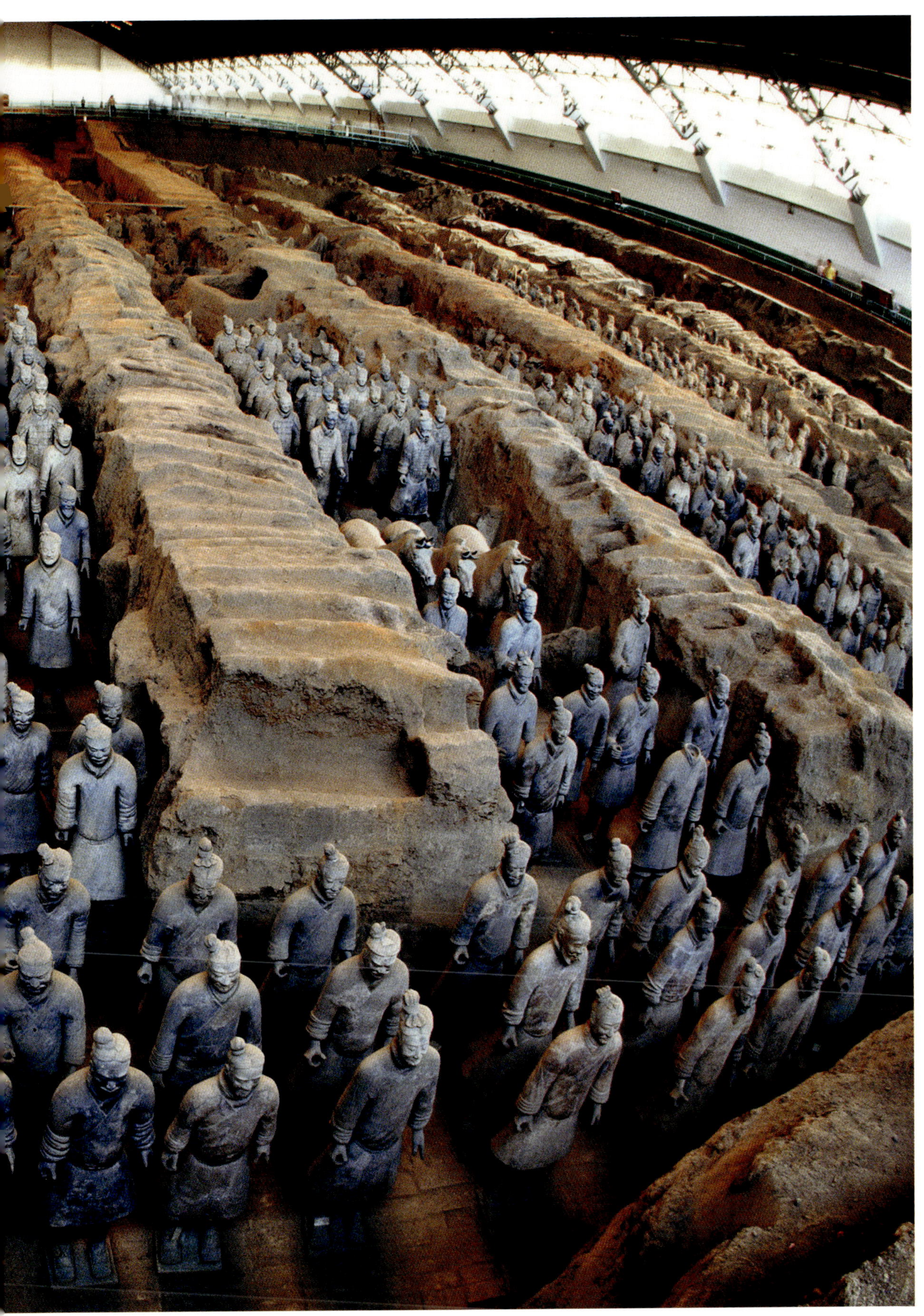

previous spread **Pit 1 of Qin Shihuang's tomb complex.**

and entertainers; imperial carriages, stables, an armoury and even an artificial lake supplied with waterfowl. A man who could claim All-under-Heaven as his property would only be satisfied in death with a similar dominion.

Despite its imperial splendour, the First Emperor's burial can be partially understood in the ongoing evolution of burial practices in ancient China. During the centuries from the Spring and Autumn period (771–475 BCE) to the first empires, burials of the elite had undergone significant change. Nobles of the central states had been buried in pits with the riches of their position, such as fine jades and intricate bronzes, as well as the bodies of servants and slaves interred to accompany them. But by the Han dynasty these practices had given way to increased representation of earthly existence in bewildering and quotidian detail, including food, clothing, books, utensils and furniture, as well as models of servants and buildings.

Since the activities of the dead mirrored those of the living, items in these interments now met an extended range of needs and expectations. For example, food ensured ongoing sustenance: in addition to cooked meals of lavish variety served in lacquerware or pottery, granaries and domestic animals explicitly ensured an ongoing supply of food for tomb occupants. Nor were the dead idle: officials could be accompanied by books of laws and statutes, presumably so they could continue with their work in the other realm. Perhaps mirroring the increased bureaucratisation of the empire and its obsessive record-making, burial goods were accompanied by complete inventories (useful to the modern archaeologist).

With this diversification, tombs were no longer simple repositories for corpses and objects, but increasingly became places the dead might want to inhabit. Made of extensive and detailed stonework, they took on a structure akin to abodes of the living, with various chambers denoting locations in a real house. While the First Emperor in death was given the world, lesser mortals were given a home.

Such an array of comforts in death would encourage the dead not to wander. Inscriptions inside tombs record the concern of the living for the welfare of their deceased relatives. Since souls abroad as ghosts faced many dangers, rituals were performed to call them to return to the tomb. Spiritual protection for the tomb was also necessary, since not just the living might seek to cause harm to the contents. Door-knockers with the heads of beasts warded off baleful influences, while, by the late Han, contracts were being placed in the tombs declaring the legitimacy of a tomb's construction, and seeking to ward off rival claims to the location or to mollify deities of the Earth that might have been disturbed by intrusion into their territory.

Yet this effort also reflected the self-interest of those left behind. If wandering, the recent dead were a threat to their descendants, bringing malevolent influence in the form of illness or misfortune. As a result, families strove to ensure that the souls of their relatives were safely delivered to their destination, with elaborate funerary practices encouraging them to take up their new abodes. Ongoing placation in the form of ritual offerings at shrines located near the tombs continued to address their needs. The living endeavoured to ensure that they and their dead remained safely separated.

But tomb as residence is only part of the story, for the images inside do not suggest a fully

Partially excavated soldiers from Han Yangling Mausoleum.

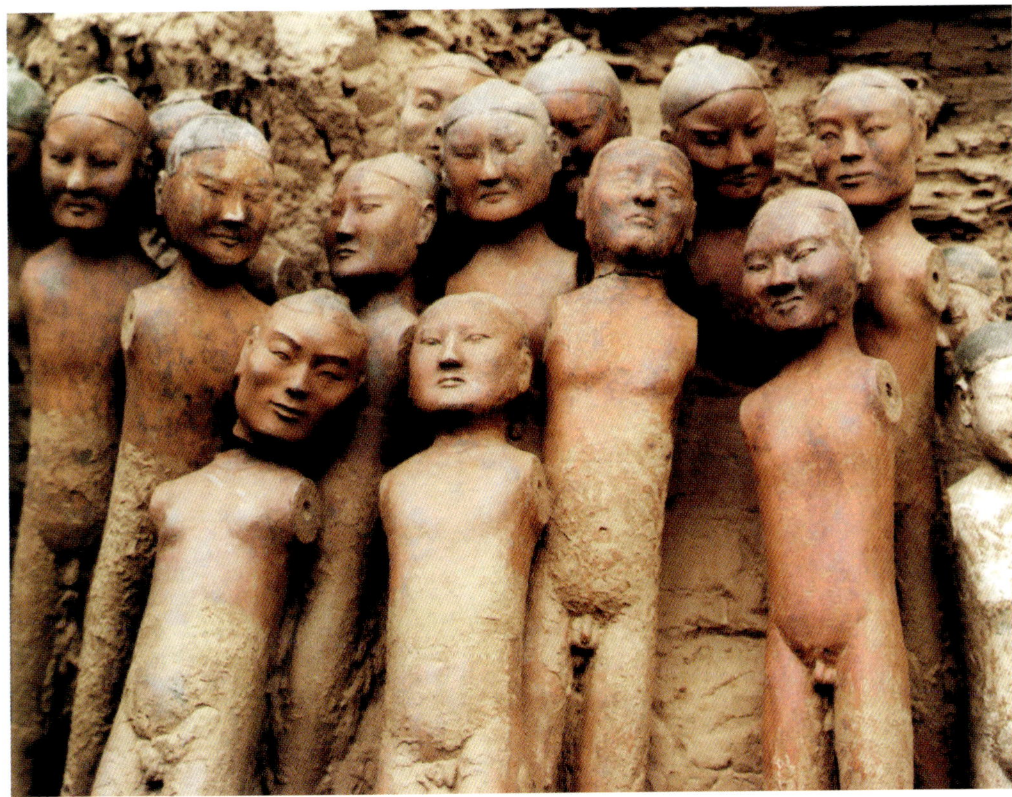

sedentary existence for the deceased. Adorning the doors and walls of tombs are depictions of a range of activities, some associated with the household, but others with the world outside, such as scenes of hunting or battle, animals in the wild, entertainers engaged in their crafts, or travel to wondrous lands populated by deities; towers housing people engaged with family or servants stretch skywards. Which relate to activities for the dead – in life or in the otherworld – and which to significant stories from histories or legends can be difficult to determine. Furthermore, regional variation across the empire's vast territory likely led to the incorporation of different local beliefs, complicating modern-day interpretation.

Did the dead remain in the tomb? Some early textual evidence allows for the existence of two or more distinct essences of an individual, equating in different ways to the concept of a soul. It might be that one essence remained with the corpse, while another embarked on a passage to an immortal paradise. Yet material evidence does not correlate closely with such understandings, which may in any case have been limited to a few among the elite. Representations in the tomb suggest multifarious possibilities in the afterlife.

The divine beings that populated a space between Heaven and Earth commonly appear on the walls of the tombs. Flying amid swirling clouds or atop mountains, these immortals (*xian* 仙) are often engaged in ascent of the route to a celestial domain. They can appear astride tigers

Ink rubbing of a Han dynasty brick decorated with a relief carving of the Queen Mother of the West on the magic mountain Kunlun.

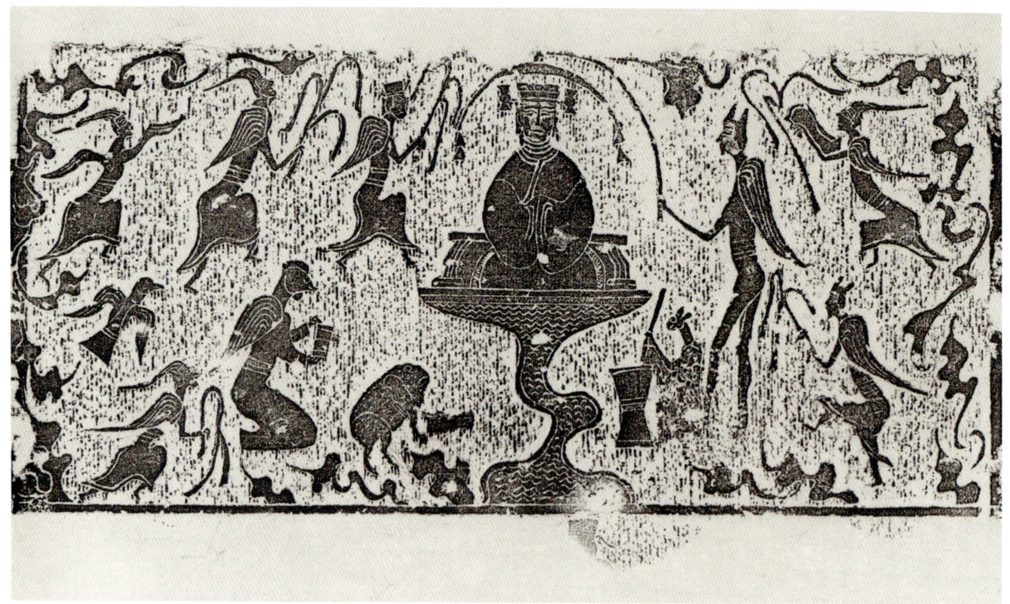

and dragons, or among the winding tendrils of a marvellous plant. Their physical features accentuate their divine nature: wings, feathered bodies and large ears denote their liminal nature with power over the worlds of life and death. Immortals often hold forth a plant or a ball of medicine, a sign of their possession of the secrets of the elixir of immortality. Dynamic portrayals of their movement through space may represent guidance for the dead in the aspiration that they, too, might transcend the mortal world and follow these immortals to the celestial realm. Popular lore recorded the names of individuals who had achieved such transcendence and departed from human society. Now in the tomb, this possibility of immortal life was held out to the dead.

Ruling over the otherworld as depicted inside the tomb was the Dowager Queen of the West. She is one of the most commonly appearing divinities in tomb art of the Han dynasty. Located uppermost in images, she is often seated, riding on a cloud or presiding over her court in the western paradise on Mount Kunlun. She is accompanied by a dragon and a tiger, and arranged about her are divine creatures of the celestial bodies: the hare and toad of the moon, and the three-legged bird of the sun. Courtiers in human form can also be found in attendance, perhaps immortals paying homage or come to report, for the otherworld increasingly took on many aspects of the worldly bureaucracy.

She dispenses the elixir of immortality as prepared by the hare of the moon in his pestle. Under the Han dynasty, the Dowager Queen of the West was associated with popular cults that sometimes blossomed into major unrest, with followers carrying tokens of her promise of everlasting life and engaging in shamanistic and divinatory practices, but in the tomb she consistently represented cosmological order and divine protection.

The movement of the dead into another

Partially excavated soldiers, animals and tomb provisions from Han Yangling Mausoleum.

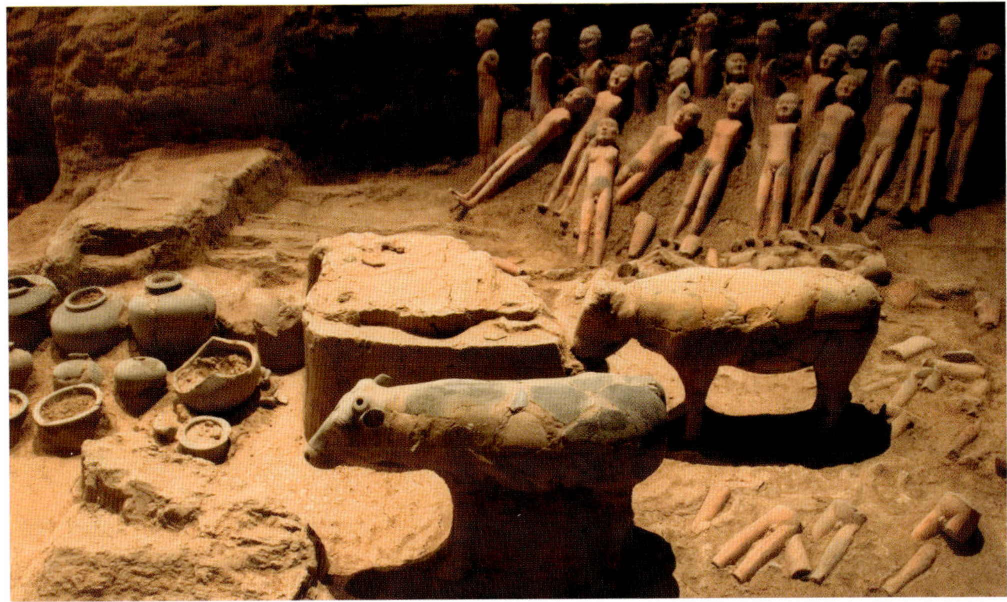

domain could also be denoted by images of the Gates of Heaven inside the tomb. Constellations could be mapped out on walls or the ceiling. The cardinal directions were represented by their relevant creatures: the black tortoise in the north, the vermilion bird in the south, the azure dragon in the east, and the white tiger in the west. Sometimes the stone doors of tombs, modelled on their wooden equivalents with lintel and panels, could be decorated with clouds and heavenly bodies to mark it as an entrance-way into a celestial realm.

Some were adorned with the semi-reptilian forms of Nüwa 女媧 and Fuxi 伏羲, primordial deities associated with the creation of humans and the beginnings of civilisation, respectively. The lower halves of their bodies are often depicted as having scaly tails akin to those of snakes or lizards, perhaps significant for their abilities to slough off old skin in a form of rebirth. Nüwa and Fuxi sometimes hold the sun and the moon, or have their tails intertwined, suggestive of their complementary natures and powers of regeneration.

The tensions between immortal paradise and underground household are indicative of multiple and changing conceptions of death, underscoring the uncertainties it held for the living. Such ambiguities are betrayed in occasional accounts of empty tombs. When he went to the tomb of the Yellow Emperor to perform ritual offerings, Emperor Wu of the Han enquired of his entourage how the tomb came to be built if this (mythical) ruler had achieved immortality. They replied that the tomb was in fact empty, holding only the Yellow Emperor's clothes and hat.

Such a transformation on the cusp of death was possible for the very few of the mortal world initiated into the secret of eternal life, a secret that proved elusive for China's First Emperor. But even for him, the tomb was to prove a liminal place, an intersection of life, death and immortality. ■

Catalogue of exhibition objects

日常生活的禮儀

Treasures of ritual in everyday life

Ancient China is steeped in myth and legend. While historical texts provide a chronology of the period before and during the Qin and Han dynasties, the material culture recovered from archaeological sites over the past fifty years offers a means to reconstruct the ritualised world of ancient China.

These remarkable objects, cast in bronze and gold, carved from jade or moulded in ceramic, attest to the power of art as spectacle. They showcase the remarkable ingenuity, or *qiao* 巧, of the makers, whose talents went beyond technical skill, demonstrating great craftsmanship and creativity at every stage of production.

The survival of much of this material is due to its association with sumptuous burials. Throughout this period, rulers would be accompanied into the afterlife by ceremonial bronzes and ceramics for ritual purposes, weapons and amulets for protection, ornaments for delight, as well as food and wine for nourishment. While the material and decorative qualities of these objects changed over time, as did the scale of production, they reveal a strand of cultural continuity that persisted over millennia.

BRONZE

The production of bronze represents a major watershed in the development of any civilisation, requiring a settled, highly organised and hierarchical community. Bronze metallurgy reached a highpoint in ancient China, with the objects, cast in ceramic moulds, demonstrating great artistic and technical achievement.

Bronze, an alloy of copper and tin, was an incredibly precious commodity in ancient China. Its use and distribution was almost entirely controlled by the ruling classes. Chinese leaders would hand out bronze in much the same way as a Western ruler might reward a loyal subject with gold.

From the beginning, bronzes were made to support the performance of the ritual and ceremony crucial to maintaining order and hierarchy in ancient Chinese society. Majestic bronzes played central roles in state rituals and ancestor worship, and were used to offer food and wine to ancestors and deities. Bronzes were replete with mana, as expressions of power and legitimacy for leaders, whose power was derived from their divine forebears.

Inscriptions on the bronzes can help identify their purpose, and range from celebrating a marriage or a military success, to pleading for a good harvest. They may also identify whom the bronze was made for, or the ancestor to whom it was dedicated.

Bronzes took pride of place in burial rituals, being prized objects that were buried with royalty and members of the upper classes. They were the ultimate manifestation of power, both in life and in death.

1. Bell (*Bo*) of Duke Wu of Qin
秦公镈（带挂钩）/ 秦公鏄（帶掛鉤）

Spring and Autumn period (771–475 BCE)
Bronze, 64.2 x 26.2cm
Excavated at Taigongmiao village, Chencangqu, Baoji, 1978
Baoji Bronze Museum, 02756/IA5.5

This is one of a set of ritual bells cast for Duke Wu of Qin, who reigned from 697 to 678 BCE. The bells are tangible evidence of the political ambition of the Qin rulers, which culminated in the achievements of the First Emperor. Each bears a 135-character inscription that documents the lineage of the Qin dukes and asserts their right to rule. The inscription begins: 'The Duke of Qin states: my foremost ancestor has received the heavenly mandate, was rewarded with a residence and received his state.' The bells could be played, providing the music of ceremony and ritual.

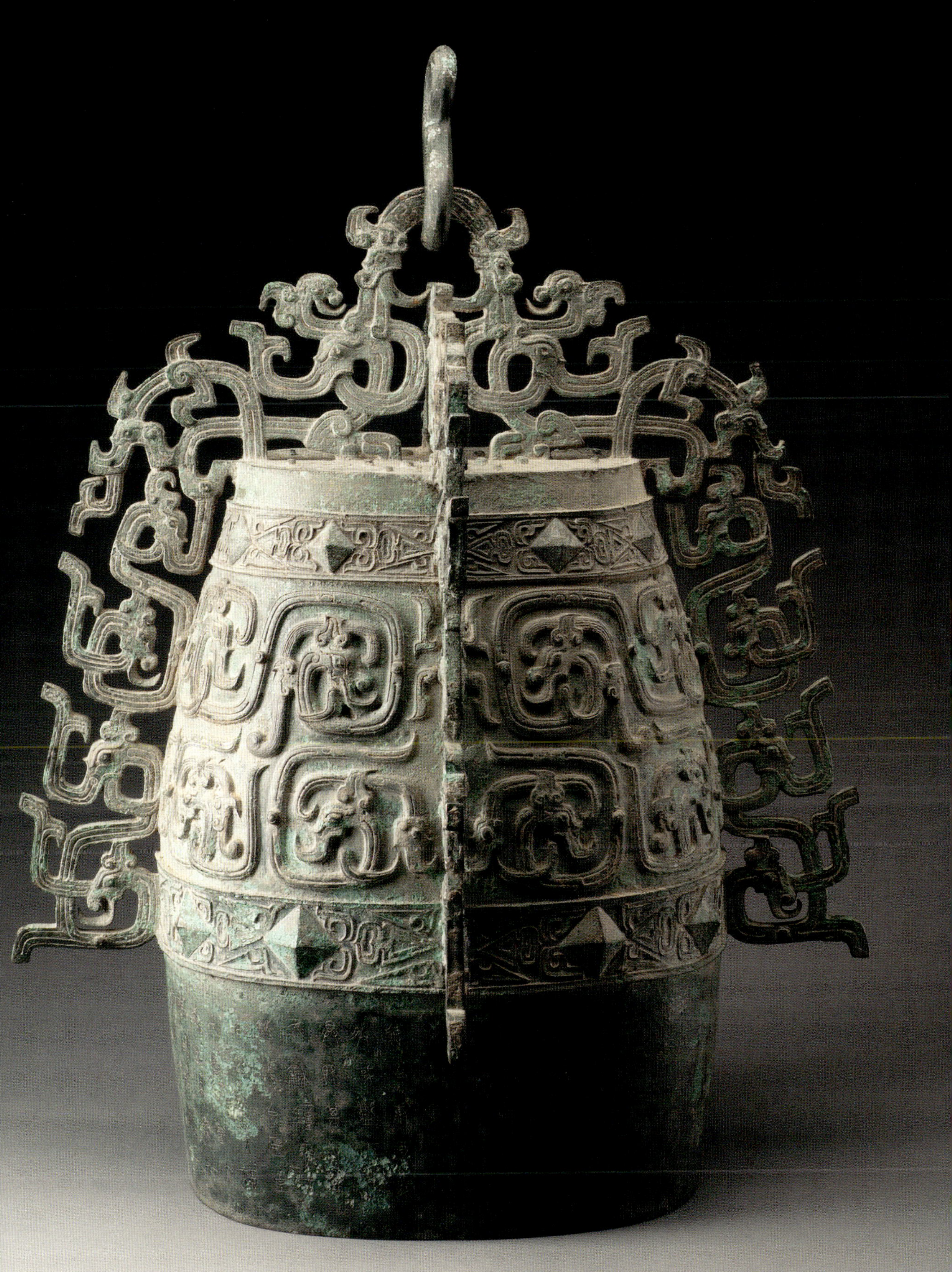

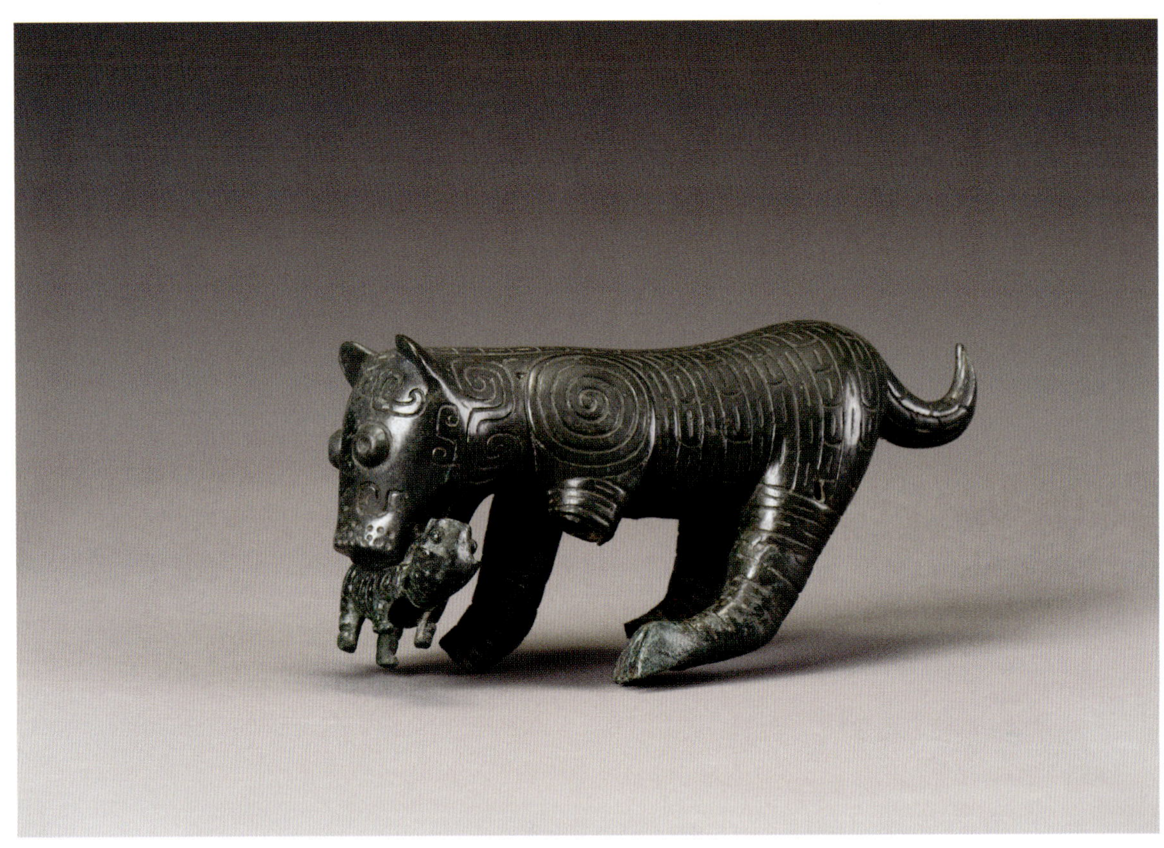

2. Tiger mother with cub in its mouth
衔子铜虎 / 銜子銅虎

Western Zhou dynasty (1046–771 BCE)
Bronze, 10 x 20cm
Excavated at Rujiazhuang, Baoji, 1988
Baoji Bronze Museum, 07648/IA11.584

The decorative features of Chinese bronzes are not incised into the surface afterwards, but are cast with the piece. The curvilinear patterns adorning this charming tiger, tenderly holding a cub in her mouth, are typical of Zhou-period bronzes.

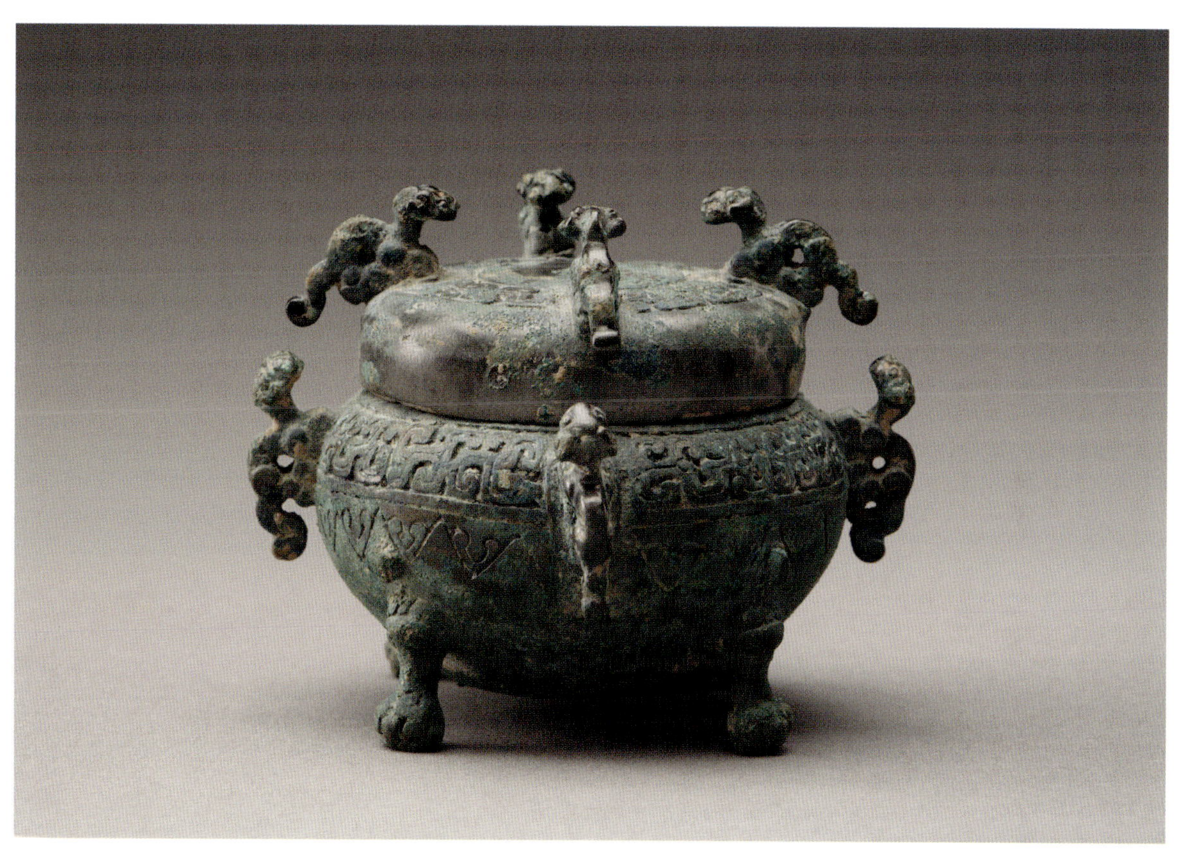

3. **Four-legged cauldron (*Ding*) decorated with eight beasts**
八兽带盖小鼎 / 八獸帶蓋小鼎

Spring and Autumn period (771–475 BCE)
Bronze, 5.7 x 4.5cm
Excavated at Shangguodian in Fengxiang, 2001
Fengxiang County Museum, 总1002

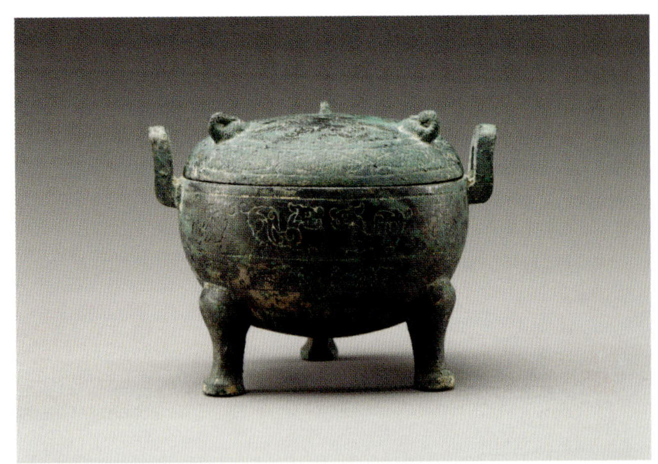

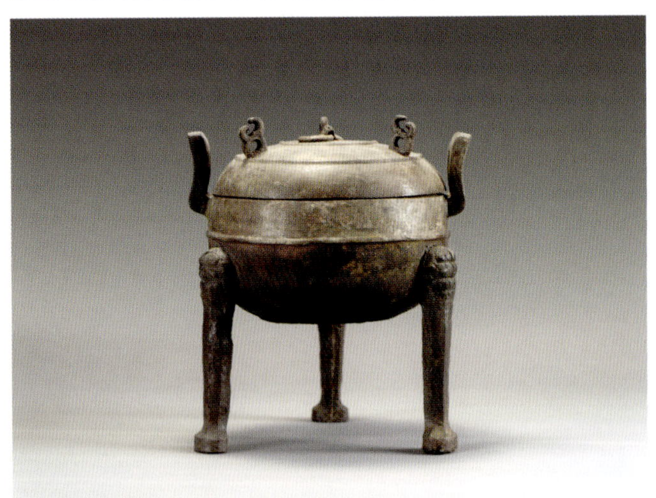

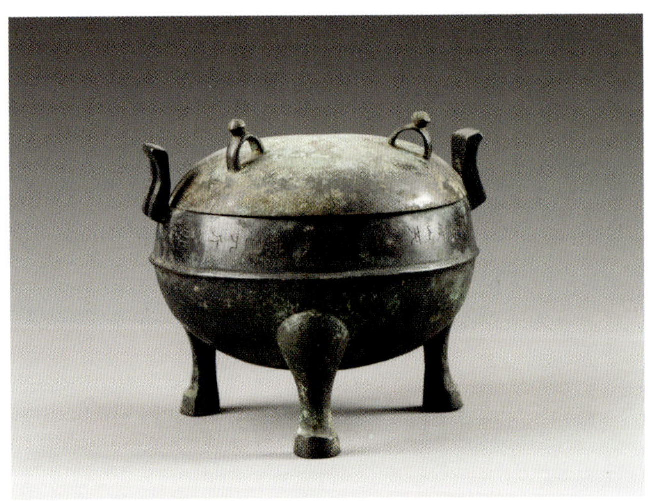

4. **Three-legged cauldron (*Ding*)**
三足带盖小鼎 / 三足帶蓋小鼎

Spring and Autumn period (771–475 BCE)
Bronze, 6.5 x 6cm
Collected in 2001
Fengxiang County Museum, 总1003

This small, refined vessel decorated with incised motifs of fish, birds and tigers differs from typical bronzes of the period. It was possibly made by a neighbouring state and acquired by the Qin as booty.

5. **Three-legged cauldron (*Ding*)**
带盖铜鼎 / 帶蓋銅鼎

Warring States period (475–221 BCE)
Bronze, 27 x 27.8cm
Excavated at Juanling, Shanyang, Shangluo, 1998
Shangluo City Museum, 总0710 D198

6. **Three-legged cauldron (*Ding*) with inscriptions**
成山铜鼎 / 成山銅鼎

Han dynasty (206 BCE–220 CE)
Bronze, 17 x 19.5cm
Collected in 1975
Fengxiang County Museum, 总0080

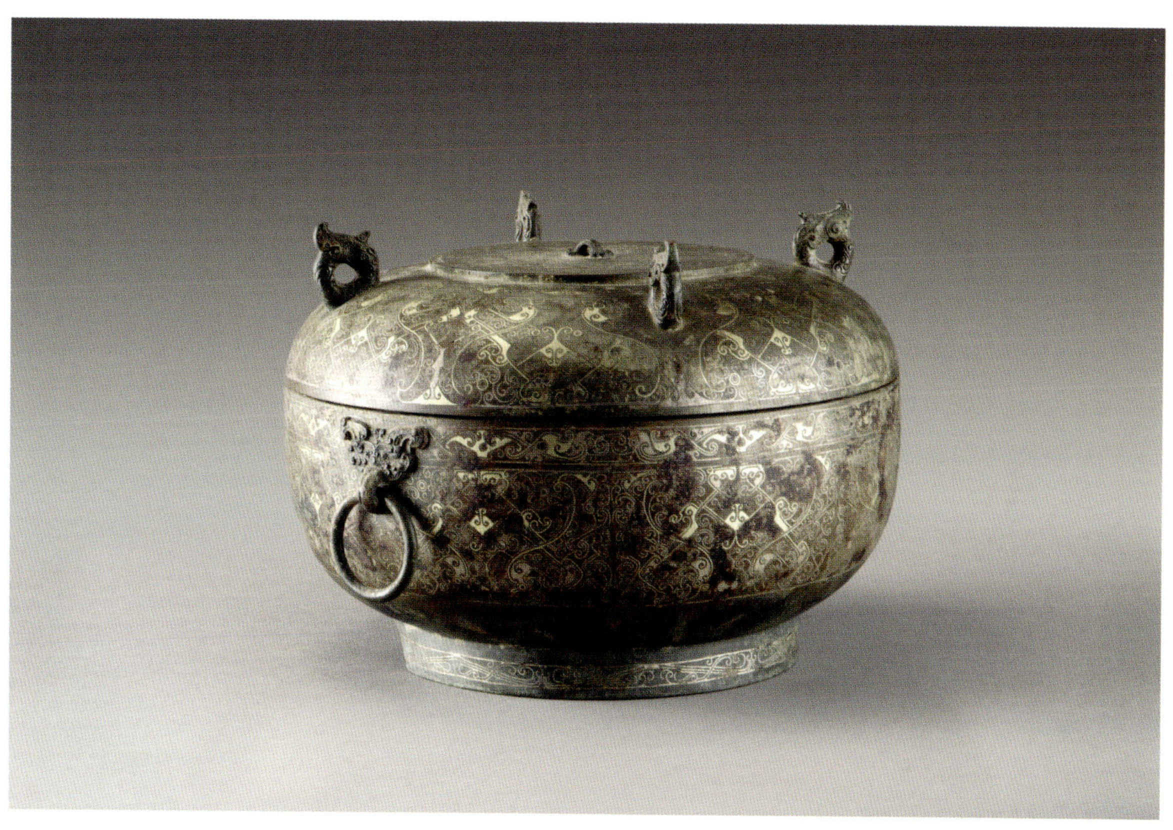

7. Tureen (*Gui*) with lid
错金银青铜簋 / 錯金銀青銅簋

Warring States period (475–221 BCE)
Bronze, inlaid with gold and silver, 15.5 x 19.2cm
Mizhi County Museum, 0001

During the Warring States period, the Bronze Age was coming to an end. Other materials, such as colourful lacquer-work, began to challenge the status of bronze. Craftsmen responded by creating ever-more luxurious bronze vessels, such as this tureen, inlaying them with decorative features in gold and silver.

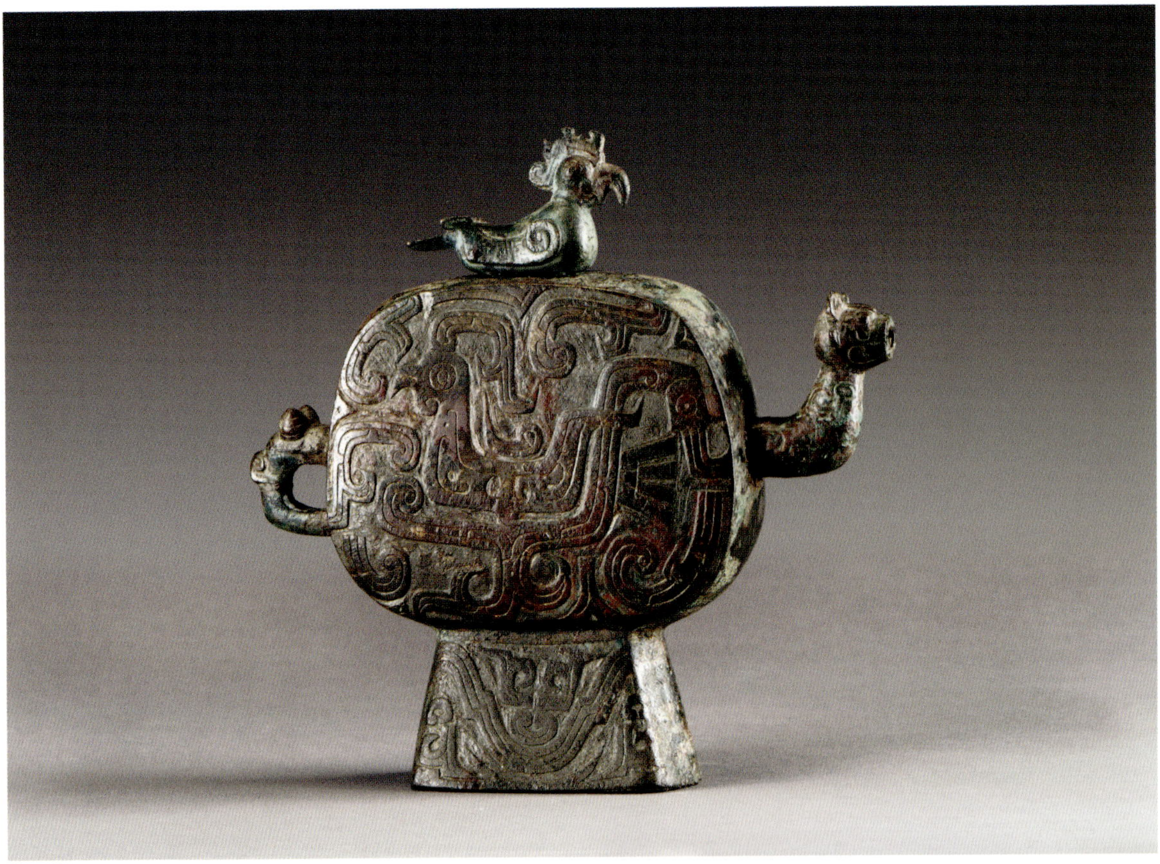

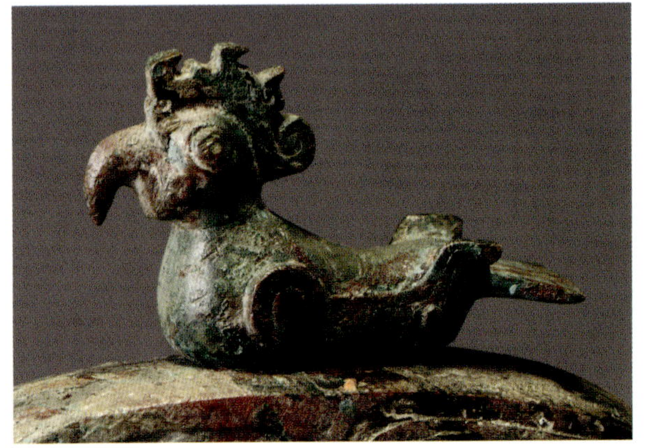

8. **Kettle (*He*) with phoenix and bird decorations**
凤鸟纹铜盉 / 鳳鳥紋銅盉

Spring and Autumn period (771–475 BCE)

Bronze, 20 x 21cm

Excavated at Bianjiazhuang, Longxian, Baoji, 1986

Longxian County Museum, 86LBM5:13 (10L3347)

A phoenix sits atop this kettle, which is also decorated with cast forms of the same mythical creature, symbolising just rule. Kettles were used together with flat basins for hand-washing in preparation for ritual or ceremonial feasts. The kettles were gradually replaced by washers over time.

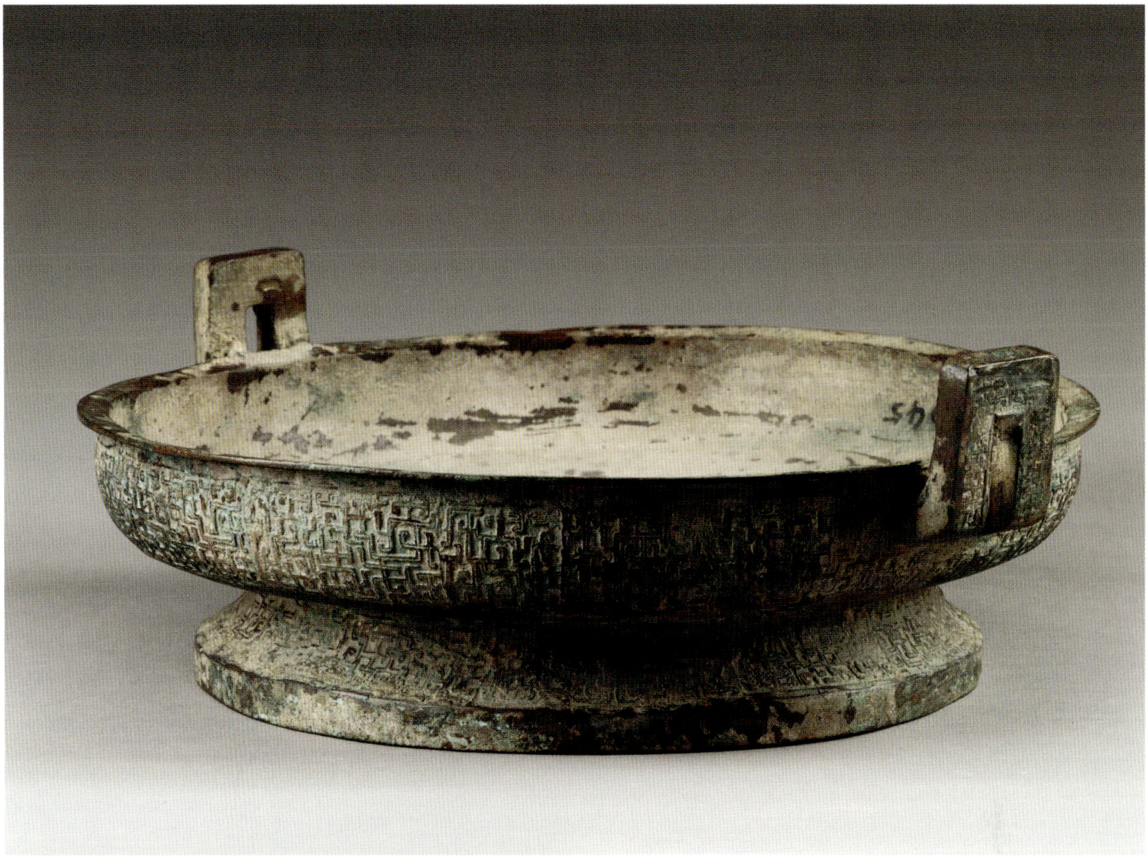

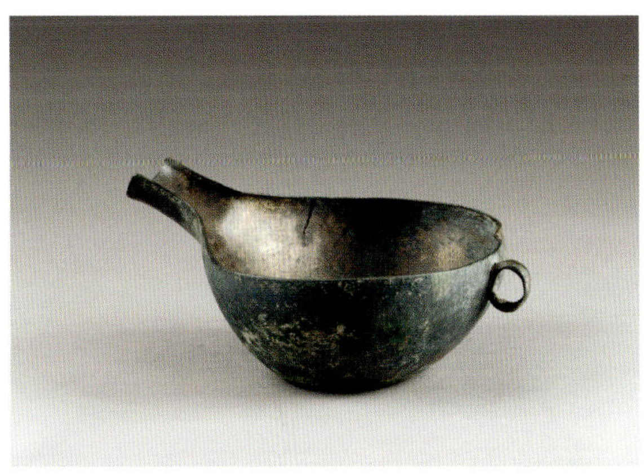

9. **Basin (*Pan*)**
双耳铜盘 / 雙耳銅盤

Spring and Autumn period (771–475 BCE)
Bronze, 12.8 x 36.5cm
Collected in 1973
Fengxiang County Museum, 总0030

10. **Washer (*Yi*)**
铜匜 / 銅匜

Warring States period (475–221 BCE)
Bronze, diameter 18cm
Excavated at Gaowangsi village, Fengxiang, Baoji, 1977
Fengxiang County Museum, 总0321

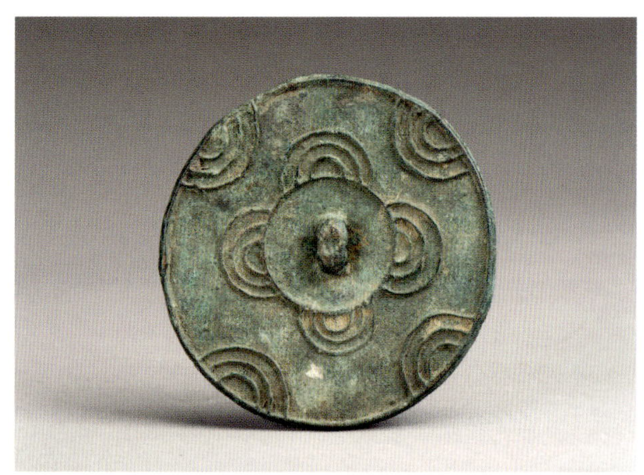

11. **Mirror**
同心弧铜镜 / 同心弧銅鏡

Warring States period (475–221 BCE)
Bronze, diameter 8.4cm
Collected at Shenmu, Yulin, 1989
Yulin Institute of Cultural Heritage Conservation, 0103

Bronze mirrors were often placed in tombs, as it was believed that their reflective surfaces could dispel evil. While the front surfaces were highly polished, the backs were decorated with cast patterns; in this case, a symmetrical arrangement of circular lines.

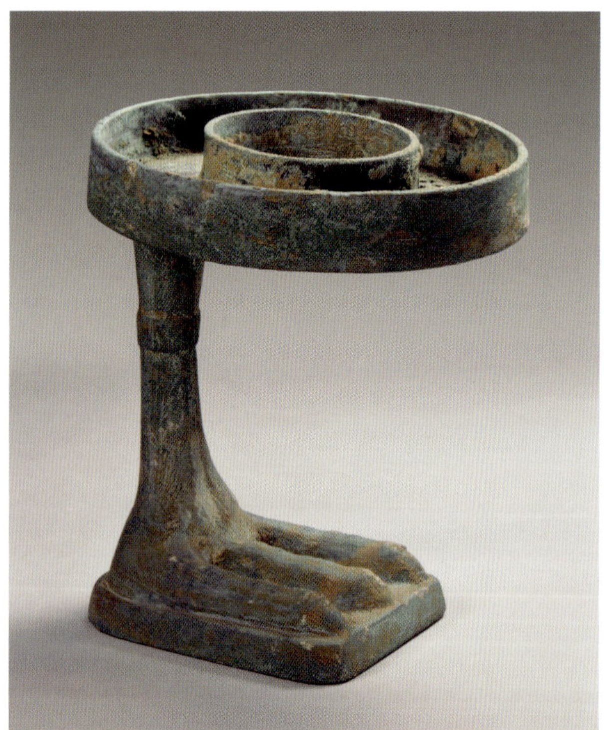

12. **Goose-foot lamp**
雁足形铜灯 / 雁足形銅燈

Warring States period (475–221 BCE)
Bronze, 13.5 x 11.7cm
Excavated at the Beijiao Economic and Technological Development Zone, Xi'an, 1995
Shaanxi Provincial Institute of Archaeology, 001050

Lamps such as these continued to be popular during the Qin and Han dynasties. A circular tray, which would have contained lighting oil or held candlesticks, sits atop a modelled leg and foot of a goose. The leg is delicately decorated with feathery patterns.

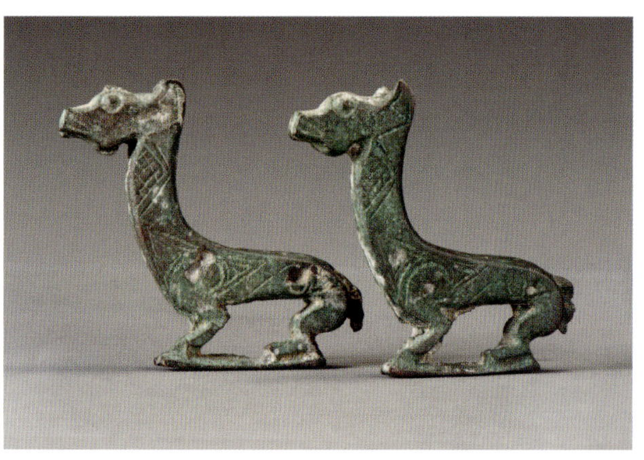

13. **Two bronze deer**
铜鹿饰件 / 銅鹿飾件

Warring States period (475–221 BCE)
Bronze, 9.5 x 11cm
Excavated at Jinggou village, Ansai, Yan'an, 1983
Donated by Zhou Faqing
Yan'an City Cultural Relics Research Institute, 214-2; 214-3

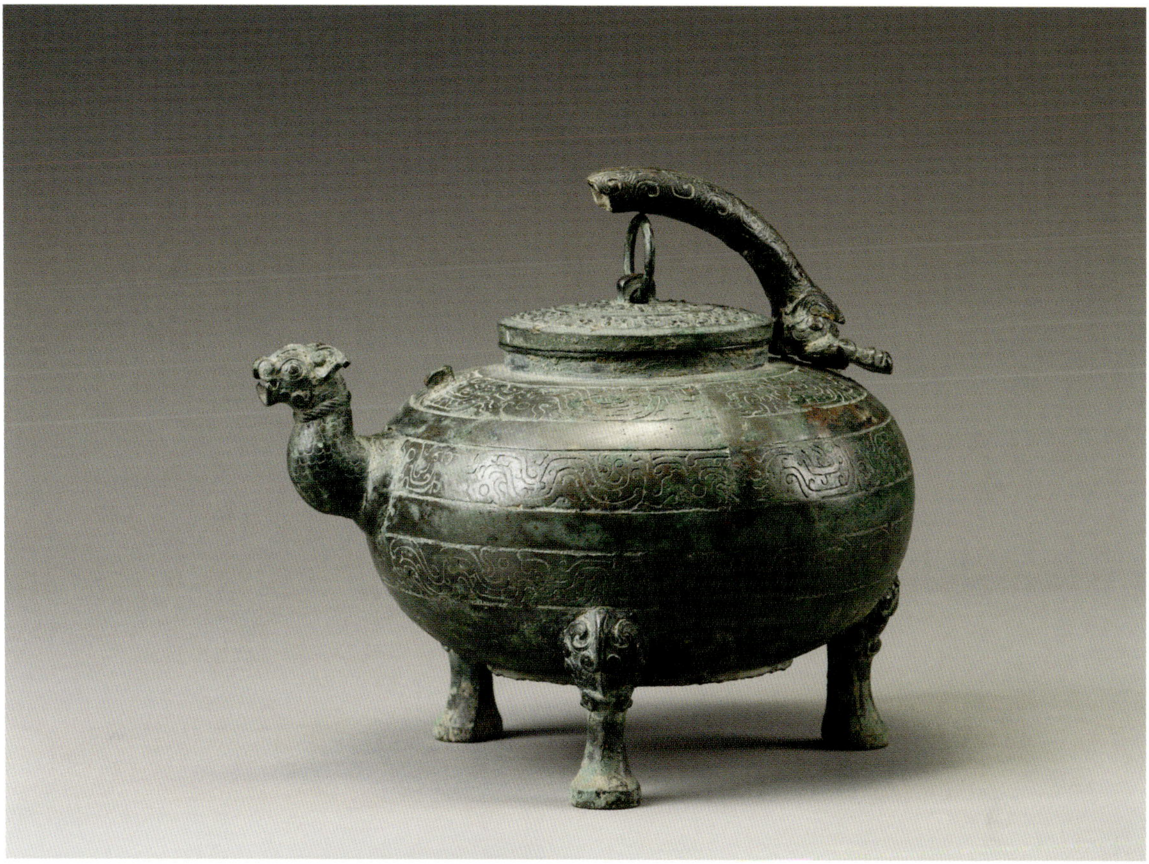

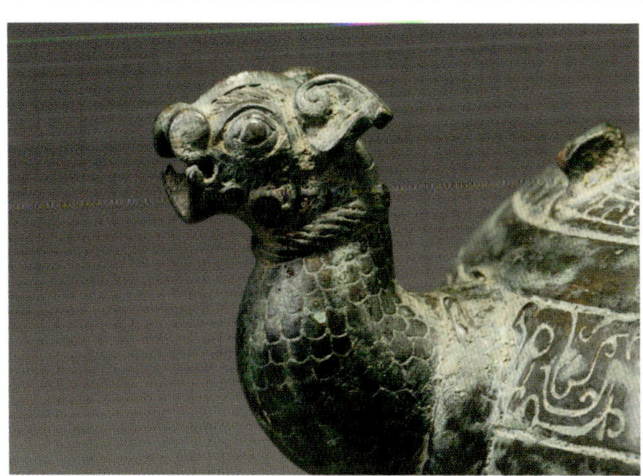

14. Kettle (*He*)

盉

Warring States period (475–221 BCE)

Bronze, 17 x 19cm

Excavated at Gaowangsi village, Chengguanzhen, Baoji, 1979

Fengxiang County Museum, 总0323

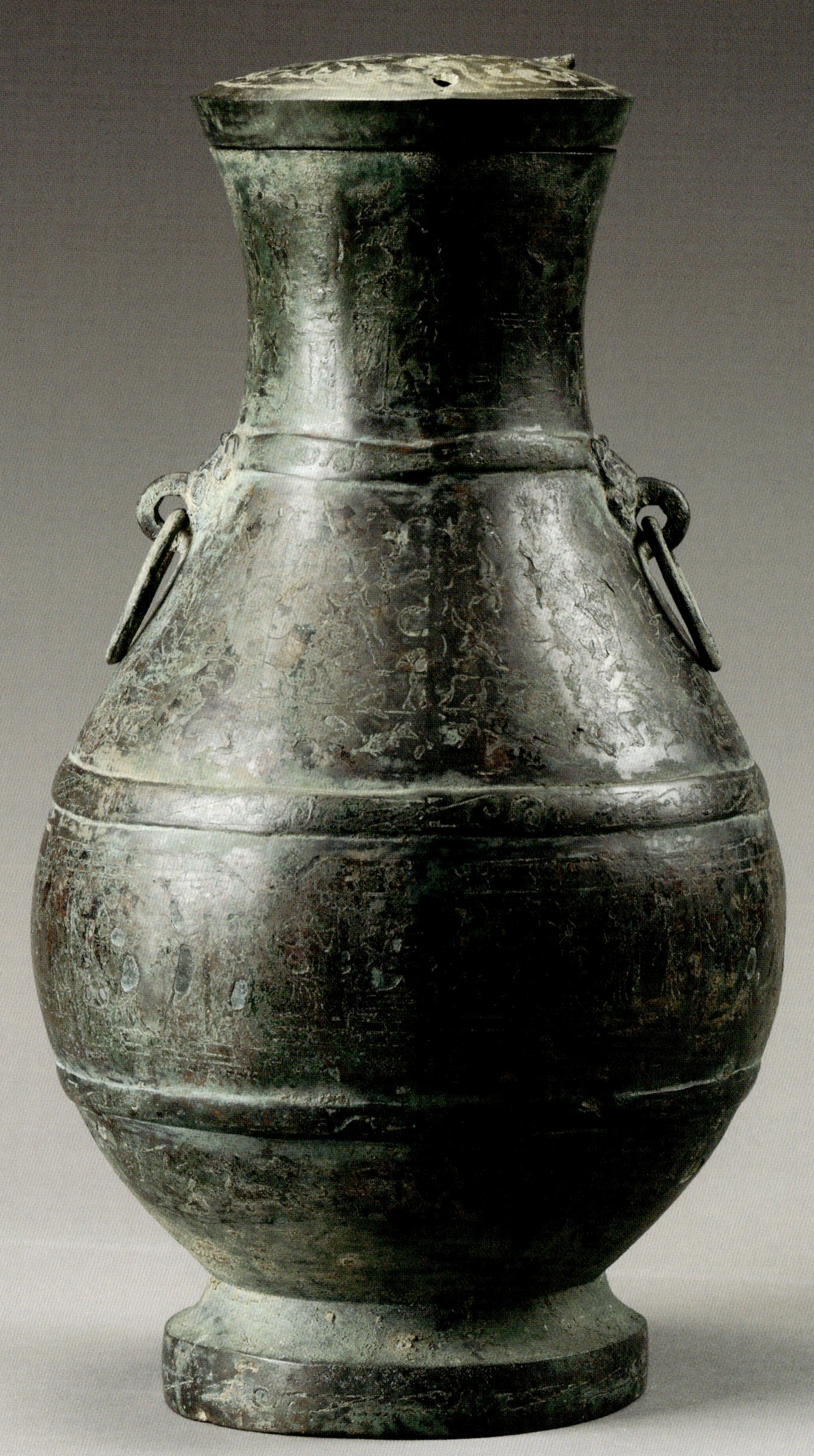

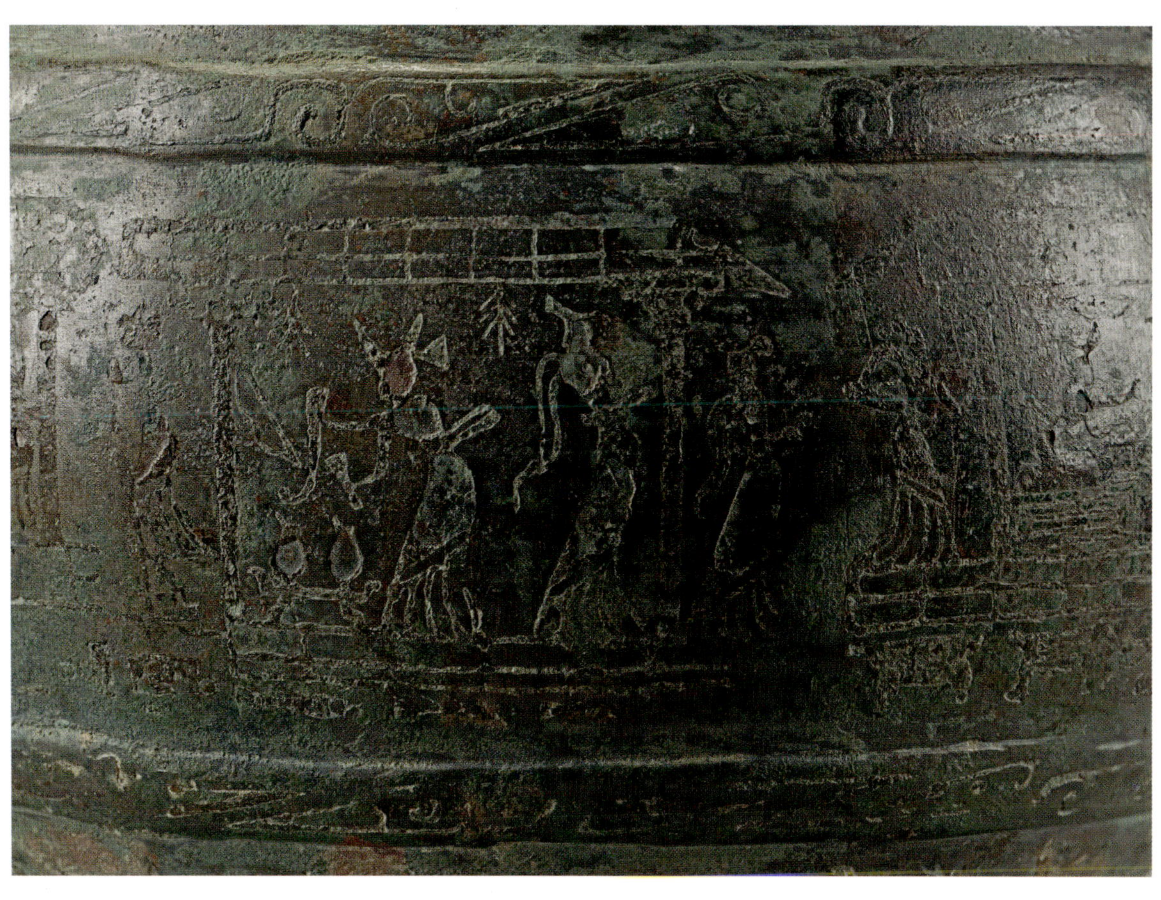

15. **Flask (*Hu*)**
狩猎纹铜壶 / 狩獵紋銅壺

Warring States period (475–221 BCE)

Bronze, 40 x 12.3cm

Excavated at Gaowangsi village, Fengxiang, Baoji, 1977

Fengxiang County Museum, 总0319

This flask is unusual, in that it is decorated with four figurative scenes showing the life of the aristocracy. Three of the scenes depict animals and hunters, armed with bows and arrows, while the detail shown above features people carrying out ritual offerings.

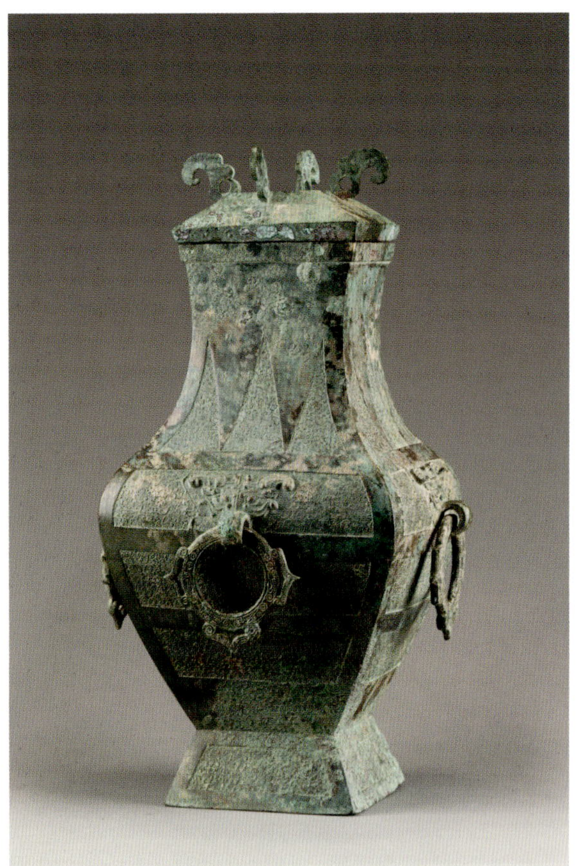

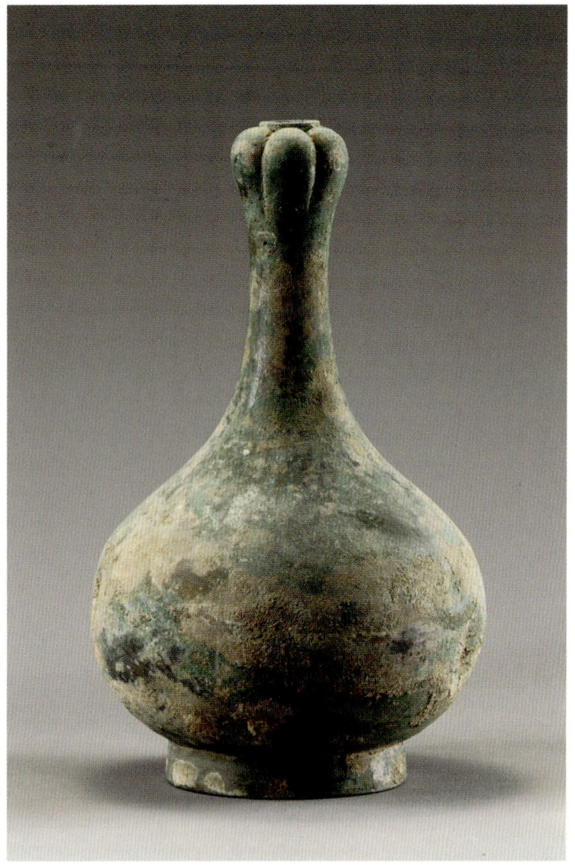

16. Rectangular flask (*Fanghu*)
四铺首衔环带盖方壶 / 四鋪首銜環帶蓋方壺

Han dynasty (206 BCE–220 CE)
Bronze, 45.8 x 23cm
Collected at Dabaiyang, Xi'an, 1972
Xi'an Museum, 3gtA131

17. Flask (*Hu*)
铜蒜头壶 / 銅蒜頭壺

Han dynasty (206 BCE–220 CE)
Bronze, height 34cm
Collected in 1981
Fengxiang County Museum, 总0558

This elegant flask appeals to a contemporary eye with its simplicity of form and garlic-shaped lip. Its lack of decoration is, however, evidence of the decline of dominance of bronze by the time of the Han dynasty.

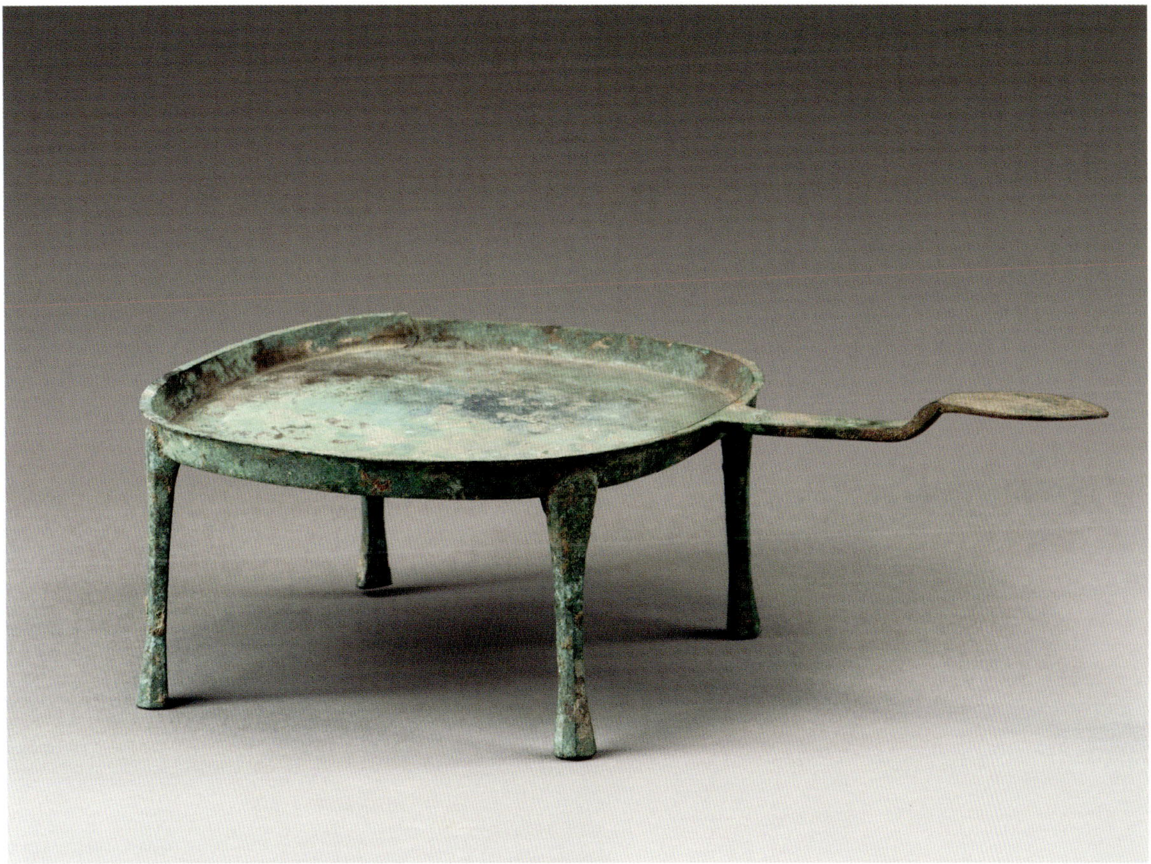

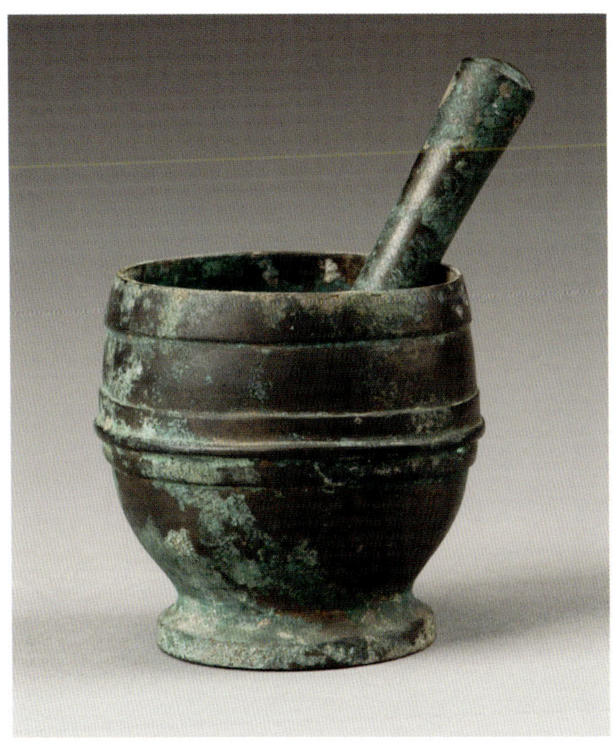

18. Hand-warmer supporter
温手炉承盘 / 溫手爐承盤

Western Han dynasty (206 BCE–9 CE)

Bronze, 2.4 x 29.8cm

Excavated from Accompanying Burial Pit 1, Accompanying Grave 1, Maoling, Xianyang, 1981

Maoling Museum, 2412

This bronze tray would once have supported a small brazier-like vessel, which when lit could be used as a hand-warmer.

19. Mortar and pestle
臼杵

Western Han dynasty (206 BCE–9 CE)

Bronze, 6.2 x 5.7cm

Excavated from Accompanying Burial Pit 1, Accompanying Grave 1, Maoling, Xianyang, 1981

Maoling Museum, 2414

CERAMICS

The Qin and Han dynasties inherited a tradition in which tombs were built as eternal dwellings. However, attitudes towards the afterlife had shifted. During the Shang and Zhou dynasties, the inclusion of bronze vessels and bells had enabled the tomb occupant to carry out ritual practices and provide food and drink for their ancestors. By the time of the Qin and Han dynasties, tombs were created as microcosms of the universe. Ancestors remained important, but were joined by many local spirits, as well as star deities and immortals, alongside whom the tomb occupant asserted their position.

While bronze was the favoured medium of the Zhou dynasty, lacquers and ceramics were increasingly used by the time of the Qin and Han dynasties. Funerary ceramics tended to imitate ritual bronzes, and were painted, lacquered or incised with designs to do so. Vessels and containers filled with food and drink provided sustenance for the dead in the afterlife.

By the Han dynasty, a wider selection of ceramic surrogates of new types and functions was produced, reflecting new ideas about ancestors and the afterlife.

20. Flask (*Hu*)
彩绘双耳陶壶 / 彩繪雙耳陶壺

Spring and Autumn period (771–475 BCE)
Painted pottery, 32 x 8.6cm
Excavated at Bianjiazhuang, Dongnanzhen, Longxian, Baoji, 1987
Longxian County Museum, 86LBM32:4 (10L3219)

The striking geometric patterns on this painted ceramic flask closely emulate the cast patterns on Zhou-period bronzes. The unusual shape of this vessel imitates a bronze design from the Spring and Autumn period. Its two 'ears' are in the shape of a monster's ears, from which two rings are suspended.

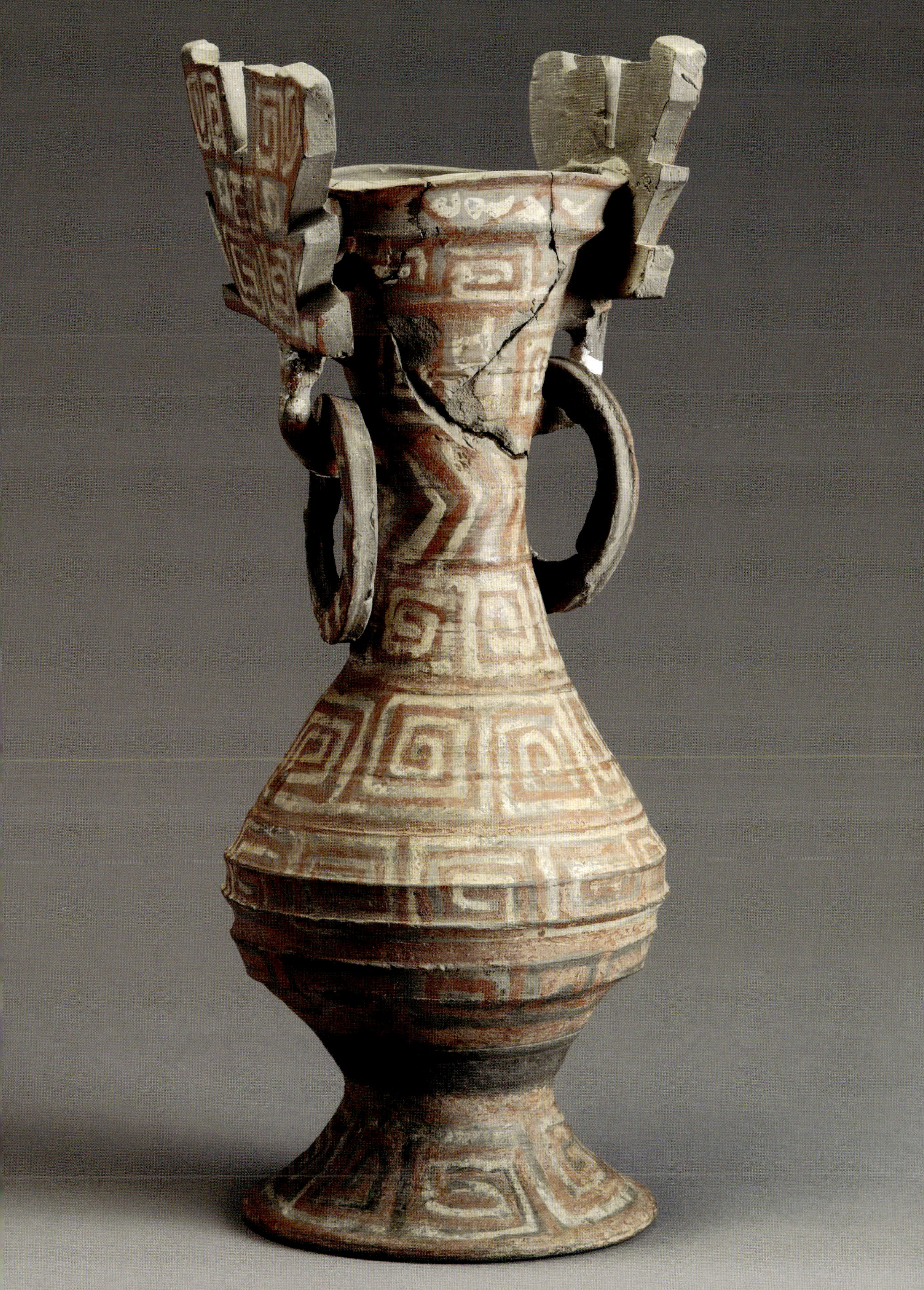

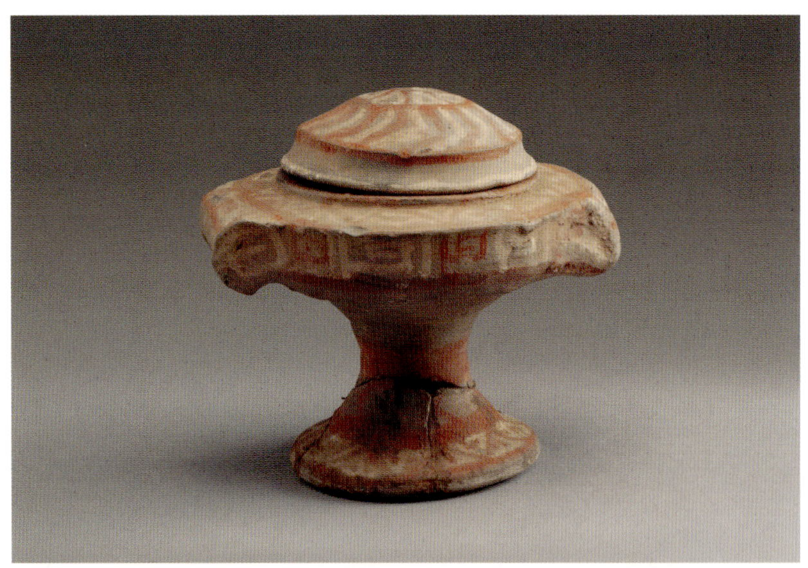

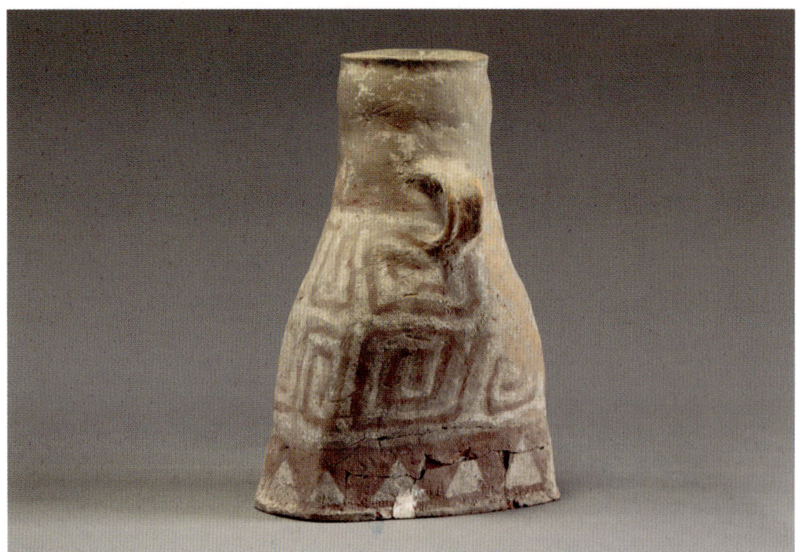

21. Bowl with stem (*Dou*) with cover
彩绘陶豆 / 彩繪陶豆

Spring and Autumn period (771–475 BCE)

Painted pottery, 11.8 x 8.4cm

Excavated at Bianjiazhuang, Dongnanzhen, Longxian, Baoji, 1986

Longxian County Museum, 86LBM32:9 (10L3224)

22. Flask (*Hu*)
彩绘陶壶 / 彩繪陶壺

Spring and Autumn period (771–475 BCE)

Painted pottery, 26.7 x 9cm

Excavated at Dianzi village, Chengguanzhen, Longxian, Baoji, 1992

Longxian County Museum, 09L2523

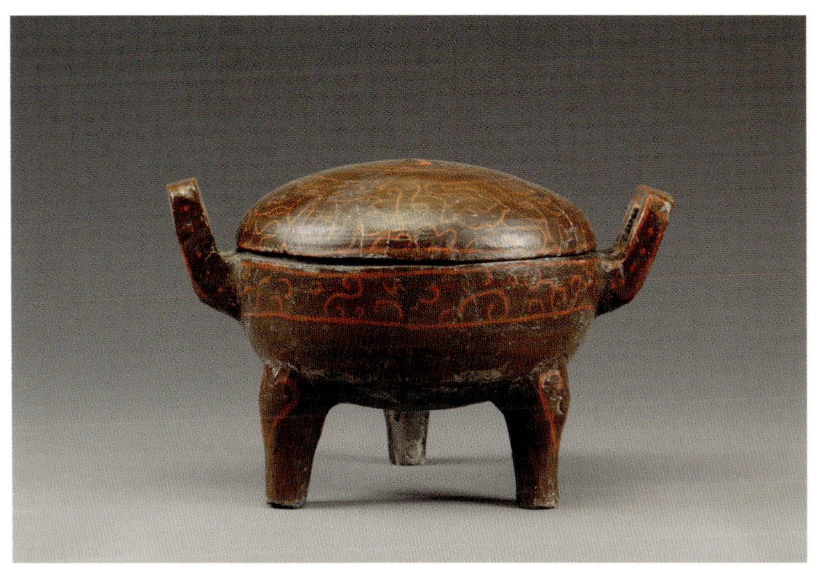

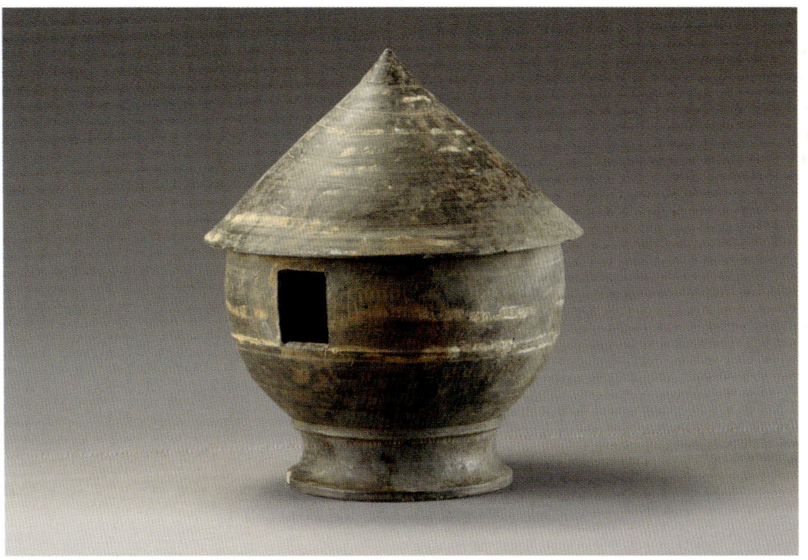

24. Miniature granary
彩绘陶仓 / 彩繪陶倉

Warring States period (475–221 BCE)

Pottery, 23 x 12.5cm

Excavated at Dianzi village, Chengguanzhen, Longxian, Baoji, 1991

Longxian County Museum, 陇店*M252:1*

Granaries, a food-storage facility, were some of the earliest pottery architectural models produced for burial rituals. In the real world, granaries represented strength, security and survival, and it is likely that they were intended to fulfil the same function in the afterlife.

23. Three-legged cauldron (*Ding*)
陶胎漆鼎

Warring States period (475–221 BCE)

Lacquered pottery, 17.4 x 17.5cm

Excavated at Xisijiyuan village, Luonan, Shangluo, 2000

Shangluo City Museum, 总*0701 C355*

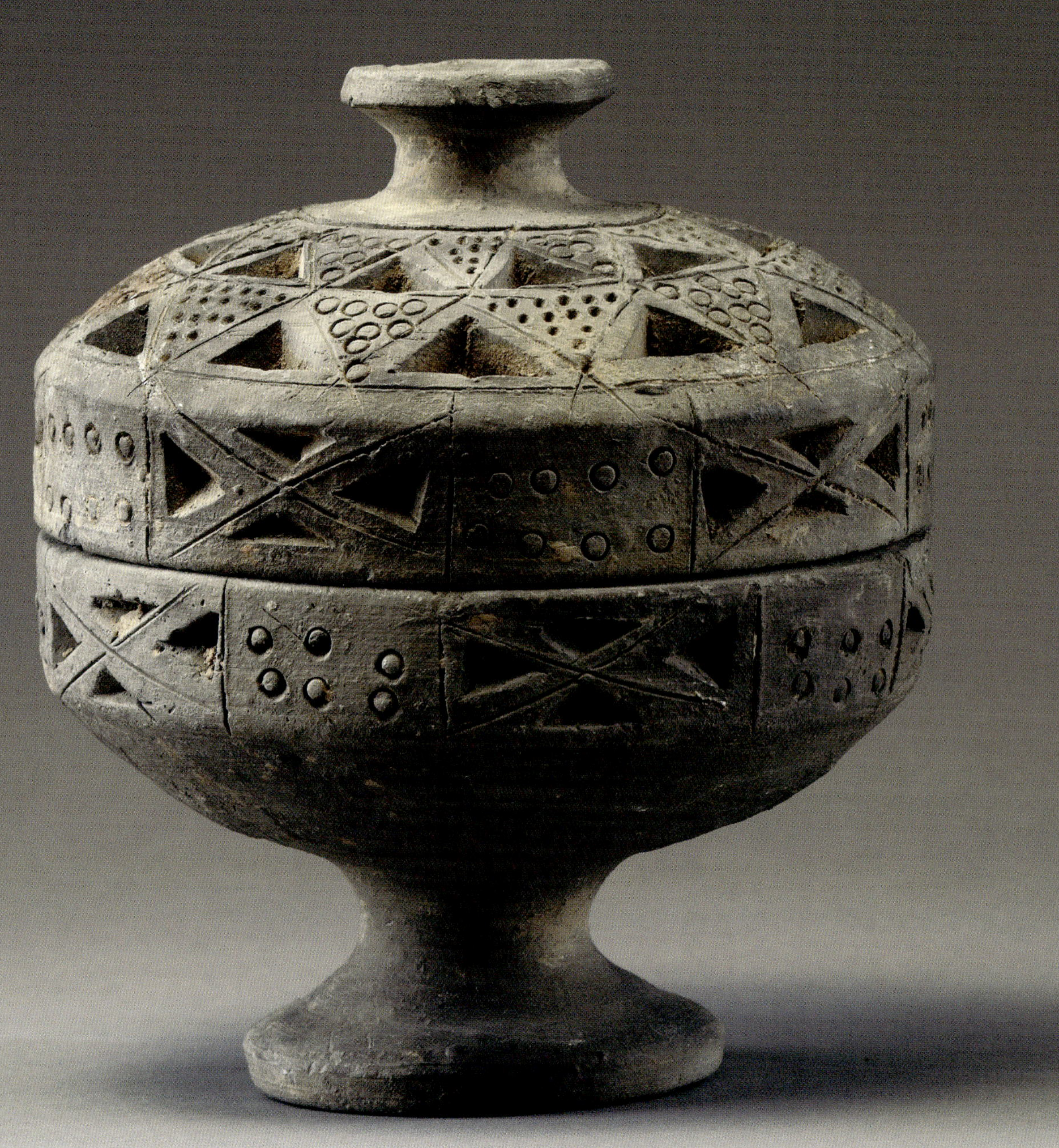

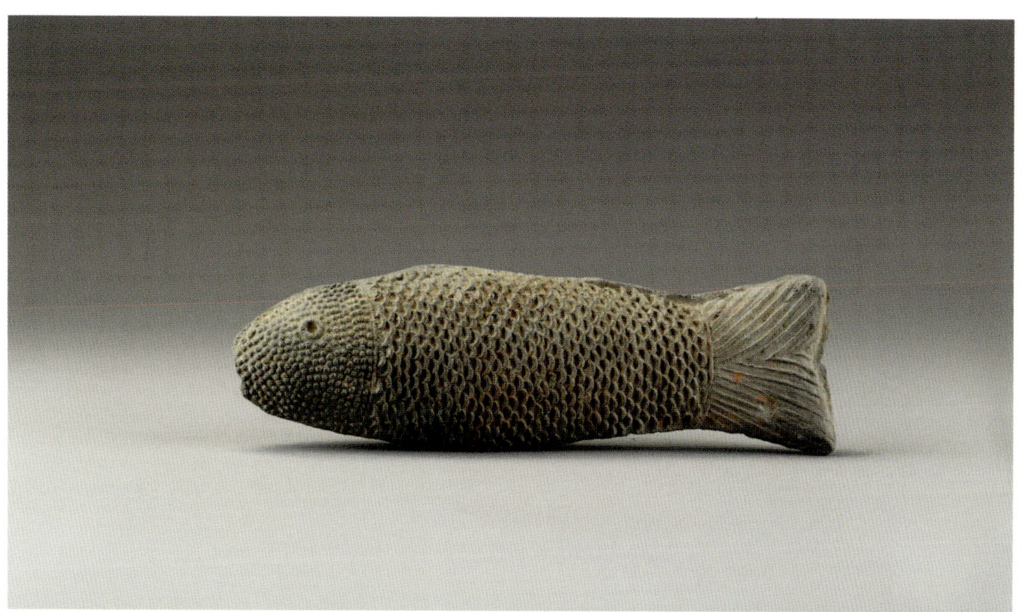

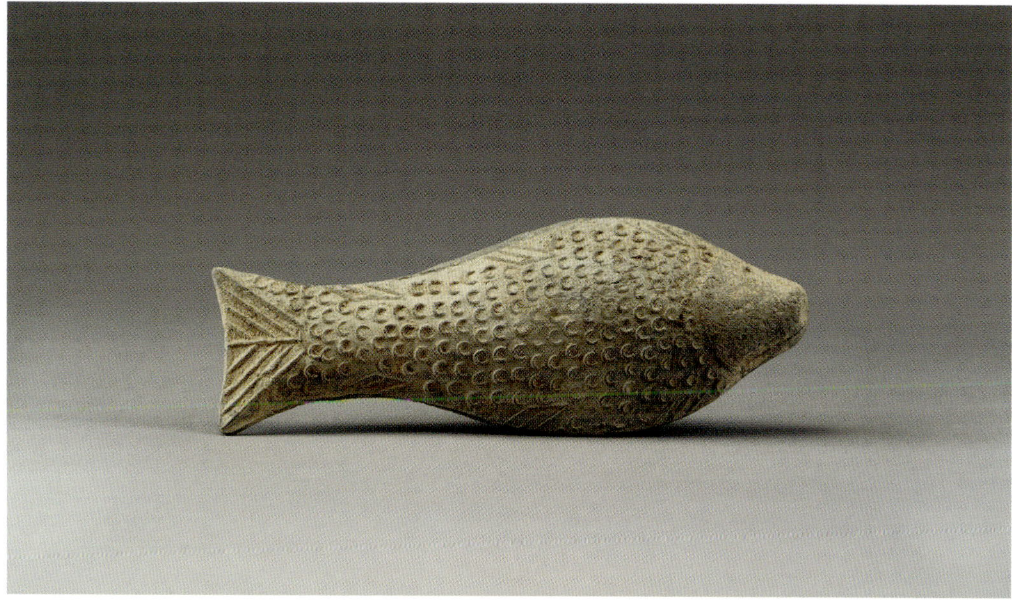

26. Pottery fish
陶鱼 / 陶魚

Qin dynasty (221–206 BCE)
Pottery, lengths 17cm; 18.5cm
Collected in 2013
Xi'an Museum, LK1258; LK1271

These pottery fish were made by joining together two halves that had been pressed into moulds. They may have held a stone within, causing them to rattle when shaken, and may have been intended as toys for children.

25. Censer
灰陶熏炉 / 灰陶薰爐

Qin dynasty (221–206 BCE)
Pottery, 15.2 x 13.6cm
Collected in 2011
Xi'an Museum, QM948

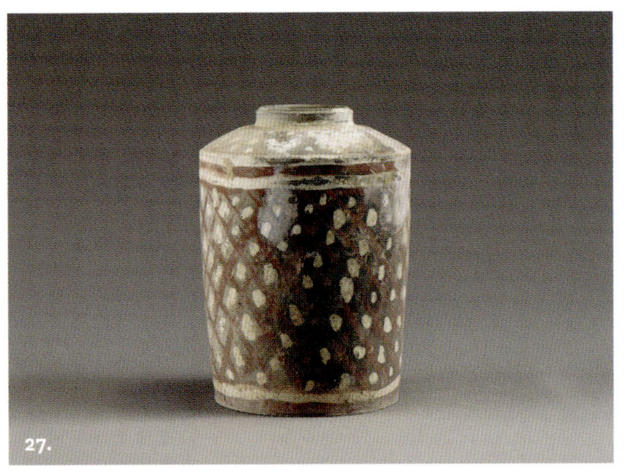
27.

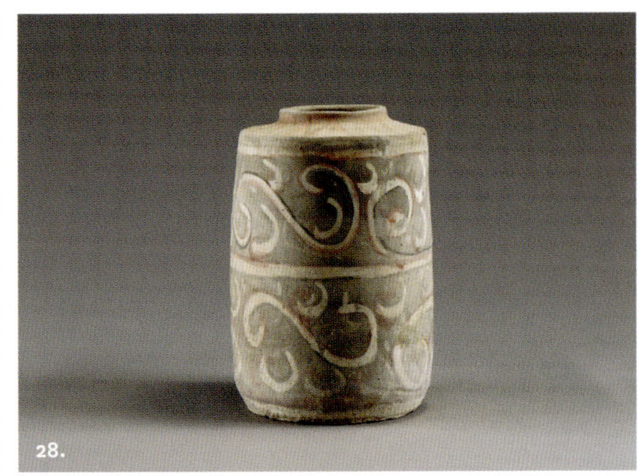
28.

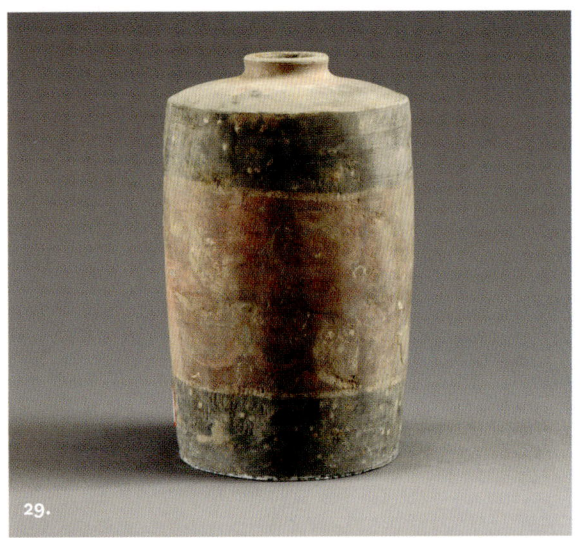
29.

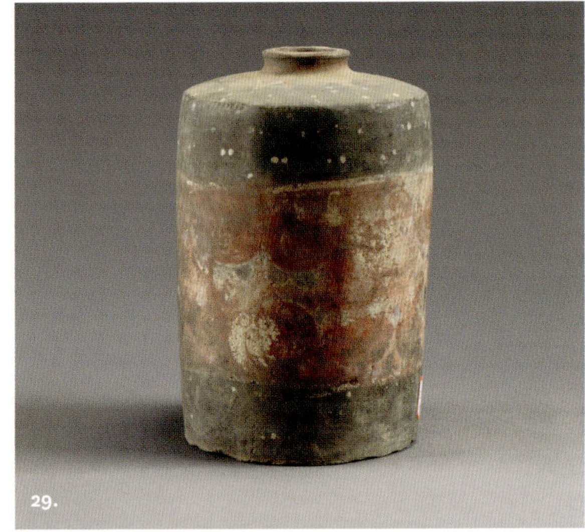
29.

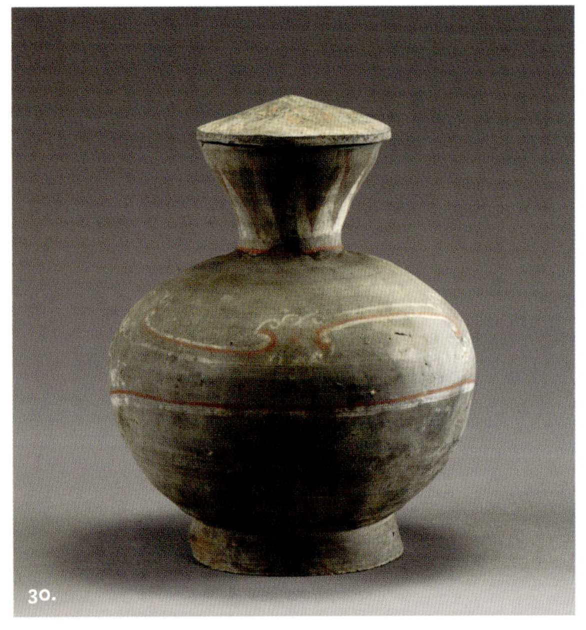
30.

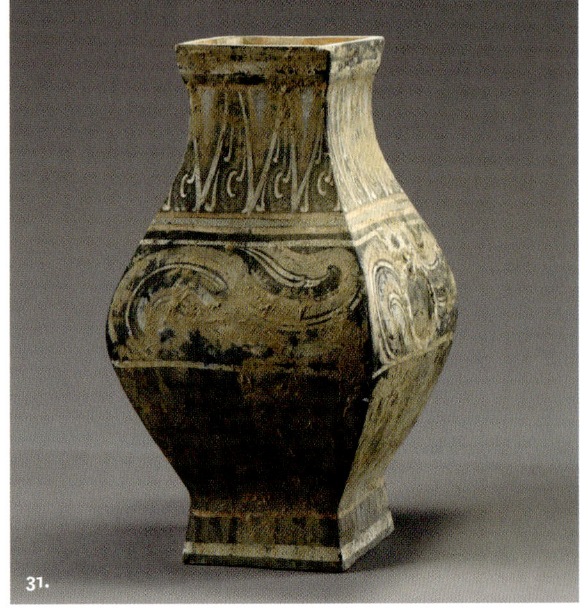
31.

The supply, storage and distribution of grain were crucial to ancient Chinese society. Taxes were paid in grain, and adequate supplies were required both to support sedentary agrarian communities and to maintain military forces. To equip the deceased for the afterlife, pottery vessels filled with grain were buried in the tomb.

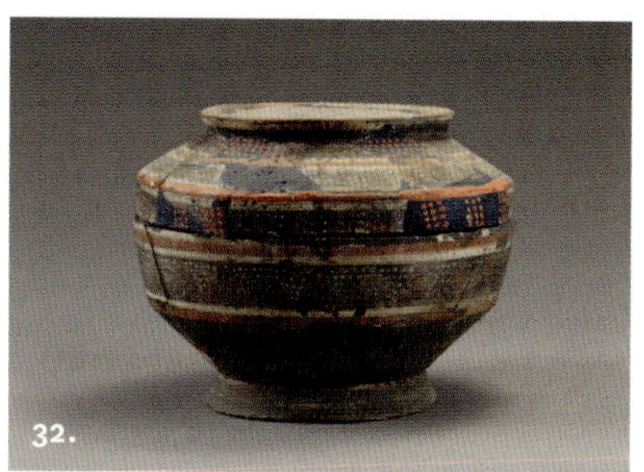
32.

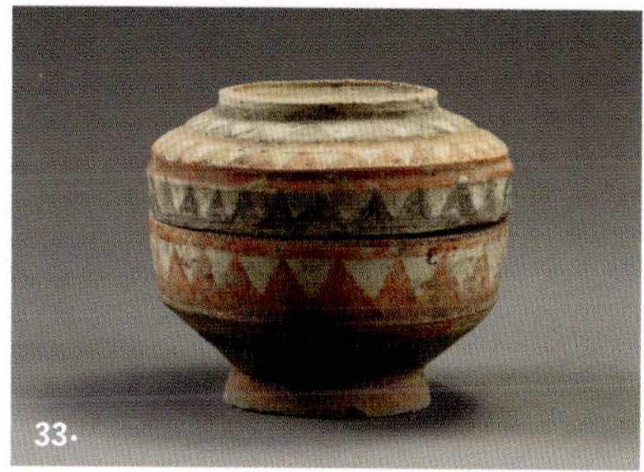
33.

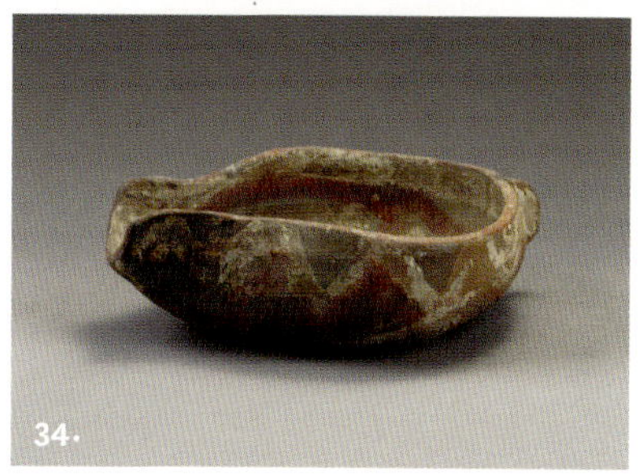
34.

27. Tubular flask for storing grain
彩绘陶仓 / 彩繪陶倉

Han dynasty (206 BCE–220 CE)
Painted pottery, 22.7 x 17.5cm
Excavated at Anjiagou village, Qiaozhenxiang, Ganquan, Yan'an, 2005
Ganquan County Museum, GQ770

28. Tubular flask for storing grain
红白彩绘陶仓 / 紅白彩繪陶倉

Han dynasty (206 BCE–220 CE)
Painted pottery, 25 x 16cm
Collected in 2013
Ganquan County Museum, GQ1456

29. Pair of tubular flasks for storing grain
彩绘陶仓 / 彩繪陶倉

Han dynasty (206 BCE–220 CE)
Painted pottery, 19 x 12.5cm
Collected in 2013
Ganquan County Museum, GQ1758; GQ1759

30. Pottery vessel (*Hu*)
彩绘陶壶 / 彩繪陶壺

Han dynasty (206 BCE–220 CE)
Painted pottery, 23 x 19.5cm
Collected in 1991
Ganquan County Museum, GQ303

31. Pottery vessel (*Fang*)
彩绘陶钫 / 彩繪陶鈁

Han dynasty (206 BCE–220 CE)
Painted pottery, 36 x 25cm
Collected in 2013
Ganquan County Museum, GQ1582

32. Pottery bowl (*He*) with cover
彩绘陶盒 / 彩繪陶盒

Han dynasty (206 BCE–220 CE)
Painted pottery, 16.5 x 21cm
Collected in 2013
Ganquan County Museum, GQ1773

33. Pottery bowl (*He*) with cover
彩绘陶盒 / 彩繪陶盒

Han dynasty (206 BCE–220 CE)
Painted pottery, 17 x 21cm
Collected in 2013
Ganquan County Museum, GQ1515

34. Pottery washer (*Yi*)
彩绘陶匜 / 彩繪陶匜

Han dynasty (206 BCE–220 CE)
Painted pottery, 4 x 12cm
Collected in 2013
Ganquan County Museum, GQ1645

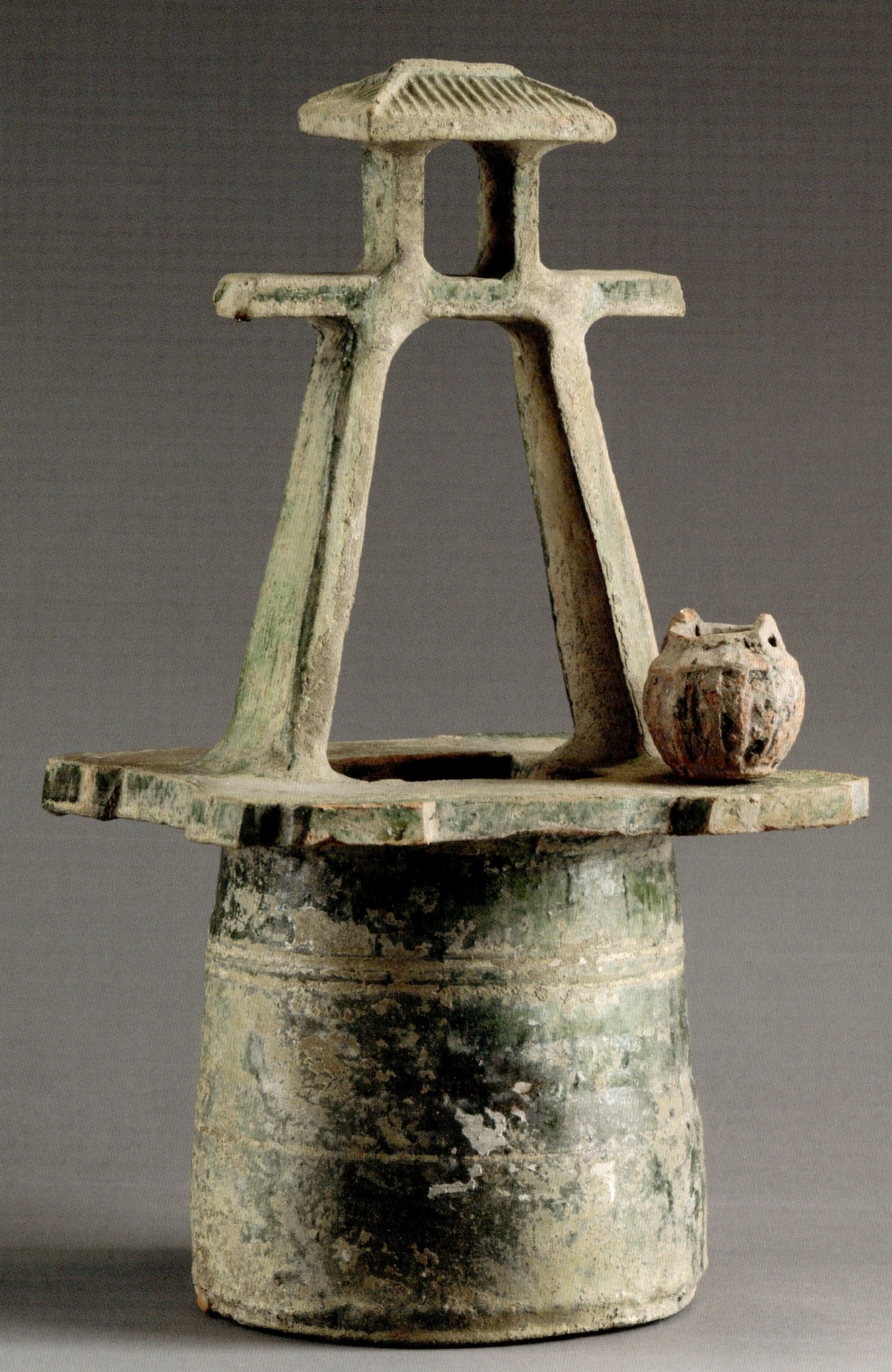

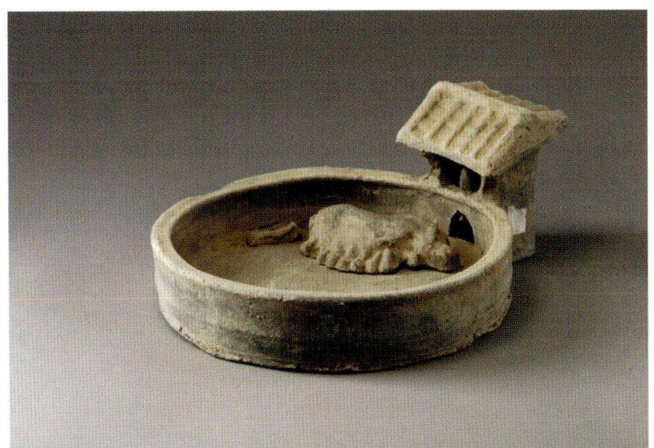

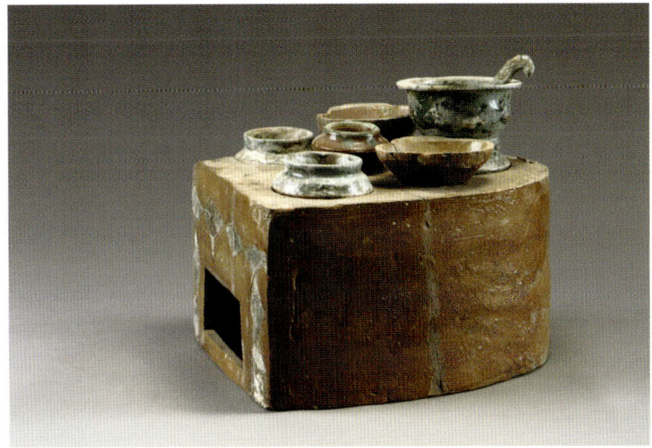

35. Glazed pottery well
绿釉陶井 / 綠釉陶井

Han dynasty (206 BCE–220 CE)
Glazed pottery, 40 x 22cm
Collected in 1966
Xi'an Museum, 3gwC115

36. Glazed pottery pigsty
灰陶猪圈 / 灰陶豬圈

Eastern Han dynasty (25–220 CE)
Glazed pottery, 10.5 x 23.3cm
Collected in 2007
Xi'an Museum, 3gwC237

Architectural models became a feature of Han dynasty funerary practice. These *mingqi* 冥/明器 (spirit objects) replicated and were intended to stand in for the real thing in the afterlife. Here, a well and a pigsty emulate in miniature two vital structures of village life, providing the deceased with water and sustenance.

37. Glazed pottery miniature stove
黄釉陶灶 / 黃釉陶竈

Han dynasty (206 BCE–220 CE)
Glazed pottery, 22 x 24cm
Collected in 2013
Ganquan County Museum, GQ1500

Mingqi worked with other tomb objects and architecture to support larger funerary ambitions, with the ultimate goal of providing sustenance for the deceased. This glazed stove enabled the ongoing preparation of food in the afterlife. As their earthly counterparts have often not survived, *mingqi* offer invaluable records of Han dynasty life.

JADE

Throughout China's history, jade has been highly esteemed. Its material qualities – hardness and durability, as well as its subtle intensity and colour – were aligned with symbolic qualities of purity, strength, nobility and integrity.

Jade was worked at least 7000 years ago. It is an extremely hard material, and cannot be carved, but must be abraded with tools. The introduction of iron tools, in around 650 BCE, enabled craftsmen to create increasingly intricate decorative styles. Consequently, the most accomplished jade, both aesthetically and technically, was produced during the Warring States period.

From the Zhou through the Han dynasties, tombs of high-ranking nobles have been found to contain copious amounts of jade, often covering the body from the neck to the knees, or, in the case of the Han dynasty, completely encasing the body in jade suits. This practice was driven by a belief in the ability of jade to both symbolically and physically protect the body from decay.

The Chinese teacher, and sometimes minister and thinker, Confucius (551–479 BCE) extolled the virtues of jade, especially as it related to the qualities of an ideal *junzi* 君子 (gentleman). For example, Confucius likened the warmth of jade to a gentleman's humanity; its durability to his wisdom; its internal radiance to his trustworthiness; and as symbols of rank and authority, to his virtue.

38. Jade and agate pendant
组玉佩 / 組玉佩

Western Zhou dynasty (1046–771 BCE)
Jade and agate, 56 x 30cm
Excavated at Qiangjia village, Fufeng, 1981
Zhouyuan Museum, Baoji City, 1587-1618

Elaborate pendant sets such as this, made from jade ornaments strung together with agate beads, were worn hung from the waist or shoulders by high-ranking individuals. The sound of tinkling that accompanied the wearing of such pendants both regulated the wearer's pace and kept evil thoughts at bay.

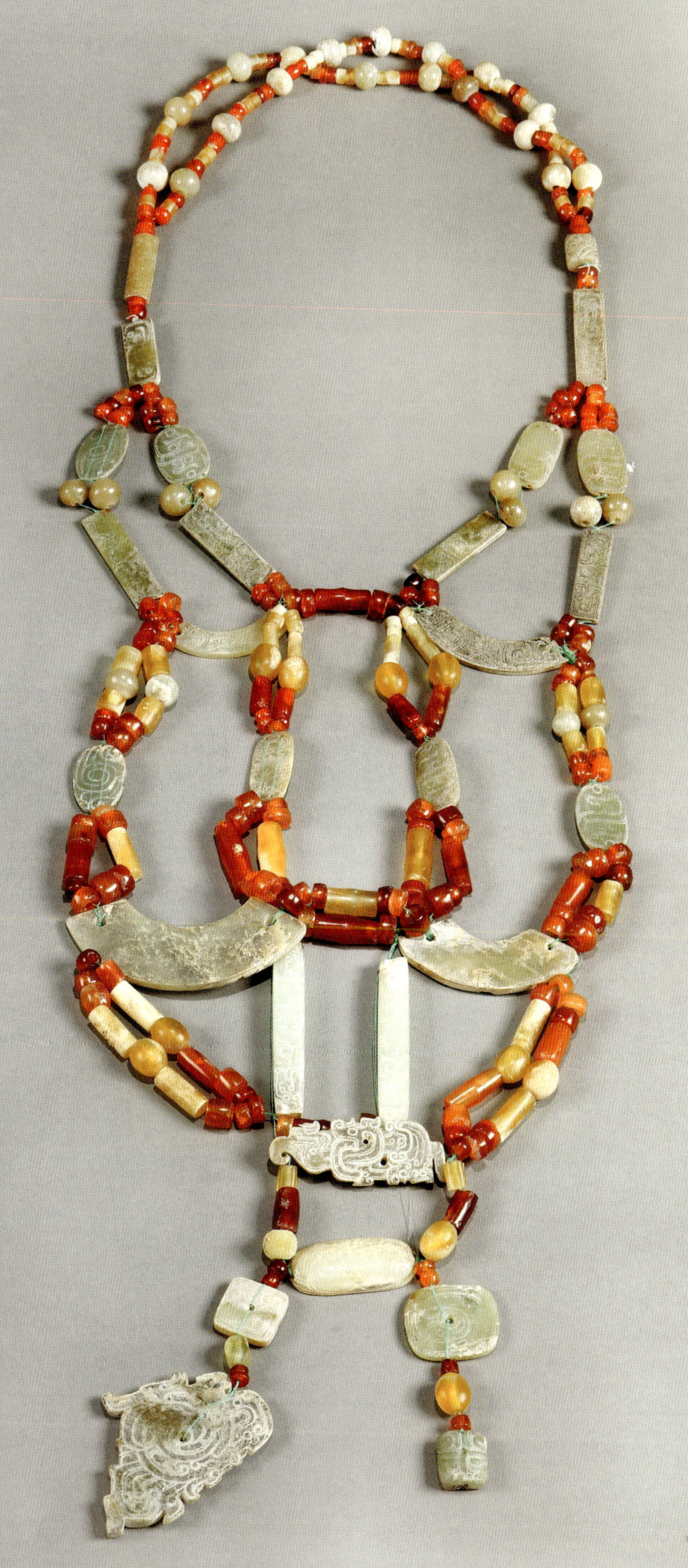

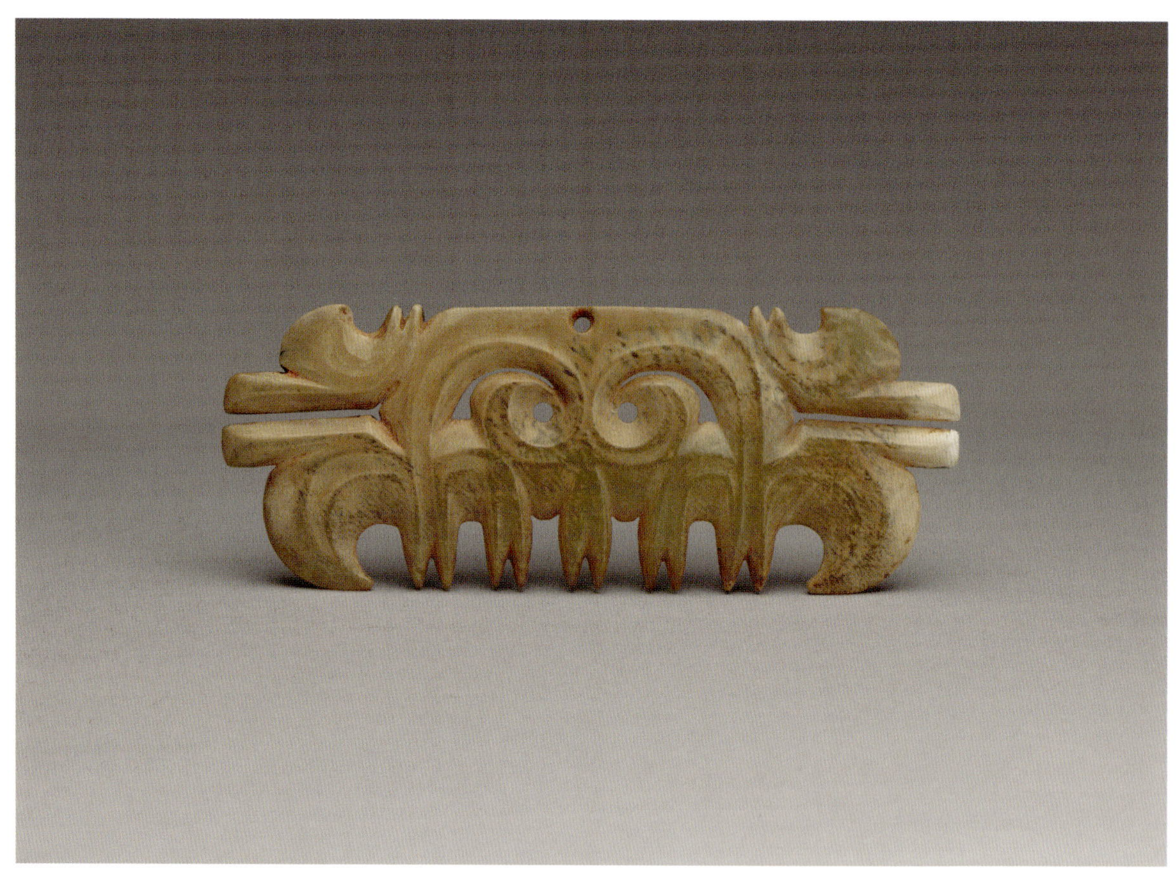

39. Owl-shaped pendant
枭形玉饰 / 梟形玉飾

Spring and Autumn period (771–475 BCE)
Jade, 4.1 x 11.3cm
Excavated at Guodian village, Guodianzhen, Fengxiang, Baoji, 2002
Fengxiang County Museum, 总1010

This pendant is carved on both sides to represent an abstracted owl's head, along with strong claws. While the owl is connected with bravery, it was also often perceived as an ill omen, and the harbinger of an unwelcome death.

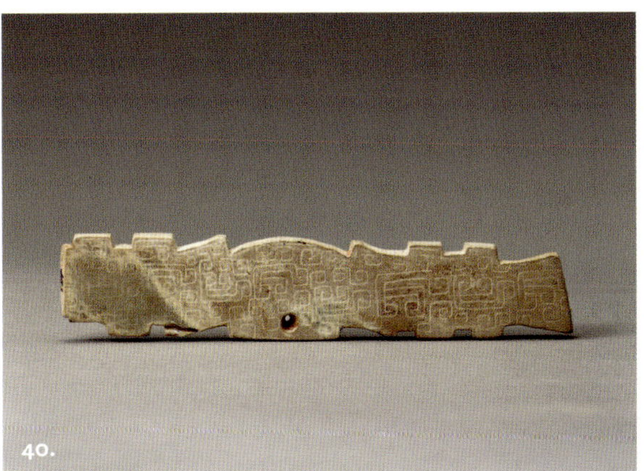

40.

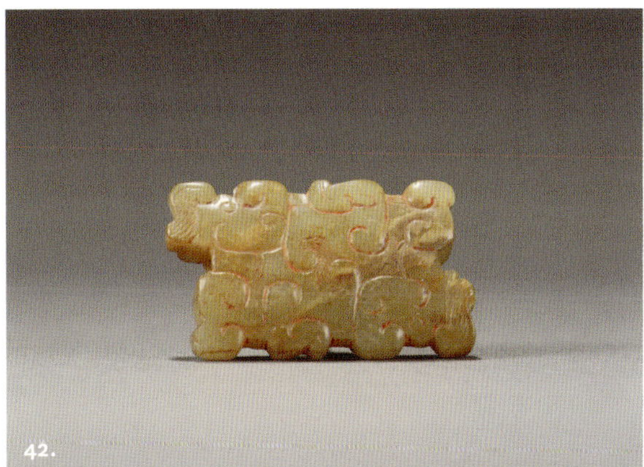

42.

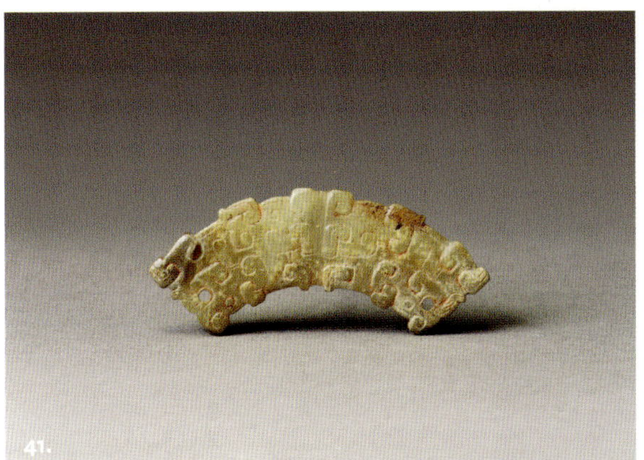

41.

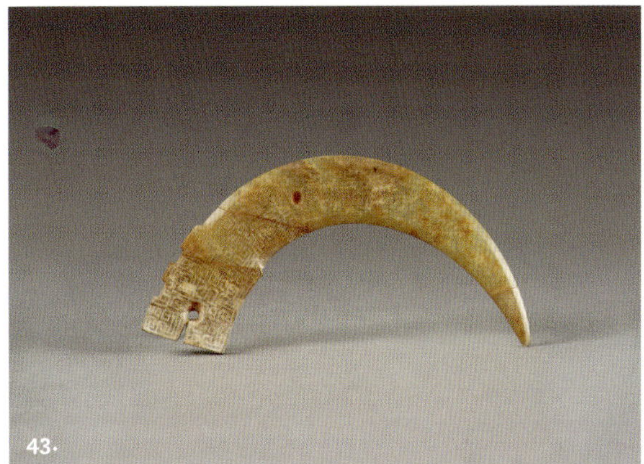

43.

40. Rectangular-shaped pendant (*Pei*)
璋形玉佩

Spring and Autumn period (771–475 BCE)

Jade, 2.5 x 12.7cm

Excavated from Tomb 2 at Yimen village, Weibinqu, Baoji, 1992

Baoji City Archaeological Team, BYM2:124

41. Arc-shaped pendant (*Huang*)
玉璜

Spring and Autumn period (771–475 BCE)

Jade, 1.8 x 6.3cm

Excavated from Tomb 2 at Yimen village, Weibinqu, Baoji, 1992

Baoji City Archaeological Team, BYM2:145

42. Elephant-shaped pendant (*Pei*)
象形玉佩

Spring and Autumn period (771–475 BCE)

Jade, 1.5 x 2.7cm

Excavated from Tomb 2 at Yimen village, Weibinqu, Baoji, 1992

Baoji City Archaeological Team, BYM2:171

43. Jade pendant (*Xi*)
玉觿

Spring and Autumn period (771–475 BCE)

Jade, 4.8 x 8.5cm

Excavated from Tomb 2 at Yimen village, Weibinqu, Baoji

Baoji City Archaeological Team, BYM2:143

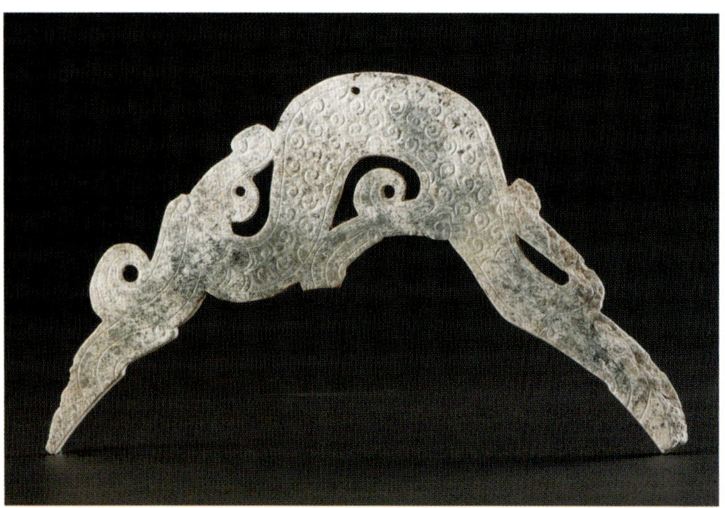

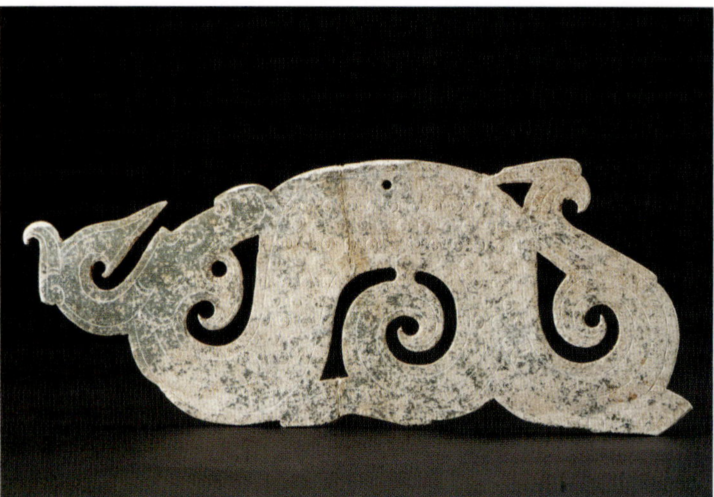

44. **Dragon-shaped pendant (*Heng*)**
龙形玉珩 / 龍形玉珩

Warring States period (475–221 BCE)
Jade, 11.5 x 20.5cm
Collected in 2008
Baoji Bronze Museum, 9643/IB1.108

45. **Dragon- and phoenix-shaped pendant (*Pei*)**
玉龙凤佩 / 玉龍鳳佩

Warring States period (475–221 BCE)
Jade, 9.4 x 18.7cm
Collected in 2008
Baoji Bronze Museum, IB1.109

Both these jades depict dragons with arched bodies and are decorated with spiral curls. They have holes pierced in them, and the one on the top could have been used to untie knots. We cannot tell, though, whether they were worn in life as part of a pendant set, or were made specifically to be worn in the afterlife. The jade in the lower photograph also features a phoenix. From ancient times, the pairing of these auspicious mythical creatures, the dragon and phoenix, was regarded as a duality, akin to the concept of *yin* 陰 and *yang* 陽.

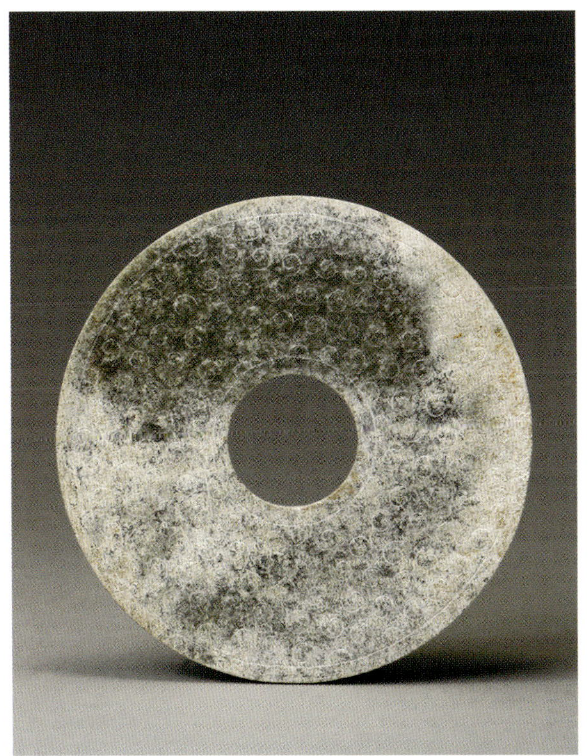

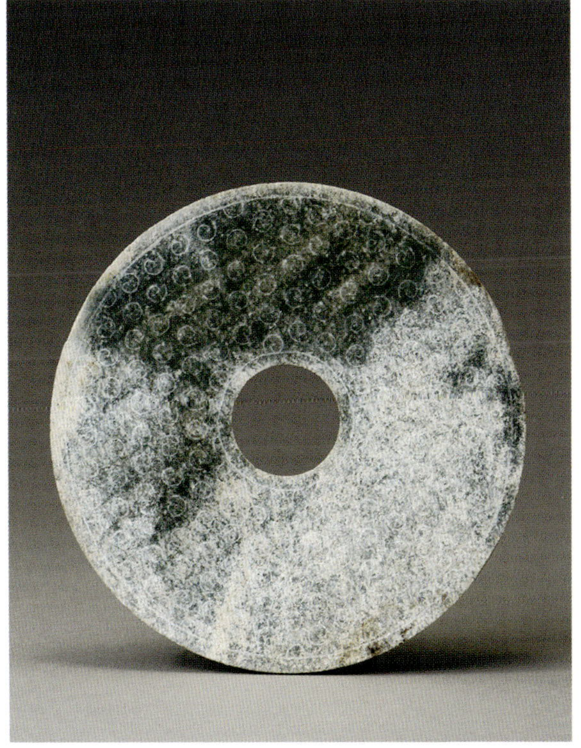

46. Ritual *Bi* discs
谷纹玉璧 / 谷紋玉璧

Warring States period (475–221 BCE)
Jade, diameters 12.2cm; 13.6cm
Collected in 2008
Baoji Bronze Museum, 9641/ IB1.106; 9656/ IB1.121

The ancient Chinese fashioned jade in the circular shape they imagined Heaven to be. Jade discs like these were used to worship Heaven, and were placed on the bodies of the dead to ensure immortality.

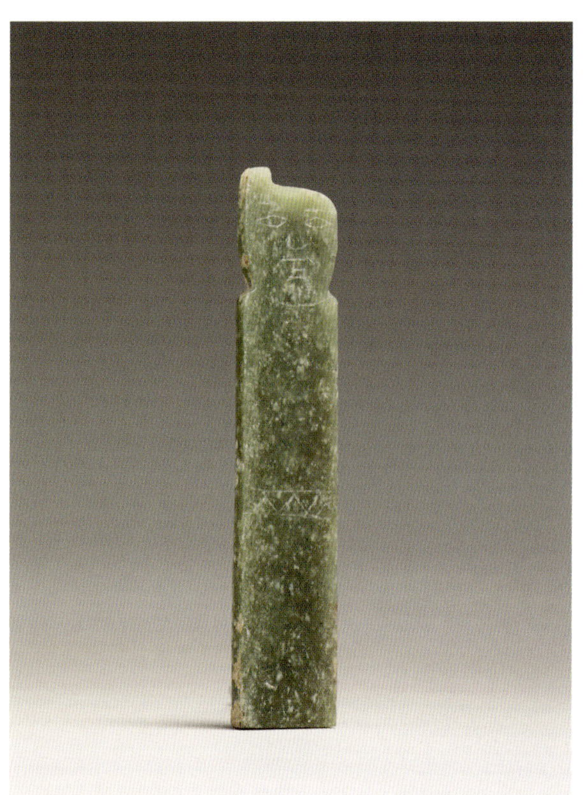

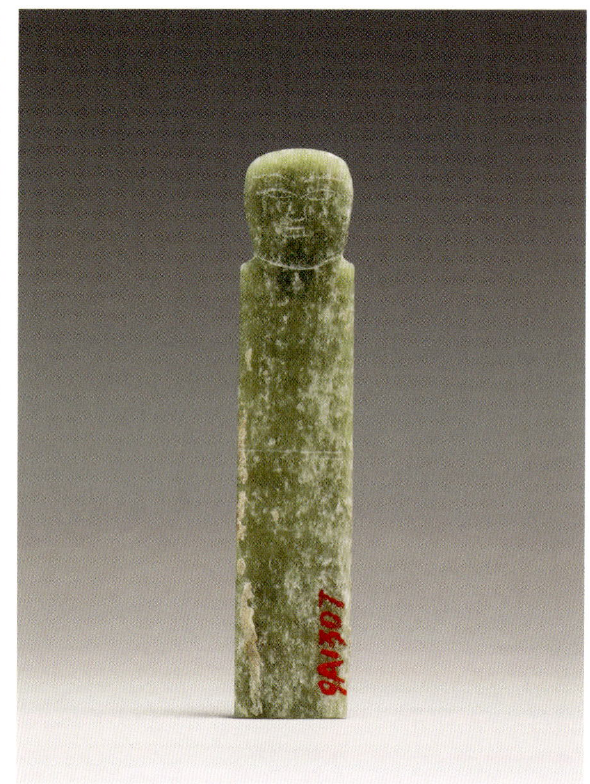

47. Male figure with topknot
玉人（男）
Female figure with flat hair
玉人（女）

Qin–Han dynasty (221 BCE–220 CE)
Jade, 12 x 2.3cm; 11.5 x 2.3cm
Excavated at Zhilian village, Xi'an, 1989
Xi'an Museum, 3gY199; 3gY201

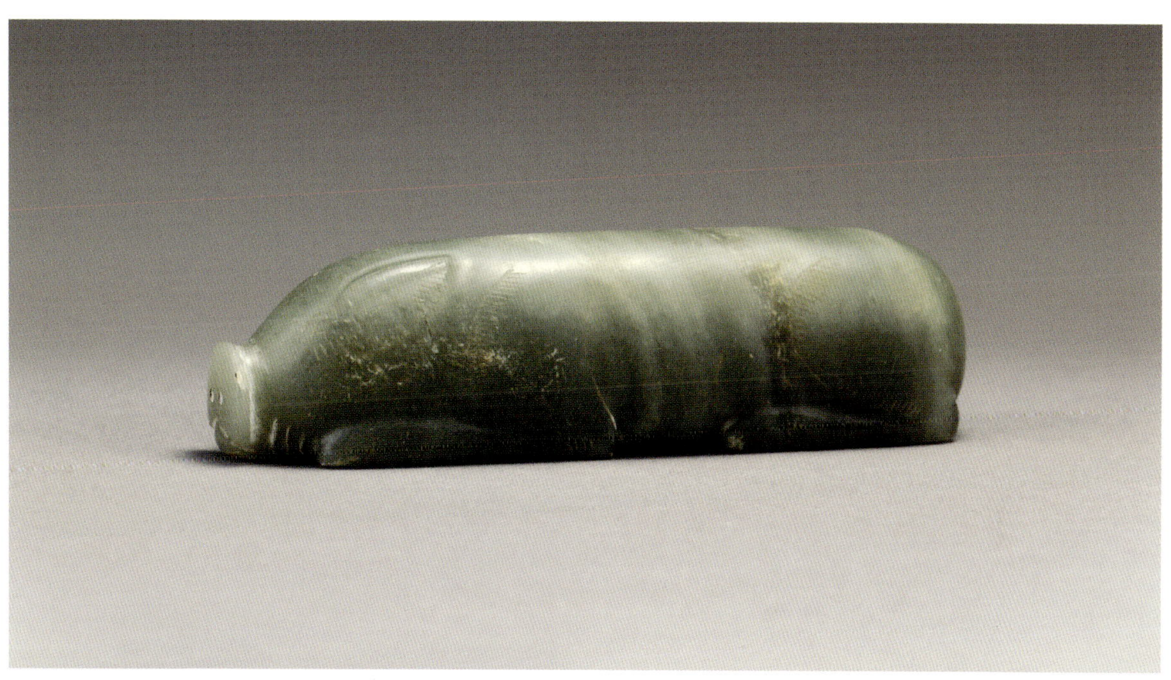

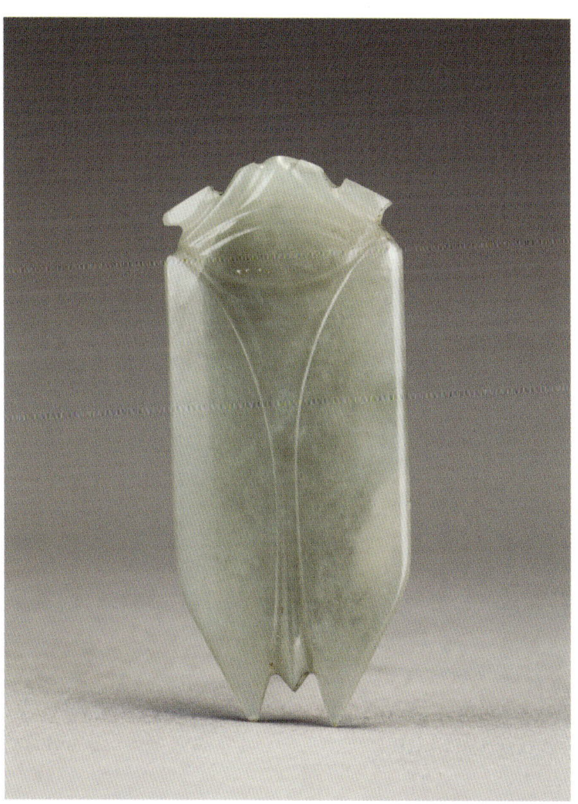

48. Jade pig
玉猪 / 玉豬

Han dynasty (206 BCE–220 CE)
Jade, 2.9 x 10.95cm
Xi'an Museum, 3gy230

49. Jade cicada
玉蝉 / 玉蟬

Han dynasty (206 BCE–220 CE)
Jade, 6 x 2.6cm
Xi'an Museum, 3gy254

During the Han dynasty, bodies of high-ranking individuals would be fully encased in jade suits. Jade pigs and cicadas such as these were used in conjunction with sets of orifice plugs to protect the body from decay and preserve its *qi* 氣, or life force.

The cicada, symbolising rebirth, was placed over, or in, the mouth; while the pig, symbolising prosperity, was placed in the hands or armpits. Both are crafted with the utmost simplicity, with just a few deep cuts creating contours suggestive of each creature.

BELTS AND GIRDLES

The humble belt hook served both practical and symbolic functions in ancient China. It came into use when the Chinese adopted cavalry warfare, which is generally believed to have been initiated by King Wuling (reigned 325–299 BCE) of Zhao, one of the Seven States of the Warring States period.

King Wuling recognised that in order to resist the frequent incursions by nomadic tribes from the north, his troops needed to be more mobile. Rather than wearing court dress during battle, as had been the custom, he decreed that his troops should copy the more practical nomadic dress, including trousers, which required belts and hooks to keep them up.

Not all belt hooks were used for tying belts; they may also have been used to carry personal items, such as pouches or knives, as there were no pockets in Chinese gowns. Sumptuary law also prescribed the dress of officials and gentry, meaning that the materials used to make belt hooks served as indicators of status.

50. Coiled snake-shaped belt hook
盘蛇形金带钩 / 盤蛇形帶鉤

Spring and Autumn period (771–475 BCE)
Gold, 1.4 x 2.6cm
Excavated from the Qin Tomb, Yimen village, Weibingu, Baoji, 1992
Baoji City Archaeological Team, BYM2:23

During the Zhou dynasty, gold was rarely exploited. Its use in China dates from the beginning of the Spring and Autumn period in 771 BCE, and was primarily influenced by contact with nomadic peoples from the steppes of western Asia. When the Chinese began to work this precious metal, they didn't shape it with hammer and anvil, but cast it, meaning this belt hook is made of solid gold.

This belt hook would have been used like a buckle, with the end of a leather belt threaded through one side. The other end of the belt would have had holes in it, which the head of the snake could be pushed through, enabling the belt to be tightened or loosened.

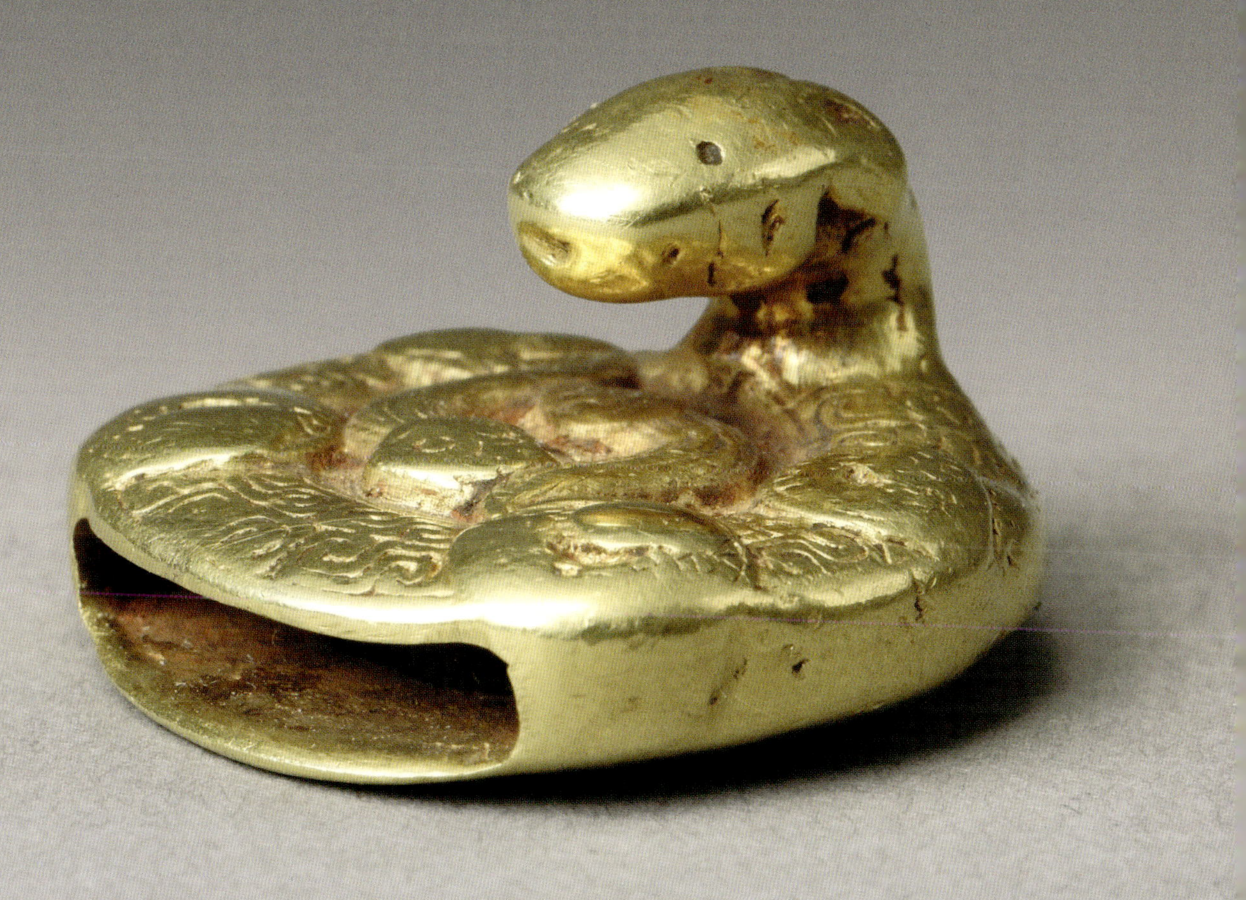

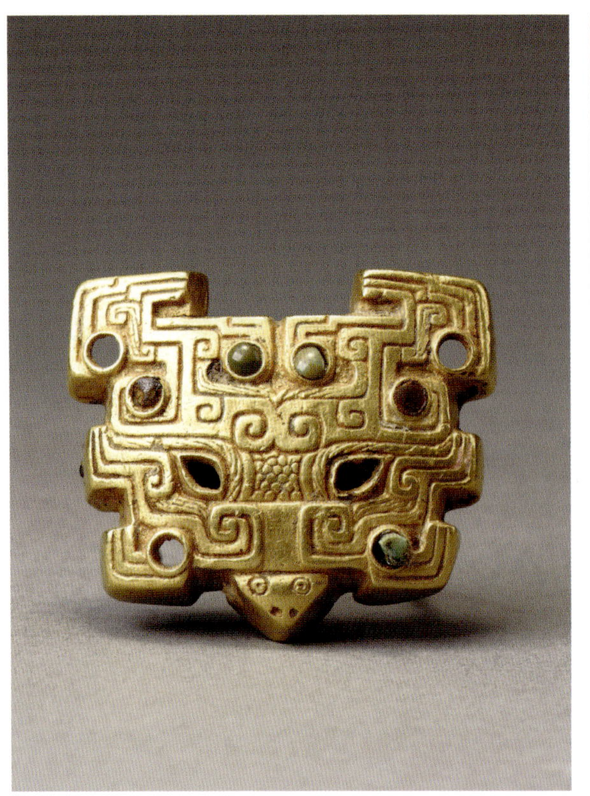

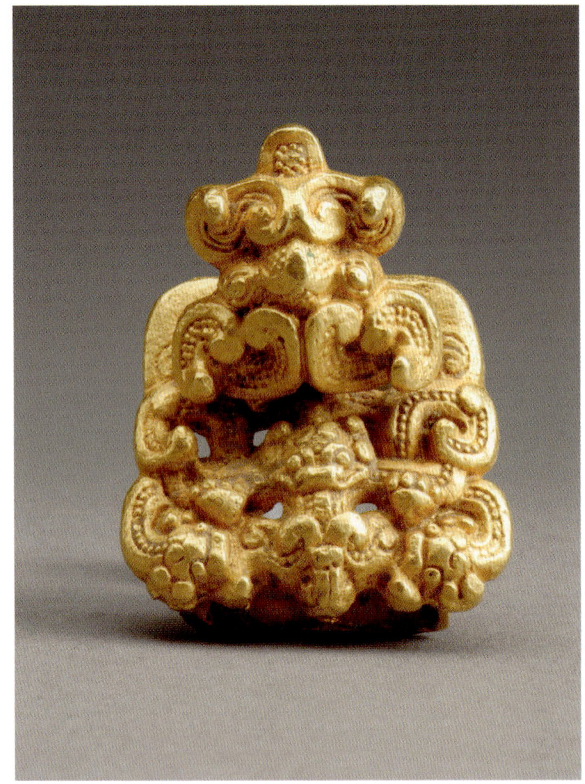

51. **Gold ornament with zoomorphic design**
兽面金方泡 / 獸面金方泡

Spring and Autumn period (771–475 BCE)

Gold and inlaid stones, 3.9 x 3.3cm

Excavated from Tomb 2, Yimen village, Weibinqu, Baoji, 1992

Baoji City Archaeological Team, BYM2:27

52. **Belt hook with dragons**
五龙金饰 / 五龍金飾

Warring States period (475–221 BCE)

Gold, 4.2 x 3.4cm

Excavated at Doufu village, Fengxiang, Baoji, 1979

Fengxiang County Museum, 总0373

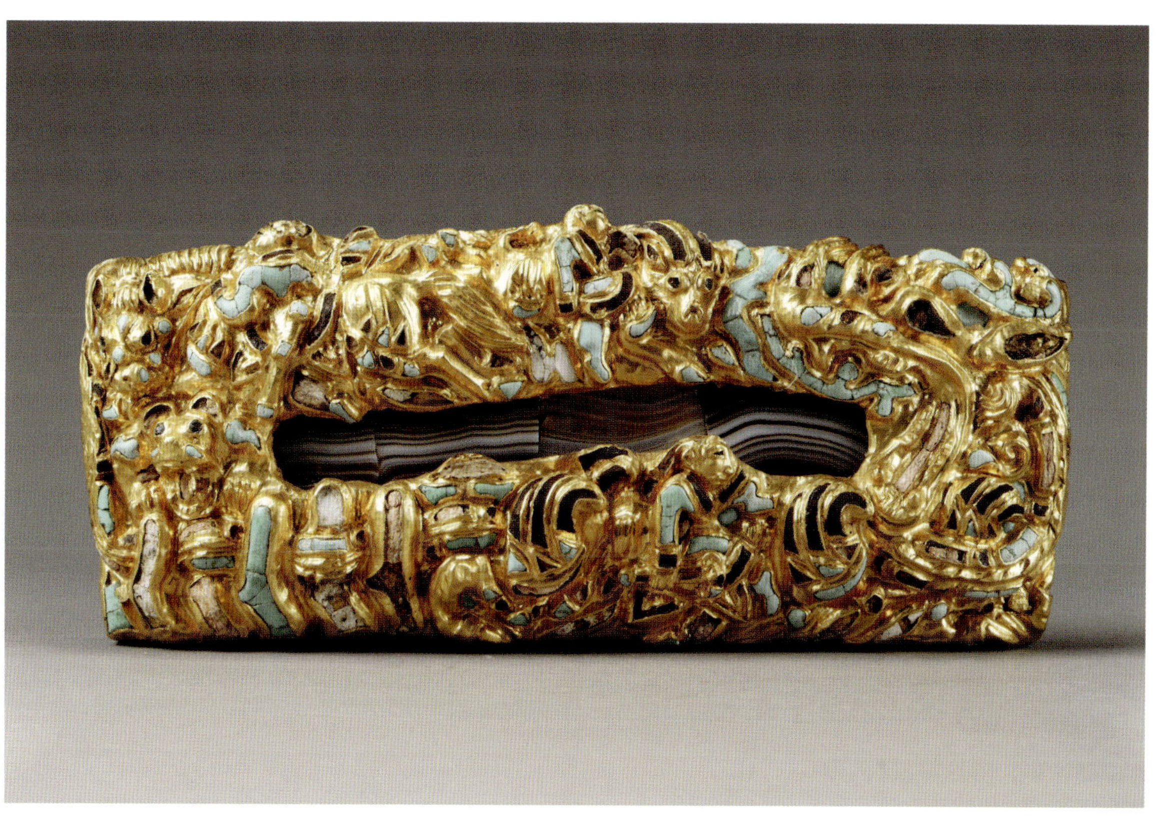

53. **Ornamental belt buckle**
金牌饰 / 金牌飾

Western Han dynasty (206 BCE–9 CE)

Gold inlaid with agate, hematite, turquoise and shell, 8 x 20cm

Excavated from Tomb 15, Matengkong, Xi'an, 2001

Shaanxi Provincial Institute of Archaeology, 005421

This remarkable belt plaque is made from a single sheet of gold inlaid with precious stones. While the design appears at first to be abstract, there are animals, both mythical and real, as well as riders, camouflaged within the swirling patterns. It is likely that this belt plaque was imported from Central Asia, as it was made by hammering the metal, rather than casting, as was typical of Chinese craftspeople.

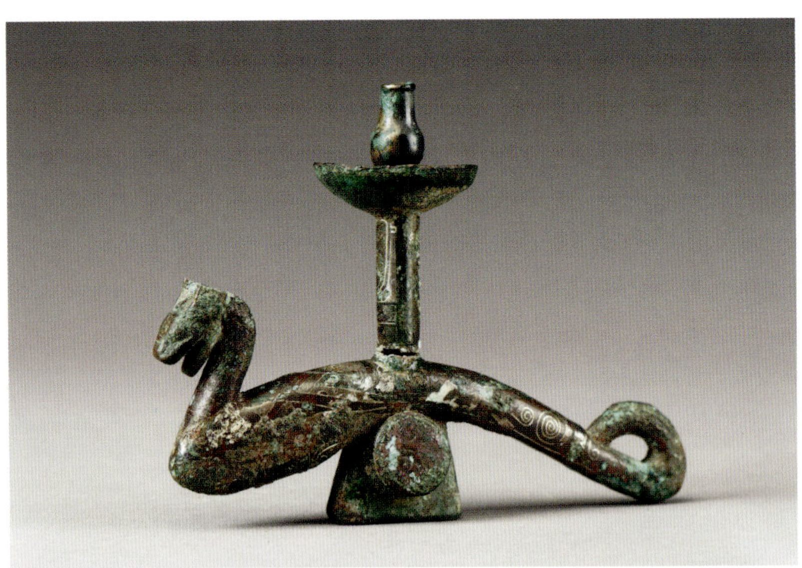

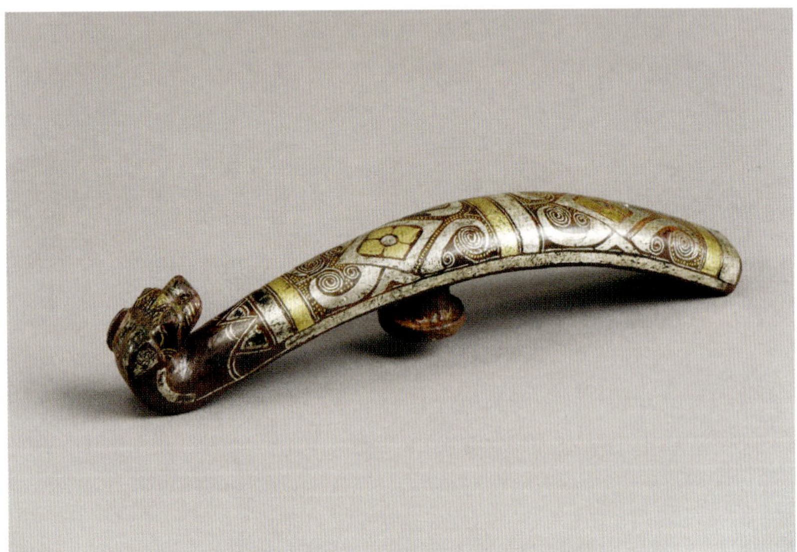

54. **Inlaid belt hook with dragon head**
龙首嵌银铜带钩 / 龍首嵌銀銅帶鉤

Warring States period (475–221 BCE)
Bronze with inlaid gold and silver, 9 x 11.6cm
Collected in 2008
Shangluo City Museum, 总3922 D3100

55. **Inlaid belt hook**
错金银铜带钩 / 錯金銀銅帶鉤

Han dynasty (206 BCE–220 CE)
Bronze with inlaid gold and silver, 2.1 x 13.5cm
Excavated at Chanba ecological district, 2004
Shaanxi Provincial Institute of Archaeology, 007280

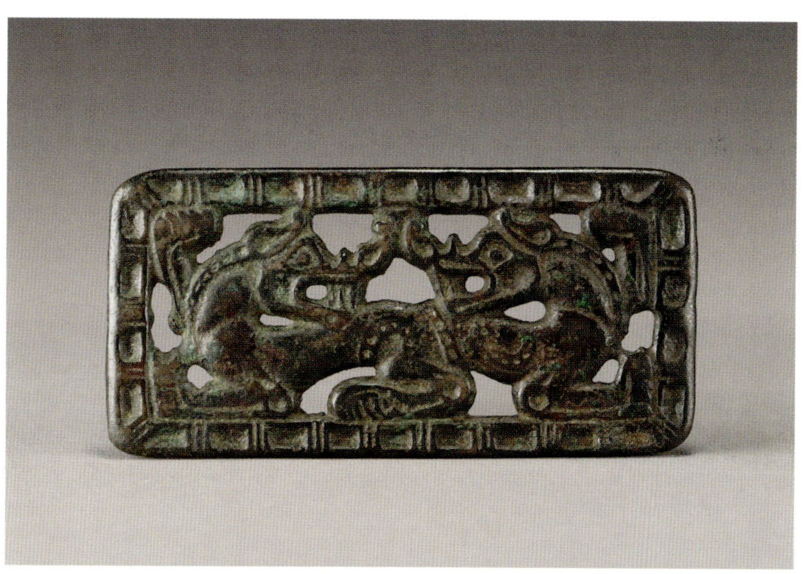

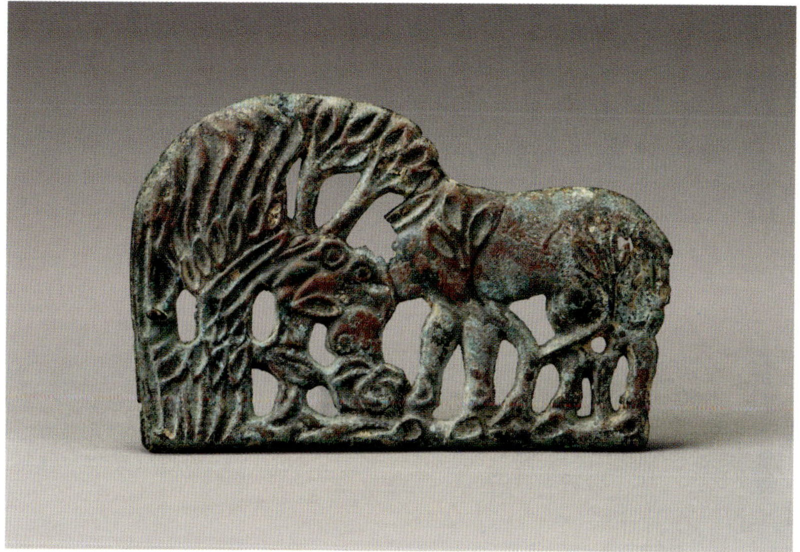

56. Belt plaque with dragon design
双龙纹镂空铜牌饰 / 雙龍紋空銅牌飾

Han dynasty (206 BCE–220 CE)
Bronze, 4.7 x 10cm
Collected at Yulin, 1974
Shaanxi History Museum, 七四93

57. Belt plaque with wrestling bulls
鹰兽相搏牌饰 / 鷹獸相搏牌飾

Han dynasty (206 BCE–220 CE)
Bronze, 8.1 x 12.6cm
Excavated at Brick and Tile Factory 2, Hongmiaopo, Xi'an, 1955
Shaanxi History Museum, 交0224

Belt plaques with figurative representations of animals were widespread among nomadic peoples from the northern steppes. They may have reached China via trade or as spoils of war, although discoveries of ceramic moulds in Xi'an dating from the third century BCE suggest they were also produced locally.

TOOLS AND WEAPONS

Before the reign of the First Emperor, the area of China was made up of seven dominant states that were constantly at war: Qin, Qi, Chu, Yan, Han, Zhao and Wei. Consequently, historians refer to this time as the Warring States period (475–221 BCE). The state of Qin was renowned for its military skills; indeed, the First Emperor created his empire through overcoming the rival states by force.

Bronze was the favoured material for weapons, and those recovered from countless tombs throughout traditional Qin homelands confirm the high degree of technical sophistication and skilled craftsmanship of the Qin peoples. They also hint at the significant resources that were invested in the production of weapons.

By the time of the Qin dynasty, Chinese knew how to apply a fine coating of chromium to weapons – known today as chrome plating. This technique, which kept the blades of weapons extremely hard, sharp and resistant to corrosion, didn't appear in Western countries until the 1920s.

Along with their technological skills in producing weapons, the success of the Qin state in warfare is attributed to their discipline, expertise with the crossbow, and their horsemanship.

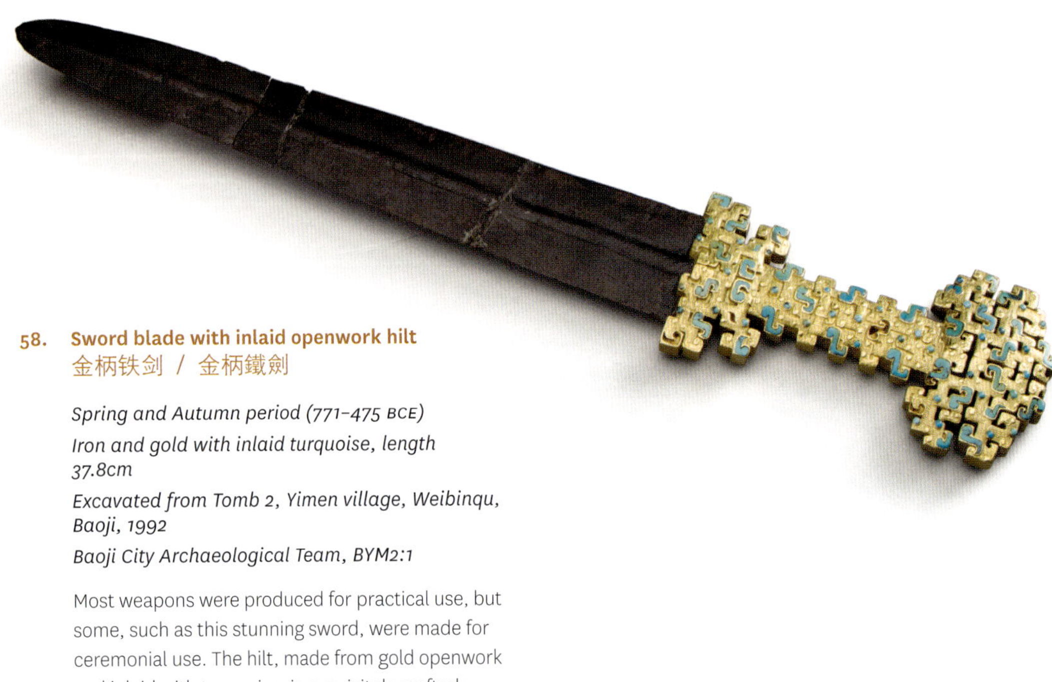

58. Sword blade with inlaid openwork hilt
金柄铁剑 / 金柄鐵劍

Spring and Autumn period (771–475 BCE)
Iron and gold with inlaid turquoise, length 37.8cm
Excavated from Tomb 2, Yimen village, Weibinqu, Baoji, 1992
Baoji City Archaeological Team, BYM2:1

Most weapons were produced for practical use, but some, such as this stunning sword, were made for ceremonial use. The hilt, made from gold openwork and inlaid with turquoise, is exquisitely crafted, while the design of interlocking serpent-like motifs echoes the sophisticated bronzes of the period.

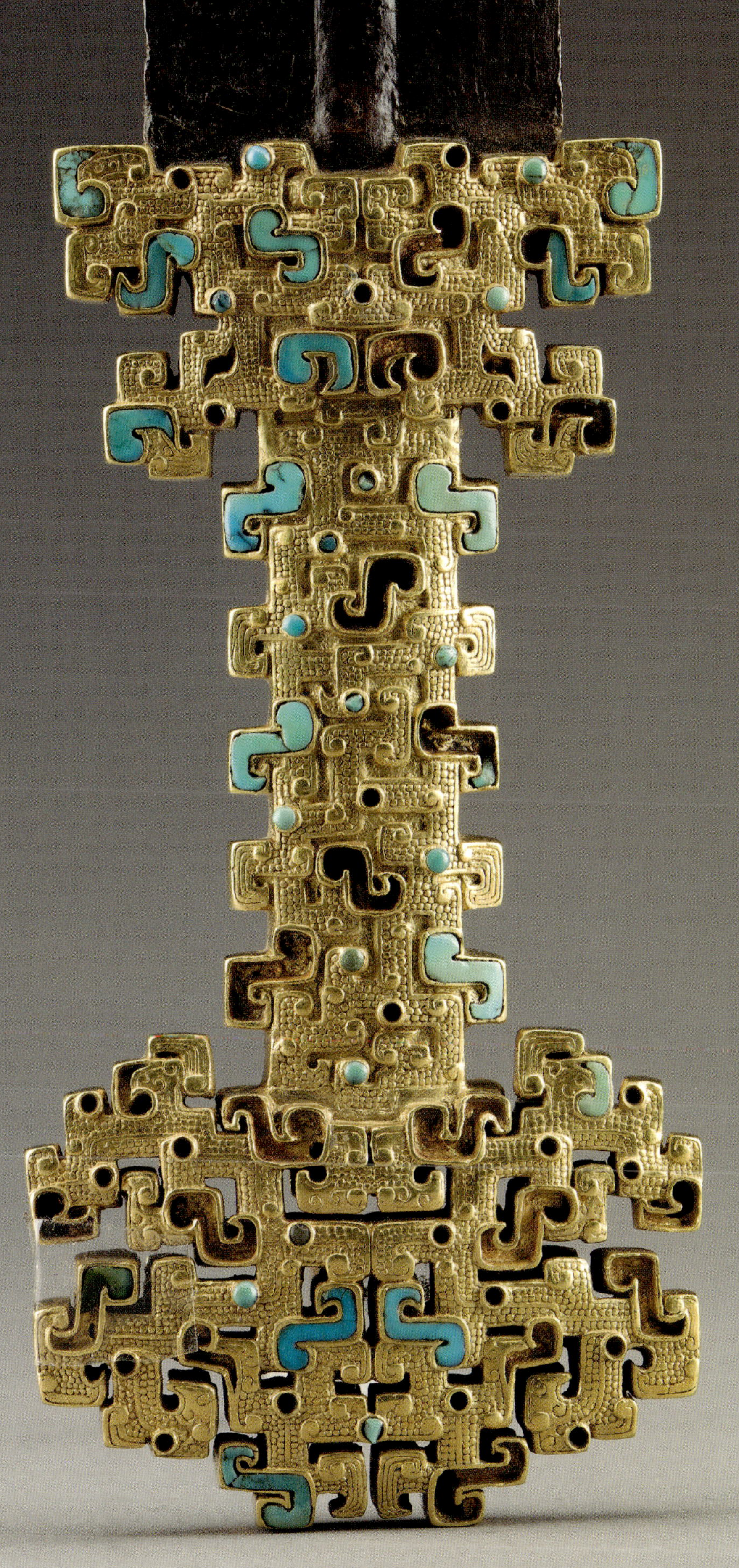

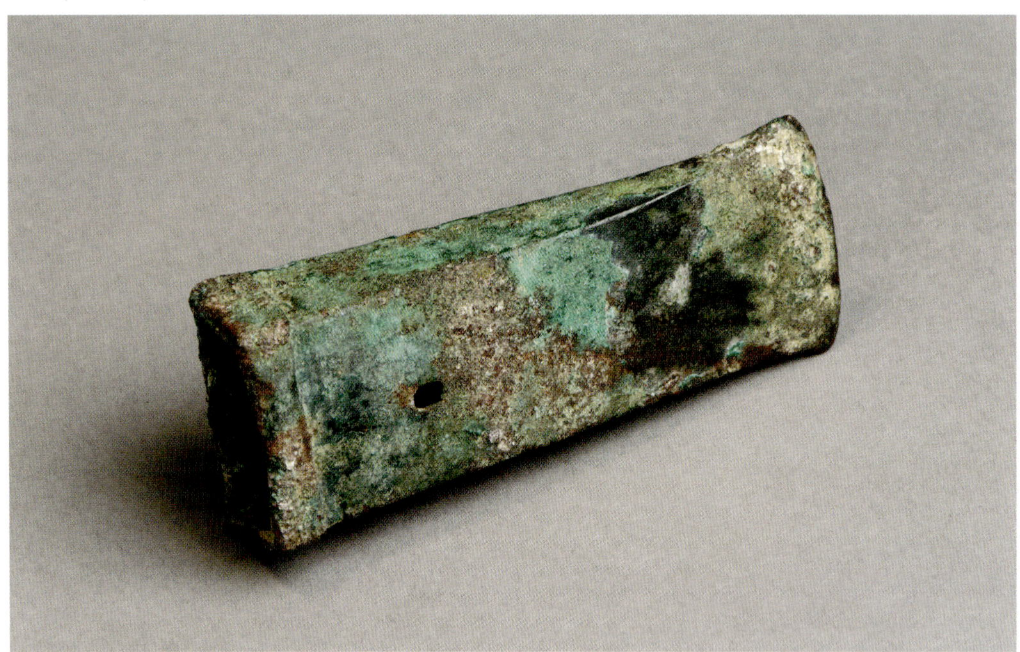

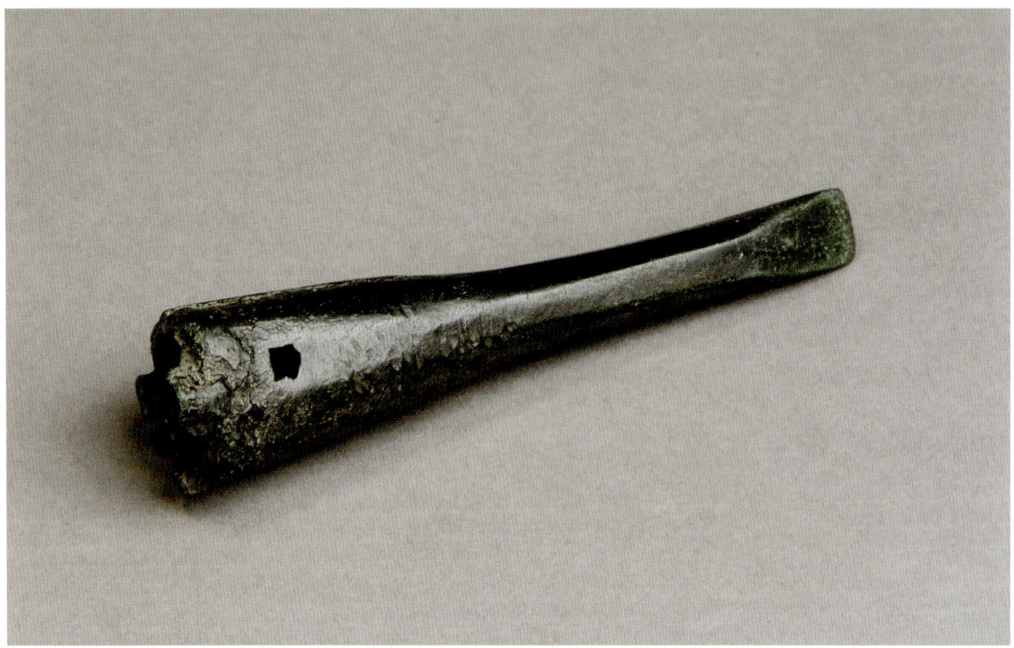

59. Bronze axe
铜斧 / 銅斧

Eastern Zhou dynasty (771–256 BCE)

Bronze, 2.5 x 8cm

Collected at Jiaochangpeng village, Machaxiang, Zizhou, Yulin

Yulin Institute of Cultural Heritage Conservation, 0924

60. Bronze chisel
铜凿 / 銅鑿

Eastern Zhou dynasty (771–256 BCE)

Bronze, 2 x 9cm

Collected at Mizhi, Yulin

Yulin Institute of Cultural Heritage Conservation, 0987

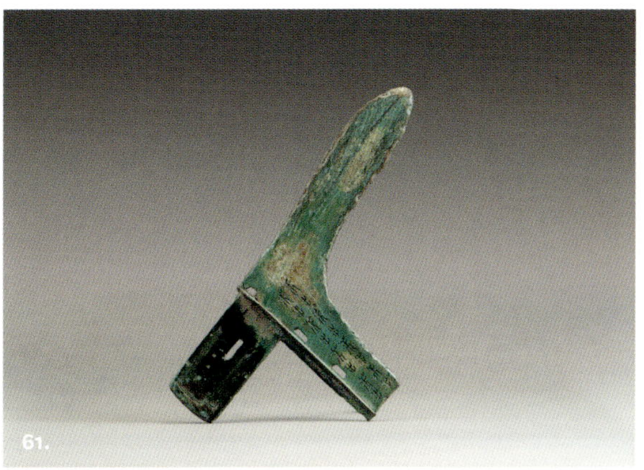
61.

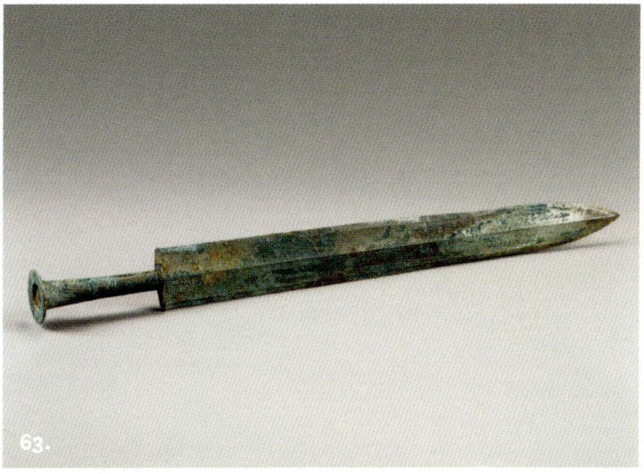
63.

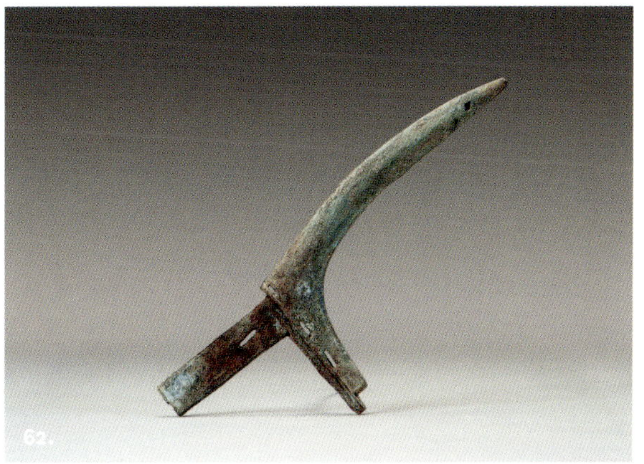
62.

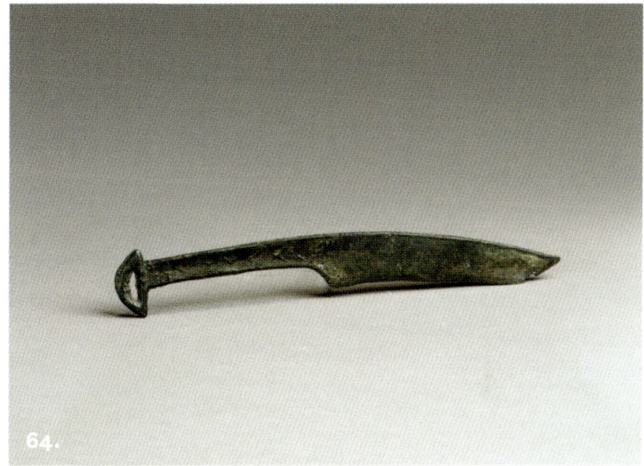
64.

One of the most common ancient Chinese weapons was the dagger axe, consisting of a bronze axe-head affixed to a wooden pole with strong leather binding. This form of weapon first appeared in the Shang dynasty, and was a key weapon of the Warring States and Qin periods. They were often inscribed, identifying the owner, maker or any significance of the particular weapon.

61. Dagger axe (Ge) with inscriptions
十六字长胡三穿戈 / 十六字長胡三穿戈

Warring States period (475–221 BCE)
Bronze, 11.5 x 23.5cm
Collected in Xi'an
Xi'an Museum, 2gt5

62. Dagger axe (Ge)
青铜三穿戈 / 青銅三穿戈

Warring States period (475–221 BCE)
Bronze, length 33.4cm
Excavated at Guchengzhen, Danfeng, Shangluo, 1996
Shangluo City Museum, 总0298 D018

The bronze swords of the Warring States period most likely evolved from the shorter dagger-like weapons used by the nomadic peoples of the northern steppes. During the Qin dynasty, swords became longer in length, enabling greater reach during combat.

63. Bronze sword
青铜剑 / 青銅劍

Warring States period (475–221 BCE)
Bronze, length 43.8cm
Excavated at Guchengzhen, Danfeng, Shangluo, 1996
Shangluo City Museum, 总0293 D013

64. Dagger
铜匕 / 銅匕

Warring States period (475–221 BCE)
Bronze, 20.5 x 2.9cm
Collected at Erlin, Yulin, 1987
Yulin Institute of Cultural Heritage Conservation, 0055

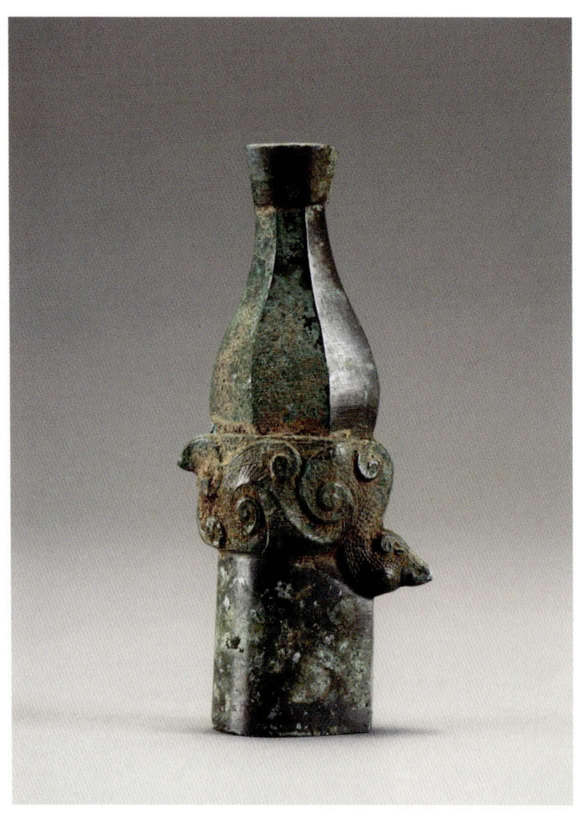

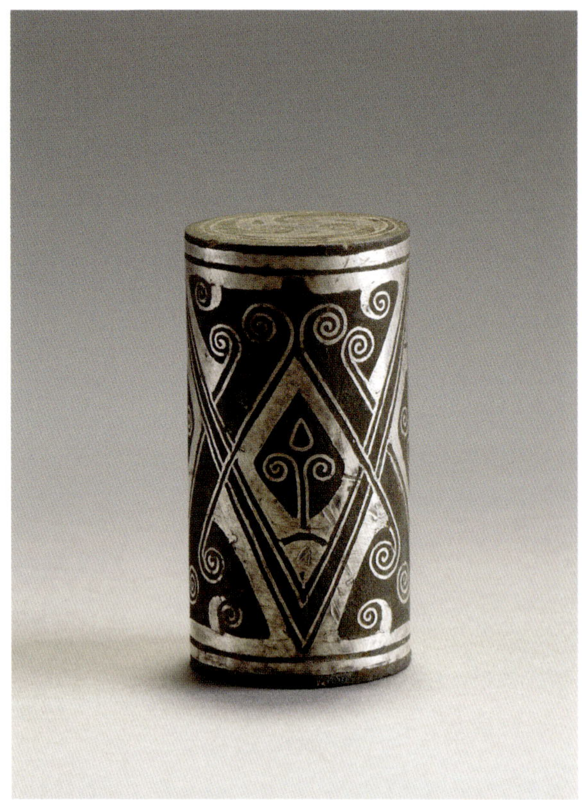

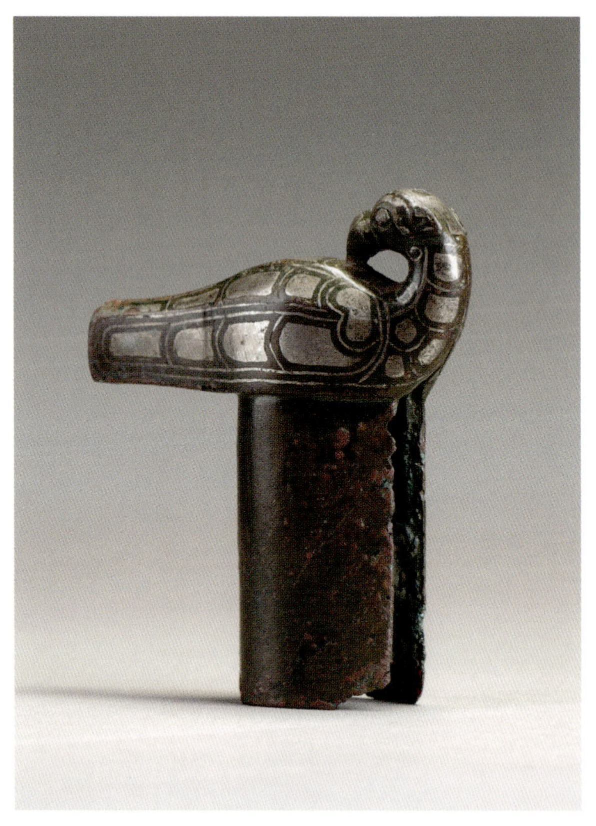

65. **Decorative weapon accessory (*Dun*)**
凤鸟纹铜镦 / 鳳鳥紋銅鐓

Warring States period (475–221 BCE)
Bronze, height 10.2cm
Excavated from Tomb M2, Juanling, Shanyang, Shangluo, 1998
Shangluo City Museum, 总0284 D004

66. **Decorative weapon accessory (*Dun*)**
错银铜镦 / 錯銀銅鐓

Warring States period (475–221 BCE)
Bronze, 5.9 x 3.1cm
Excavated from Shouling Mausoleum, Weicheng, Xianyang, 2007
Xianyang Institute of Cultural Heritage and Archaeology, 2735

67. **Finial form of a bird of prey**
错银鸠形杖首 / 錯銀鳩形杖首

Qin dynasty (221–206 BCE)
Silver and bronze, 7.2 x 8.5cm
Collected at Dabaiyang, Beijiao, Xi'an, 1967
Xi'an Museum, 3gtD45

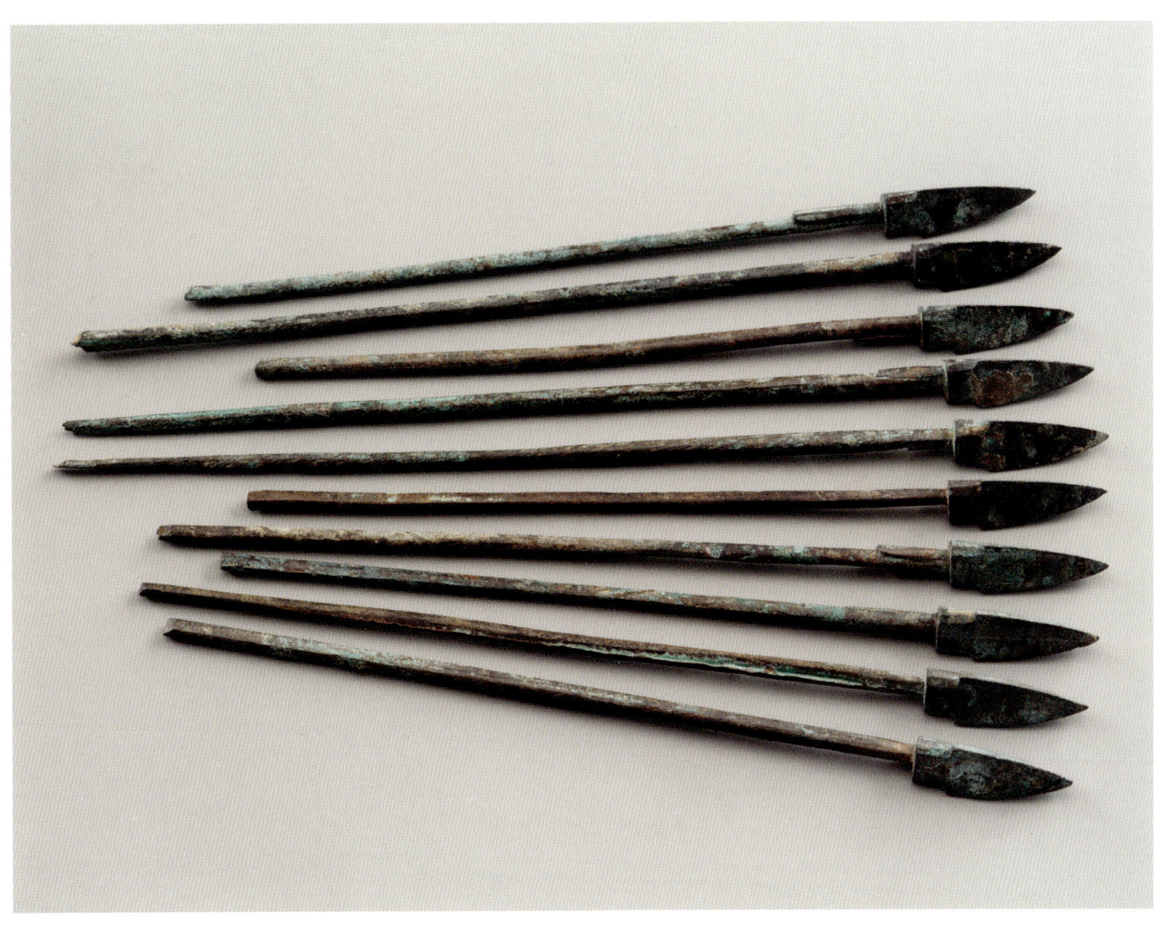

68. Arrowheads
青铜箭镞 / 青銅箭鏃

Qin dynasty (221–206 BCE)

Bronze, lengths 11.3–16.3cm

Excavated from Pit 1, Qin Shihuang tomb complex, 1975

Emperor Qin Shihuang's Mausoleum Site Museum, 001464

The Chinese invented the *nu* 弩, or crossbow, before 450 BCE. During the First Emperor's reign, the weapon was enhanced, and it played a key role in the defeat of nomadic neighbours. Qin crossbows were allegedly able to fire arrows over distances of 150–800 metres, depending on the size and height of the archer.

Over 40,000 arrowheads have been excavated from the Terracotta Army's Pit 1. Each archer would have carried sets of 70, 100 or 114 arrows in hemp quivers on their back.

CHARIOT FITTINGS

Artefacts excavated from royal burial sites have enabled historians to date the use of chariots in China to the thirteenth century BCE during the Shang dynasty (*c.*1600–*c.*1046 BCE). In this period they became widely used, both as military vehicles and as status symbols. The practice of burying worldly goods such as chariots and horses with deceased rulers began during the Shang dynasty, and continued through to the Qin and Han dynasties.

While the wooden chariot structures have long since perished, the fixtures and fittings remain. The lavish care bestowed on these apparently functional objects speaks to the importance of the chariot and the horse in ancient China.

69. Headstall ornaments
鎏金铜饰 / 鎏金銅飾

Warring States period (475–221 BCE)
Gilt bronze, overall diameters 5.1–5.7cm
Excavated at Beiganhe village, Fengxiang, Baoji, 1985
Fengxiang County Museum, 总0702

The use of chariots in warfare reached its height during the Warring States period. A typical chariot had two wheels and a single pole on which to harness two or four horses. Towards the end of this period chariots were replaced by cavalry, and the increased use of the crossbow and mass infantry.

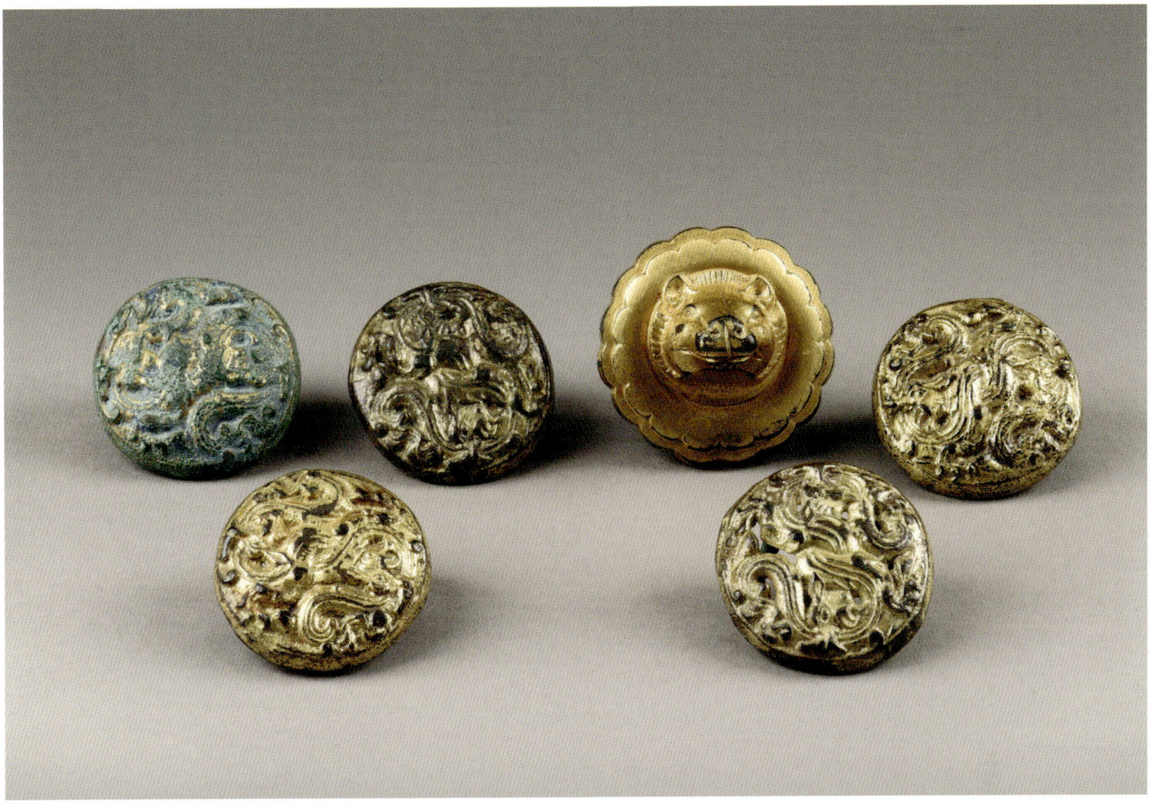

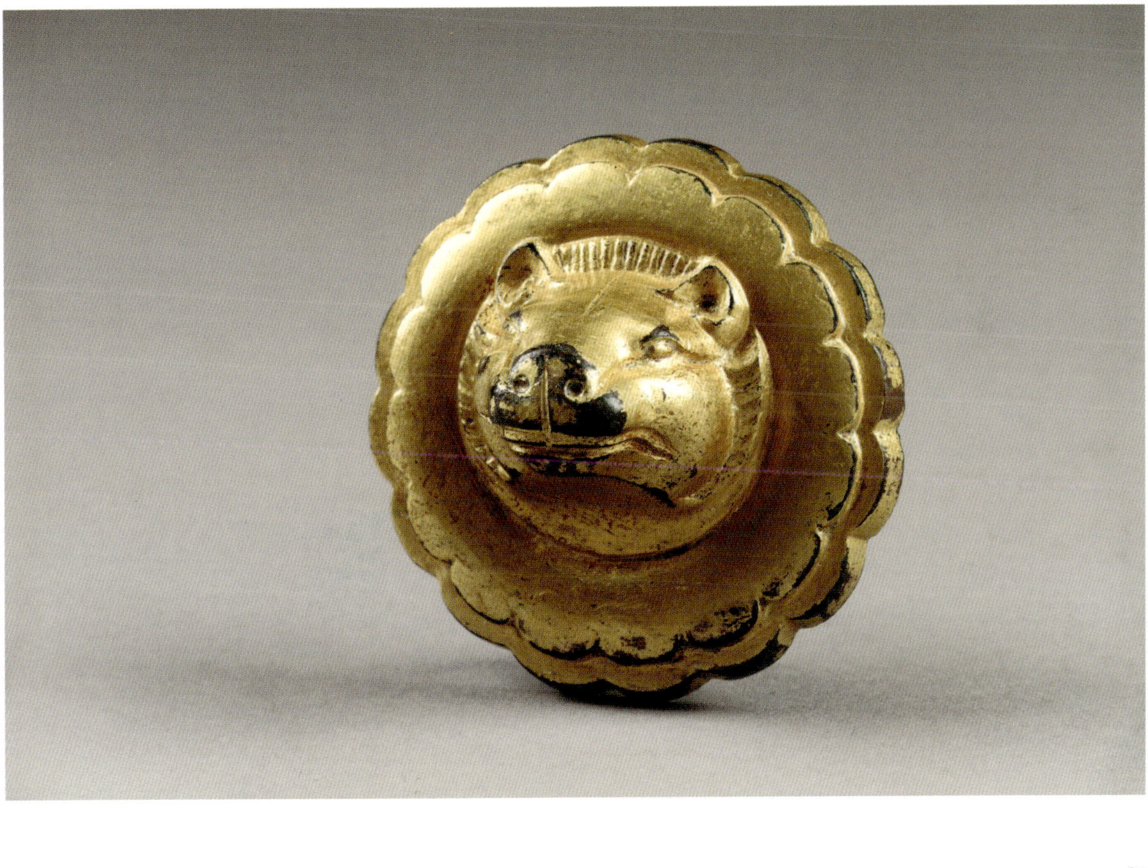

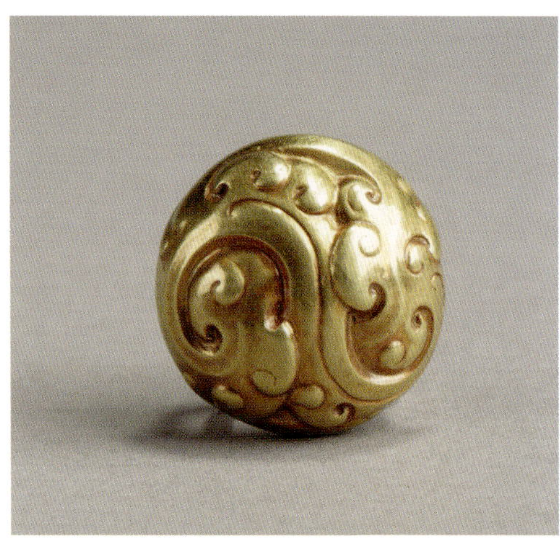

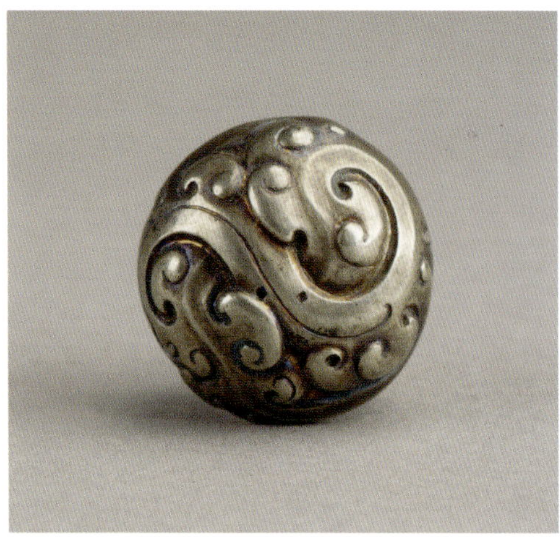

70. Headstall ornaments
金节约，银节约 / 金節約，銀節約

Qin dynasty (221–206 BCE)

Gold and silver, diameters 2.5cm

Excavated at the Bronze Horse and Chariot Pit, Qin Shihuang tomb complex, 1979; 1978

Emperor Qin Shihuang's Mausoleum Site Museum, 004476; 004507

While two half-size bronze chariots, each driven by four horses, were discovered at the First Emperor's burial site in 1980 (see catalogue nos 106 and 107), over one hundred full-size examples of wooden chariots have also been excavated from the warrior pits.

These rosettes would have decorated the horse's harnessing. Made from precious metals, gold and silver, and decorated with swirling cloud-like patterns, they attest to the extravagant attention given to horse and chariot ornamentation during Qin's reign.

71. Ornaments for horses and chariots
车马饰/ 車馬飾

Western Han dynasty (206 BCE–9 CE)

Gilt bronze, measurements vary: 1.65–8.55cm

Excavated from the Accompanying Burial Grave Garden, Han Yangling, Xi'an, 1998

Han Yangling Museum, YG0993; YG0994; YG0978(10/13–13/13); YG0981(5/6–6/6); YG1005; YG1006; YG1001; YG1002; YG0977(5/7–7/7) (clockwise from top left)

By the time of the Han dynasty, the use of chariots in warfare had been superseded by cavalry and infantrymen. Chariots remained important as transport vehicles, with improvements being made to their speed and agility. Their continued presence at royal burials suggests that they also retained their symbolic function as markers of status.

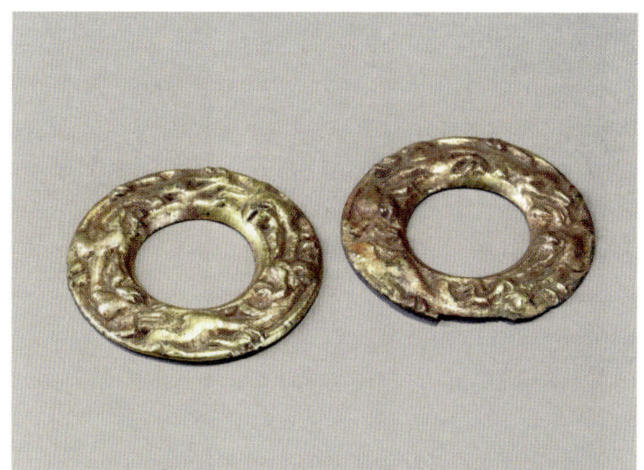
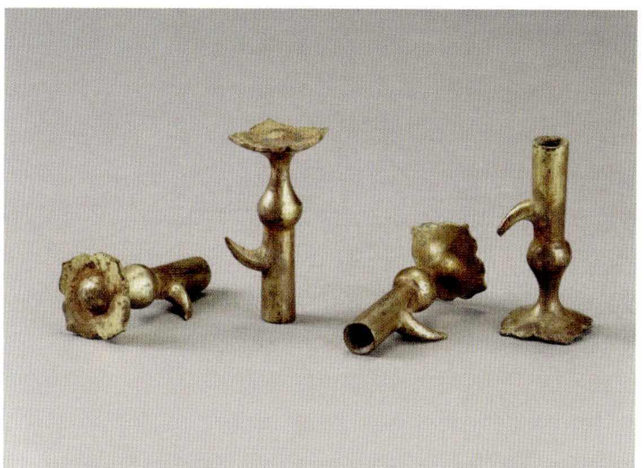
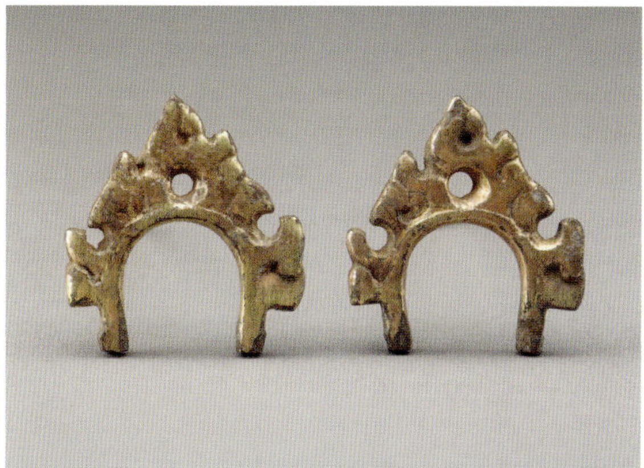
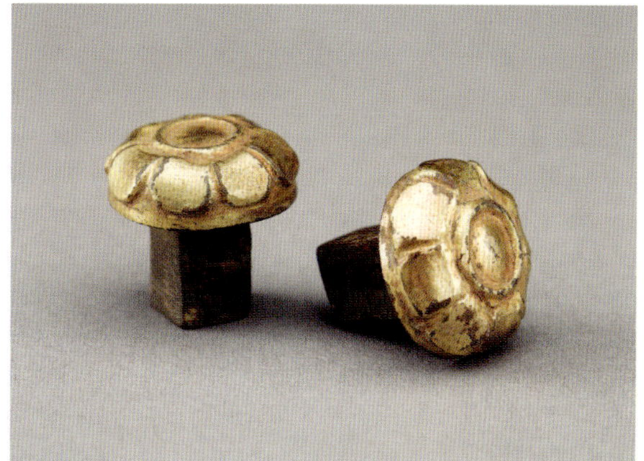
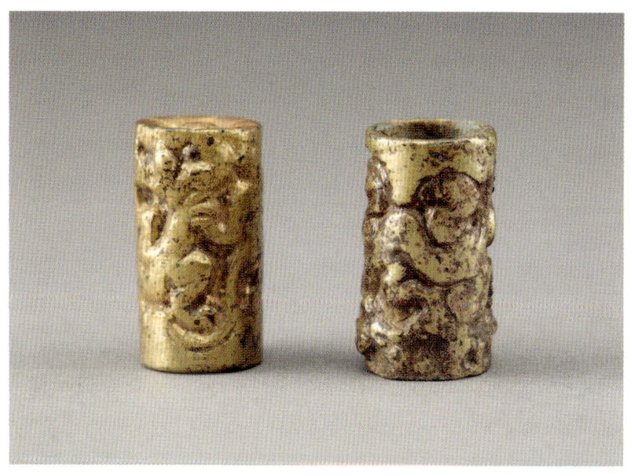
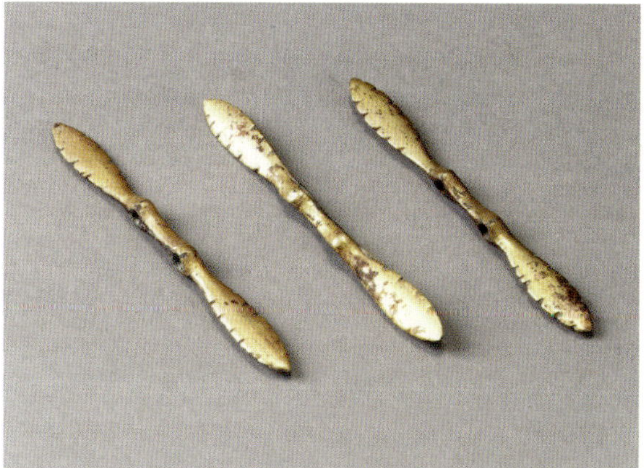

ARCHITECTURE

Buildings in ancient China were largely constructed from wood and tamped earth, meaning all that remains are written descriptions and fragmentary materials, such as bronze fittings, pottery bricks and roof tile-ends.

The material remains hint at the grandeur of ancient Chinese architecture, which is confirmed by written impressions. Sima Qian, the Han dynasty historian, records that a visitor to the Qin state capital of Yong, near present-day Fengxiang, was so struck by the opulence of the buildings that he exclaimed: 'if it was built by ghosts then it would have exhausted their energy; if it was built by people then it would have caused them great suffering'.

The Qin capital was moved to Xianyang near Xi'an in the mid-fourth century BCE, where it remained until the demise of the Qin dynasty in 206 BCE. The First Emperor continued to build on this site, reportedly embarking on more than 270 palaces. According to Sima Qian, he had 'elevated walks and walled roads built to connect all the 270 palaces and scenic towers ... He filled the palaces with curtains and hangings, bells and drums, and beautiful women ...'. Apart from the women, archaeological evidence supports Sima Qian's description.

72. Architectural beam-fittings with dragon design
双面蟠虺纹楔形铜构件 /
雙面蟠虺紋楔形銅構件

Spring and Autumn period (771–475 BCE)
Bronze, 20 x 30cm; 12.5 x 46cm
Excavated at the archaeological site of Yongcheng, Yaojiagang, Fengxiang, Baoji, 1974
Shaanxi History Museum, 九一947; 九一1241

These bronze fittings were excavated in 1974 from the site of the ancient Qin capital of Yong. They were both functional and decorative, and would have reinforced the joints of wooden beams. These examples are decorated with dragon designs, drawn from the bronzes of the period.

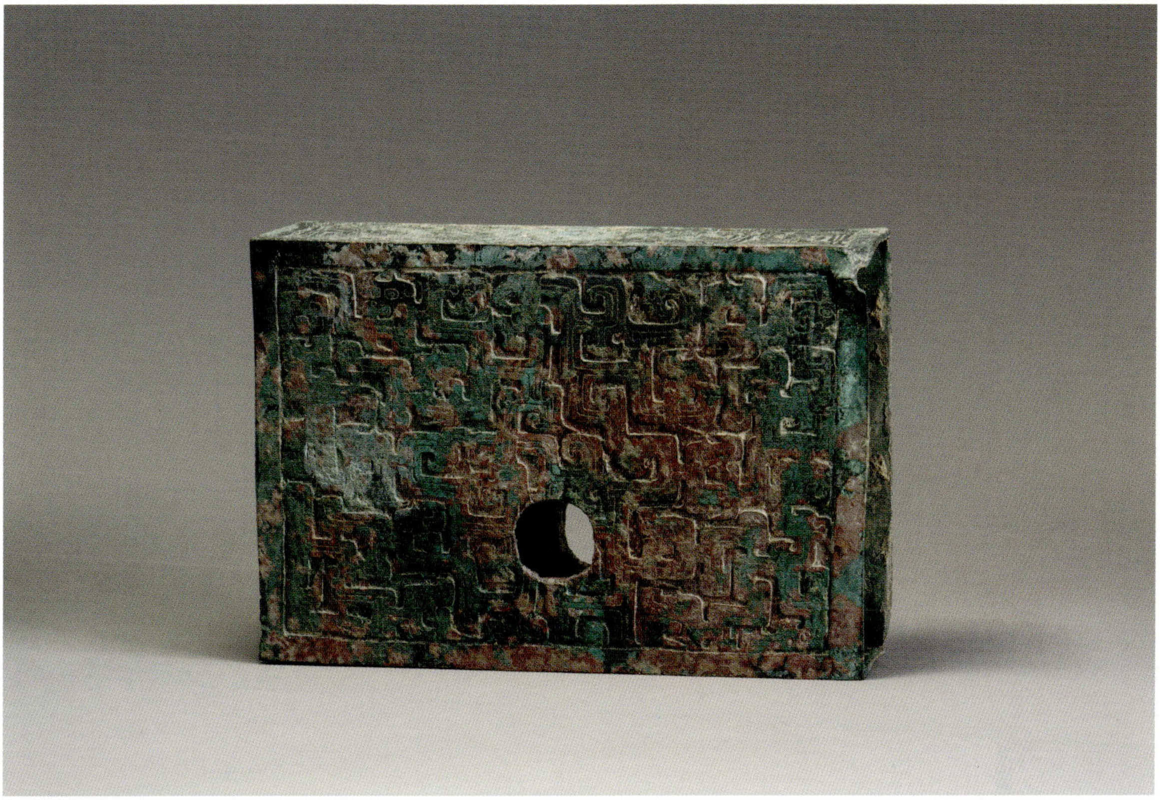

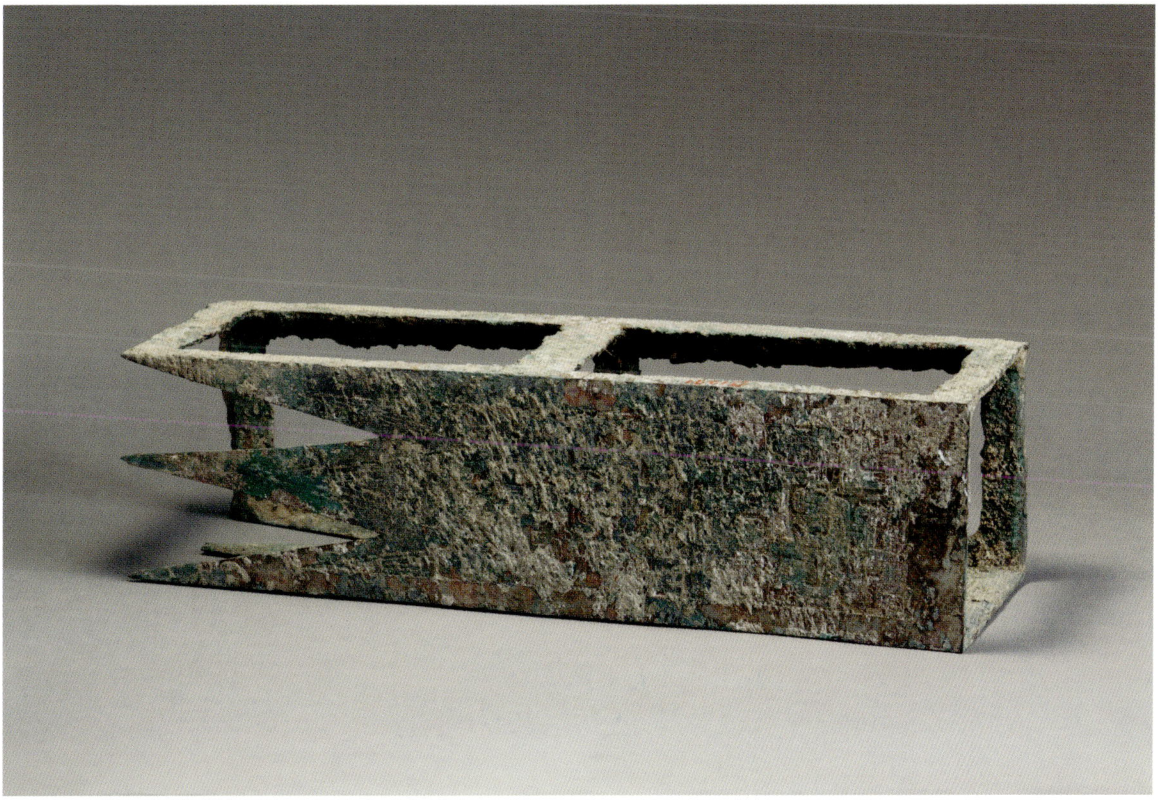

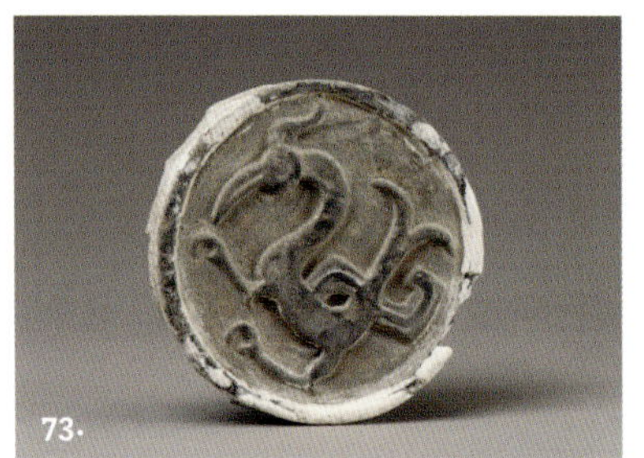
73.

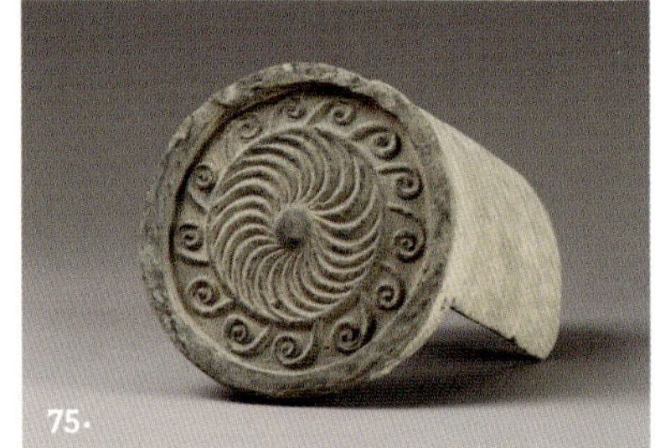
75.

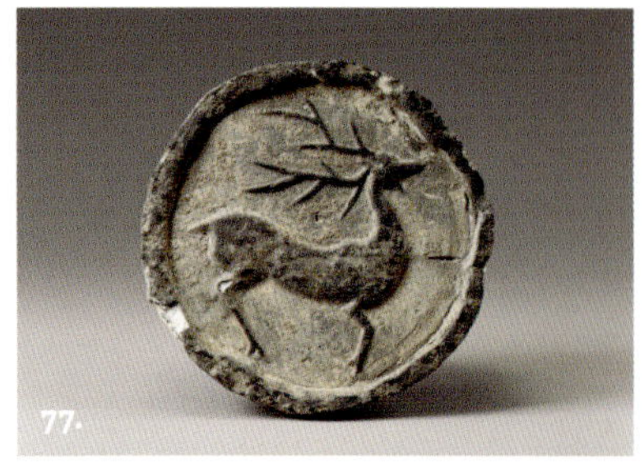
77.

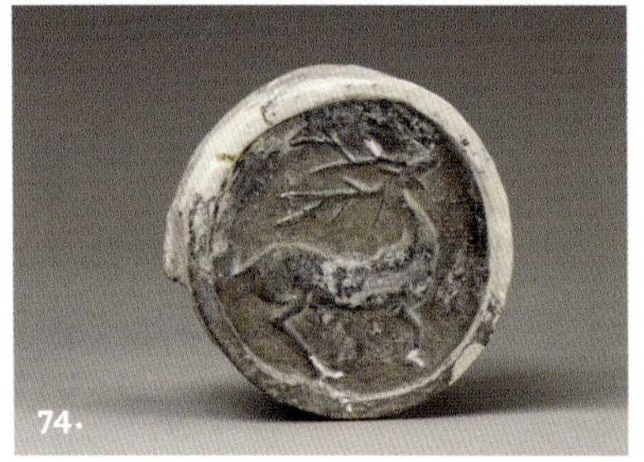
74.

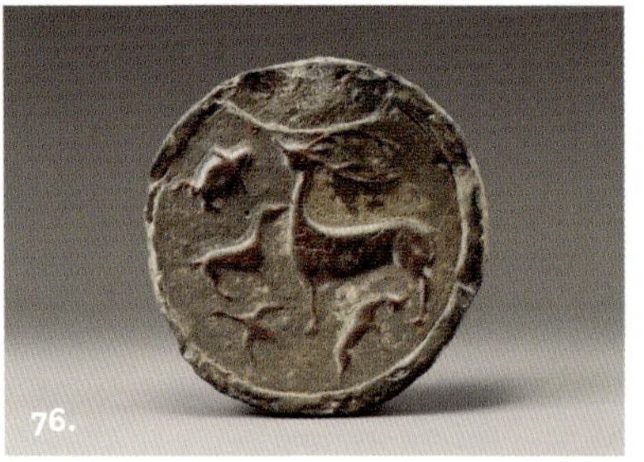
76.

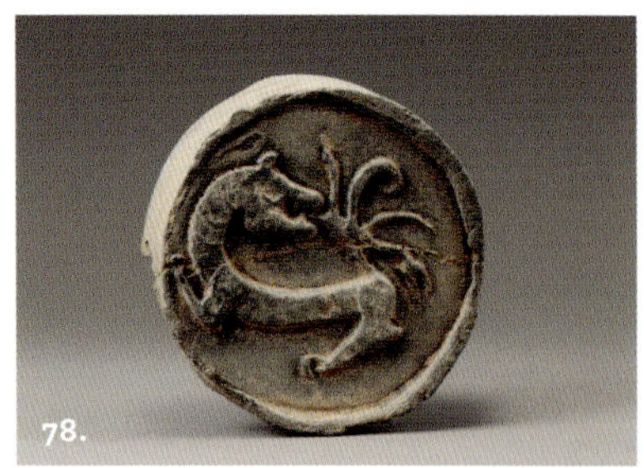
78.

Roof tile-ends protected and adorned the rooflines and eaves of ancient buildings. They frequently featured animal motifs, such as the deer (symbolising longevity) and the phoenix (representing peace), as well as abstracted patterns of such things as clouds, the sun and flowers – all auspicious signs and symbols.

73. Tile-end with phoenix motif
朱雀纹瓦当 / 朱雀紋瓦當

Warring States period (475–221 BCE)
Pottery, diameter 15.2cm
Excavated at the archaeological site of Qin Palace, Fengwei village, Fengxiang, Baoji, 1983
Emperor Qin Shihuang's Mausoleum Site Museum, 02965

74. Tile-end with deer motif
鹿纹瓦当 / 鹿紋瓦當

Warring States period (475–221 BCE)
Pottery, diameter 14.5cm
Excavated at the First Emperor of Qin's Mausoleum, Lintong, Xi'an, 1976
Emperor Qin Shihuang's Mausoleum Site Museum, 02966

75. Tile-end with cloud and floral motifs
葵纹瓦当 / 葵紋瓦當

Warring States period (475–221 BCE)
Pottery, diameter 15.3cm
Excavated at the archaeological site of the Qin capital of Yongcheng, Fengxiang, Baoji, 1982
Emperor Qin Shihuang's Mausoleum Site Museum, 02959

76. Tile-end with deer, goose, dog and toad motif
鹿雁狗蟾纹瓦当 / 鹿雁狗蟾紋瓦當

Warring States period (475–221 BCE)
Pottery, diameter 14.2cm
Collected in 1983
Fengxiang County Museum, 总0517

77. Tile-end with deer motif
鹿纹瓦当 / 鹿紋瓦當

Warring States period (475–221 BCE)
Pottery, diameter 15cm
Collected in 1977
Fengxiang County Museum, 总0426

78. Tile-end with tiger and goose motif
虎雁纹瓦当 / 虎雁紋瓦當

Warring States period (475–221 BCE)
Pottery, diameter 14.8cm
Excavated at the archaeological site of the Qin capital of Yongcheng, Fengxiang, Baoji, 2005
Fengxiang County Museum, 总1335

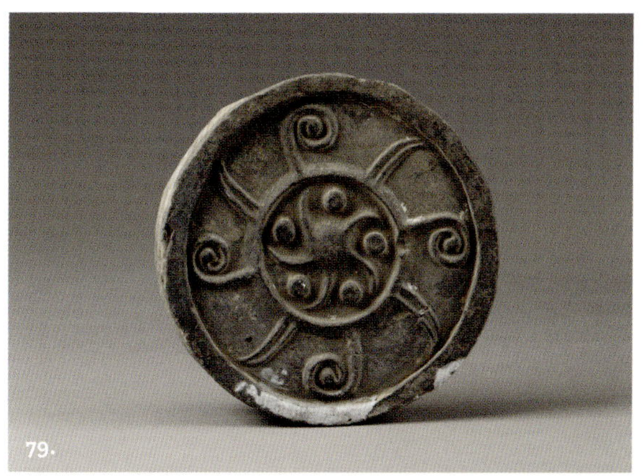
79.

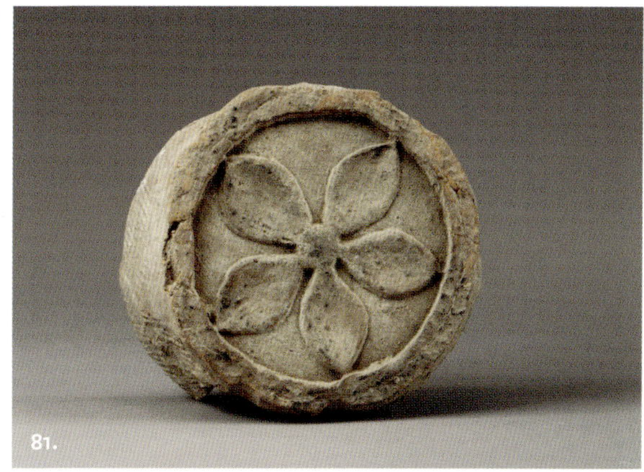
81.

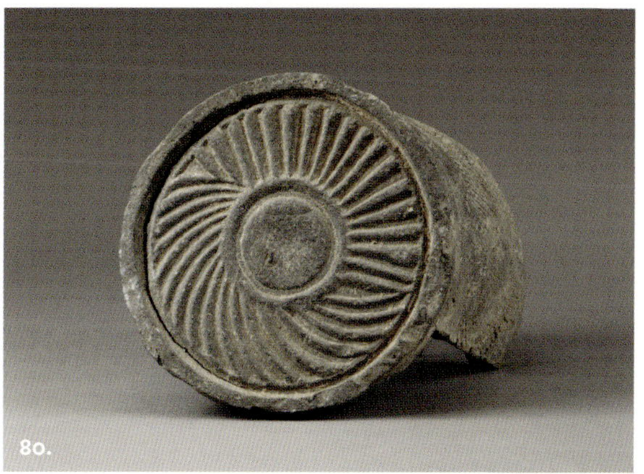
80.

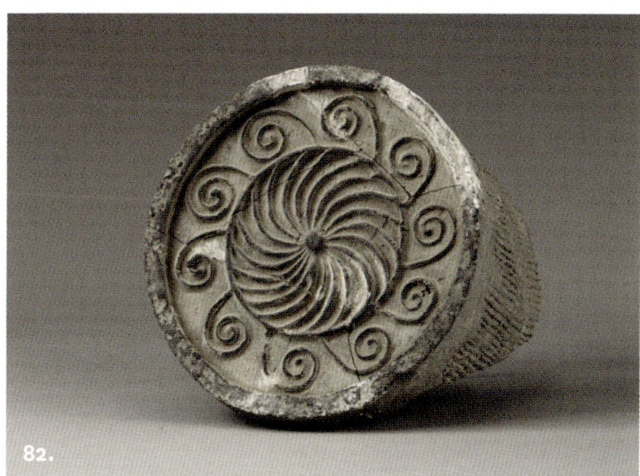
82.

79. Tile-end with cloud and floral designs
葵纹瓦当 / 葵紋瓦當

Warring States period (475–221 BCE)

Pottery, diameter 16cm

Excavated at the archaeological site of the Qin capital of Yongcheng, Fengxiang, Baoji, 1986

Shaanxi Provincial Institute of Archaeology, 004504

80. Tile-end with sun design
太阳纹瓦当 / 太陽紋瓦當

Warring States period (475–221 BCE)

Pottery, diameter 15cm

Excavated at Sunjia Nantou, Fengxiang, Baoji, 1996

Shaanxi Provincial Institute of Archaeology, 004438

81. Tile-end with floral design
叶纹瓦当 / 葉紋瓦當

Warring States period (475–221 BCE)

Pottery, diameter 16cm

Excavated at Sunjia Nantou, Fengxiang, Baoji, 1996

Shaanxi Provincial Institute of Archaeology, 004658

82. Tile-end with cloud and floral designs
卷云纹瓦当 / 捲雲紋瓦當

Warring States period (475–221 BCE)

Pottery, diameter 15cm

Excavated at the archaeological site of the Qin capital of Yongcheng, Fengxiang, Baoji, 1986

Shaanxi Provincial Institute of Archaeology, 004471

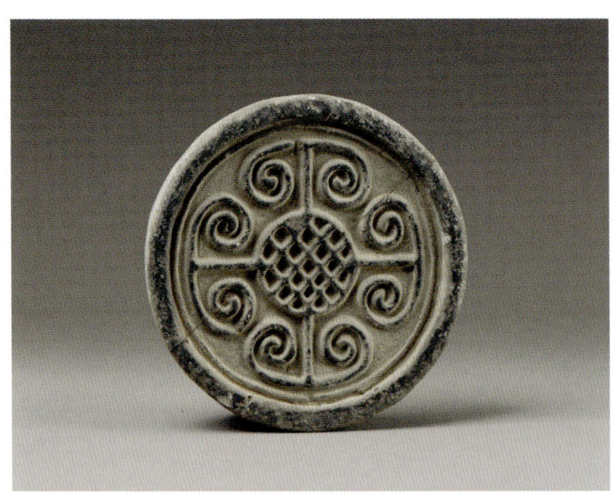

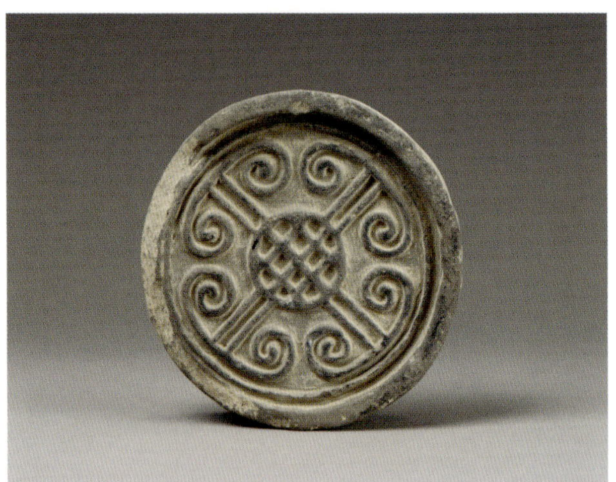

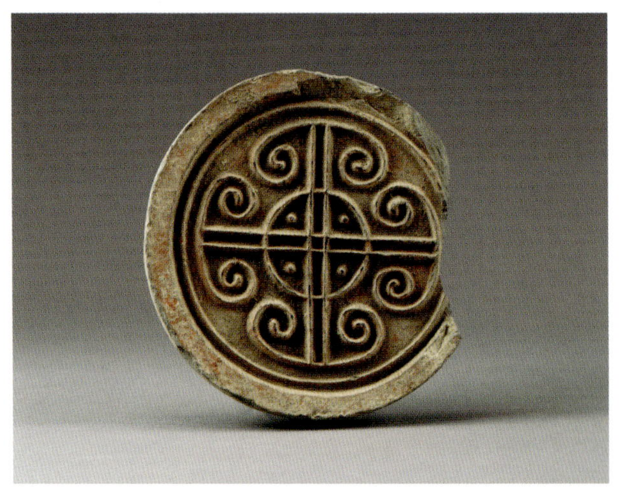

83. Tile-end with cloud design
卷云纹瓦当 / 捲雲紋瓦當

Qin dynasty (221–206 BCE)

Pottery, diameter 16.5cm

Excavated at the First Emperor of Qin's Mausoleum, 1976

Emperor Qin Shihuang's Mausoleum Site Museum, 002560

84. Tile-end with cloud design
卷云纹瓦当 / 捲雲紋瓦當

Qin dynasty (221–206 BCE)

Pottery, diameter 15.7cm

Excavated at the First Emperor of Qin's Mausoleum, 1982

Emperor Qin Shihuang's Mausoleum Site Museum, 003452

85. Tile-end with cloud design
云纹瓦当 / 雲紋瓦當

Han dynasty (206 BCE–220 CE)

Pottery, diameter 15cm

Excavated from the Dongling Mausoleum, Lintong, Xi'an, 1986

Shaanxi Provincial Institute of Archaeology, 004473

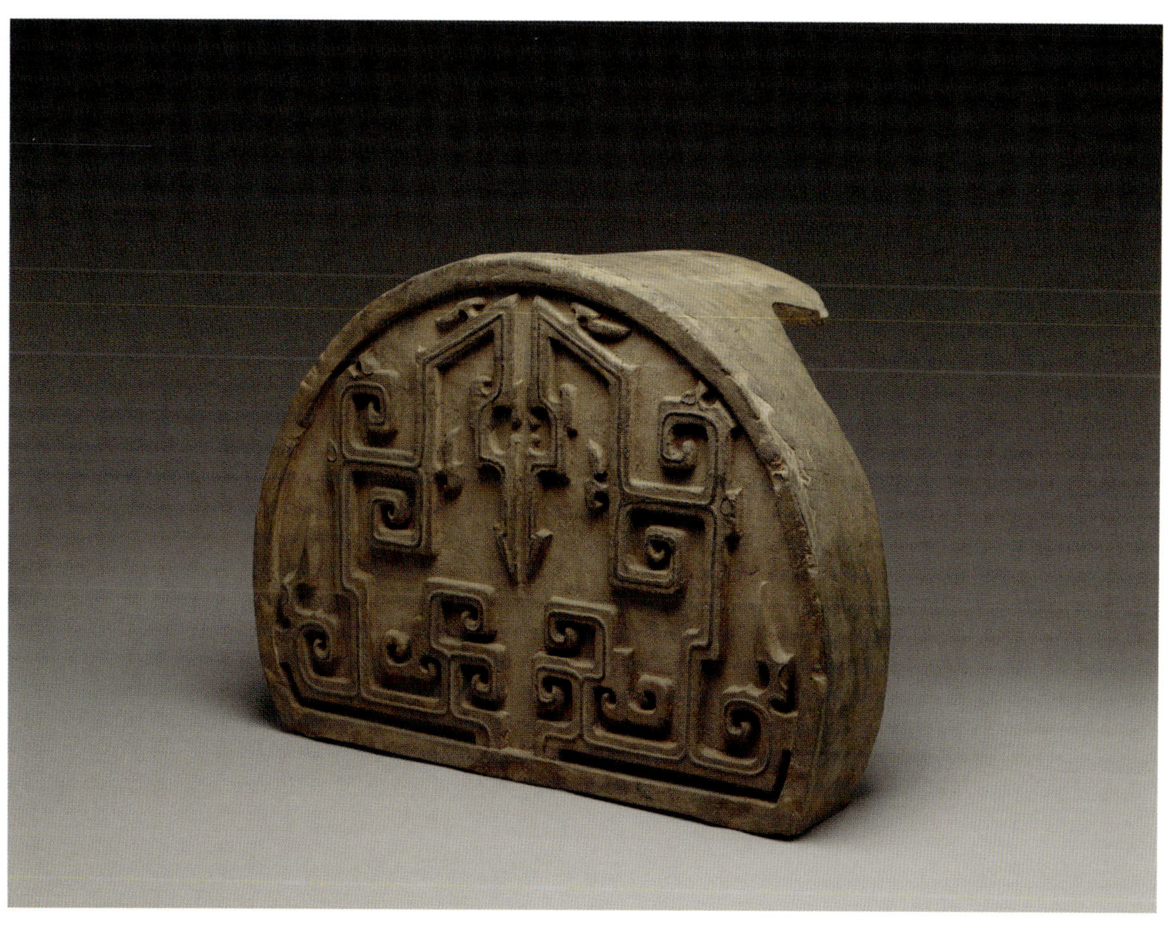

86. Large roof tile-end
夔纹大瓦当 / 夔紋大瓦當

Qin dynasty (221–206 BCE)

Pottery, 38.2 x 50.8cm

Excavated at the archaeological site of the Qin Yellow Mountain Palace, Xingping, 1993

Shaanxi Provincial Institute of Archaeology, 003001

This large roof tile-end has a geometric pattern that may represent two abstracted dragons in mirror image. The imagery is apparently closely associated with the First Emperor, and has been found on similar tiles at other Qin palace sites.

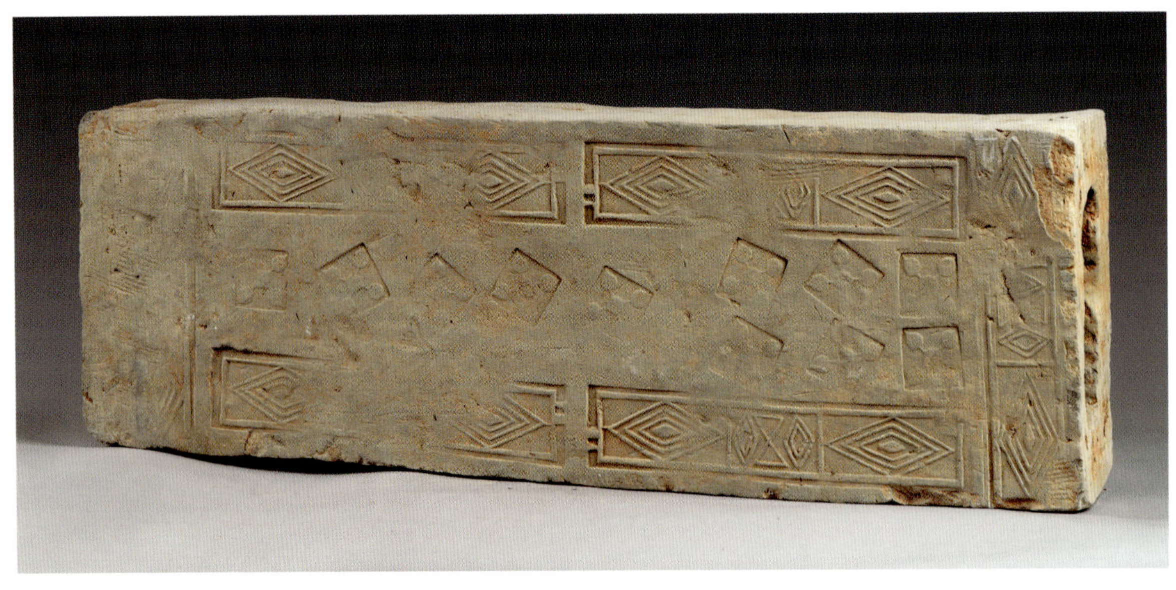

87. **Hollow brick with floral and geometric motifs**
龙纹空心砖 / 龍紋空心磚

Han dynasty (206 BCE–220 CE)

Pottery, 32.5 x 96.5cm

Excavated from a Han tomb, Wangjiazhuang, Fushuizhen, Shangnan, Shangluo, 2008

Shangluo City Museum, 总3464 C477

88. **Gate ring holders (*Pushou*)**
铺首 / 鋪首

Han dynasty (206 BCE–220 CE)

Bronze, widths 4.82cm

Excavated from a Han tomb, Donglongshan, Shangluo, 2002

Shangluo City Museum, 总3143 D2600; 总3149 D2606

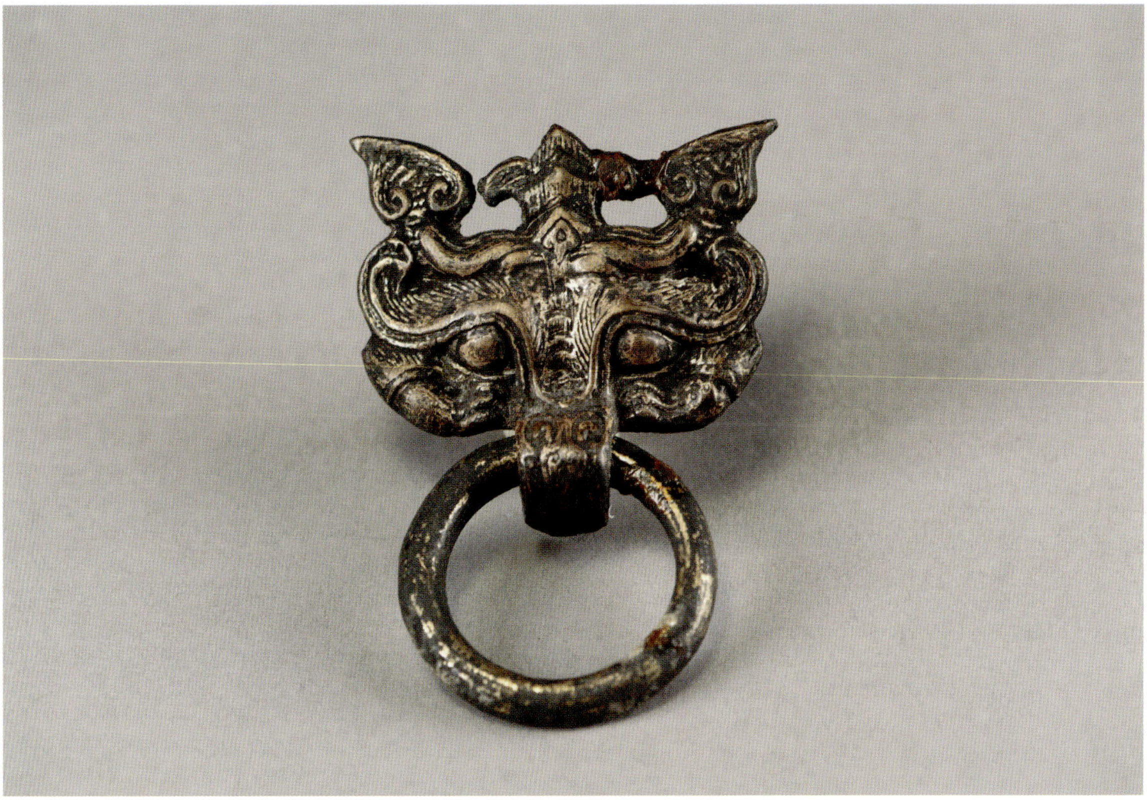

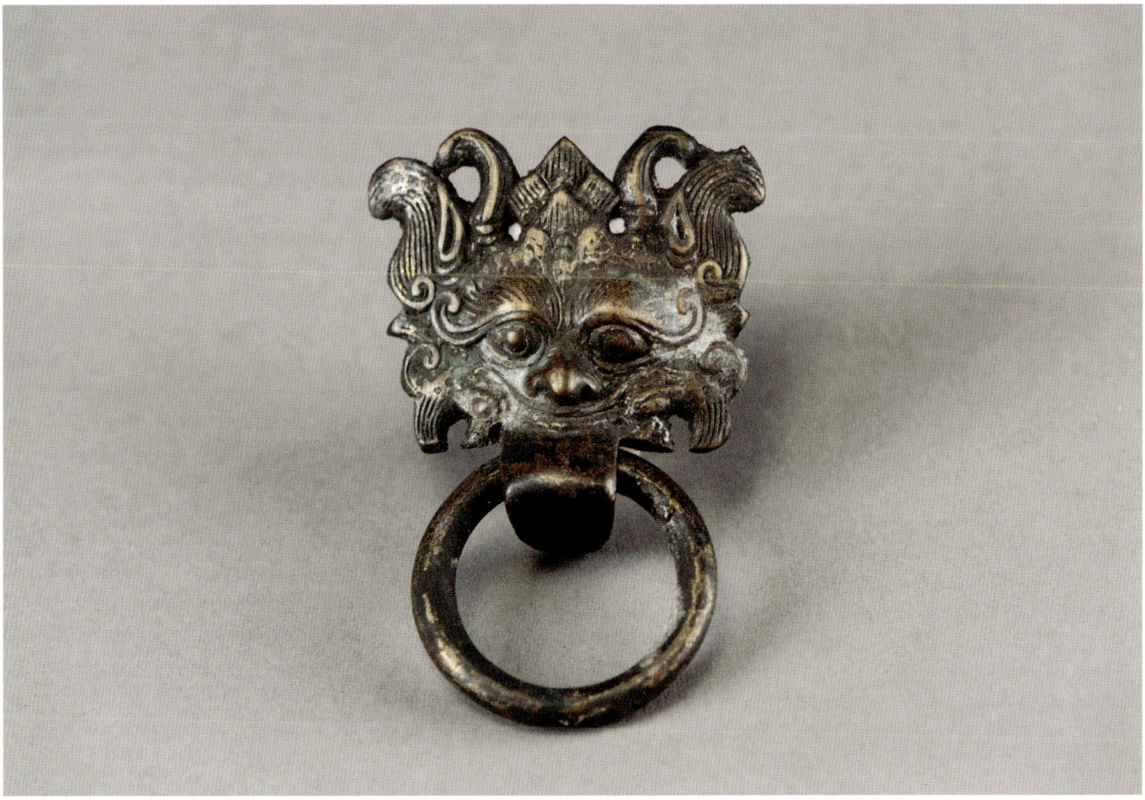

CURRENCY AND MEASURES

Immediately following the unification of the kingdom by conquest in 221 BCE, Ying Zheng 嬴政 proclaimed himself Qin Shihuang 秦始皇, or First Emperor of Qin. Along with implementing administrative and legal reforms, he set about introducing a number of controls to standardise writing, weights, measures and currency.

During the Warring States period, the Chinese spoke many different languages and Chinese script had many different forms. The First Emperor ordered everyone to use the same written form – the *xiaozhuan* 小篆 (small-seal) style of his state. Developing a common script was crucial in enabling effective communication over vast territories.

Similarly, units of weight and measurement, and currency, varied from state to state, affecting trade, as well as the amount of taxes collected by the state. Qin standards for weights and measures were imposed throughout China, and the responsibility for minting coins was centralised.

Together, these new standards facilitated better communication and trade throughout China. They also established the basis for the shared cultural and political identities of what was to become modern China.

89. Bronze measure inscribed with two edicts
两诏文铜权 / 兩詔文銅權

Qin dynasty (221–206 BCE)
Bronze, 7 x 20.8cm
Excavated at Yaowangdong, Liquan, Xianyang, 1982
Shaanxi History Museum, 八七98

Weights and measures issued during the First Emperor's reign often bear the following edict:

In the twenty-sixth year [i.e., 221 BCE], the Emperor completely unified the regional lords of All-under-Heaven. The black-headed ones [i.e., the common people] were at great peace, and he established the title of 'Emperor'. Now he commands the Chief Ministers [Wei] Zhuang and [Wang] Wan: 'As for the standards, lengths, measures, and rules that are not unified and are doubtful, clarify and unify them all.'

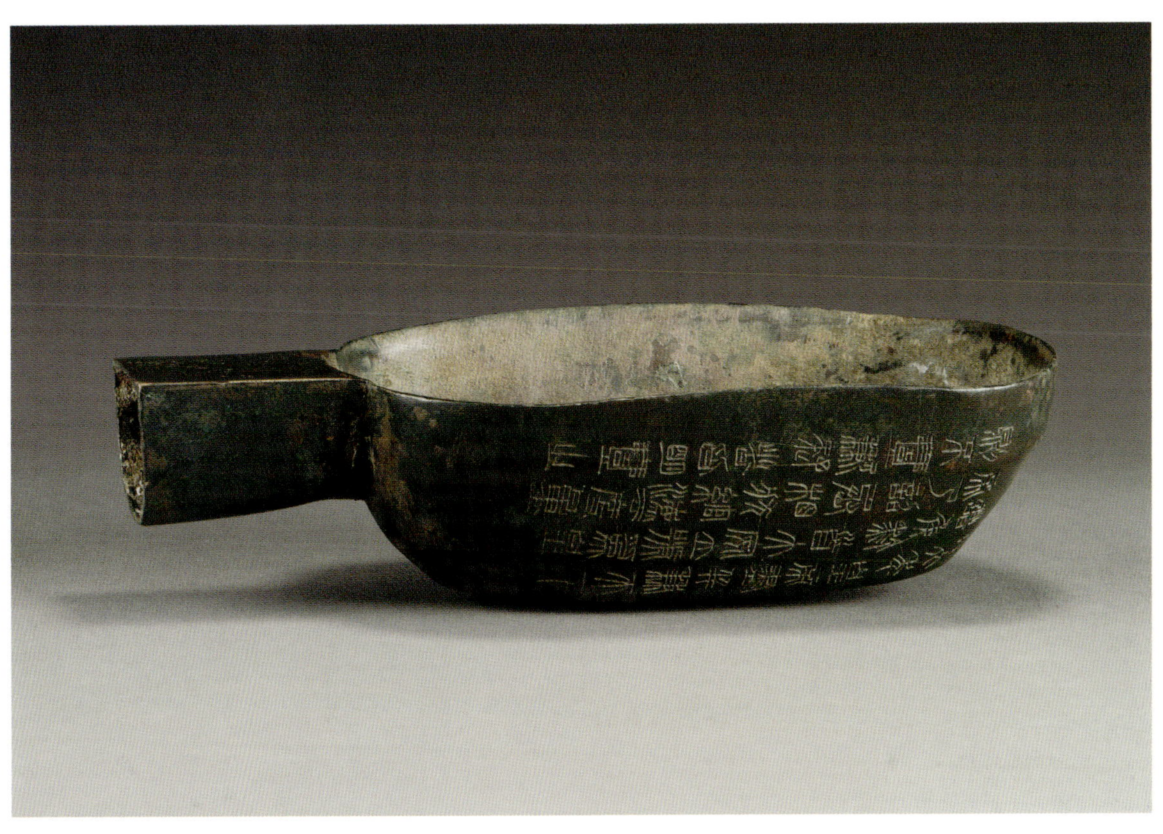

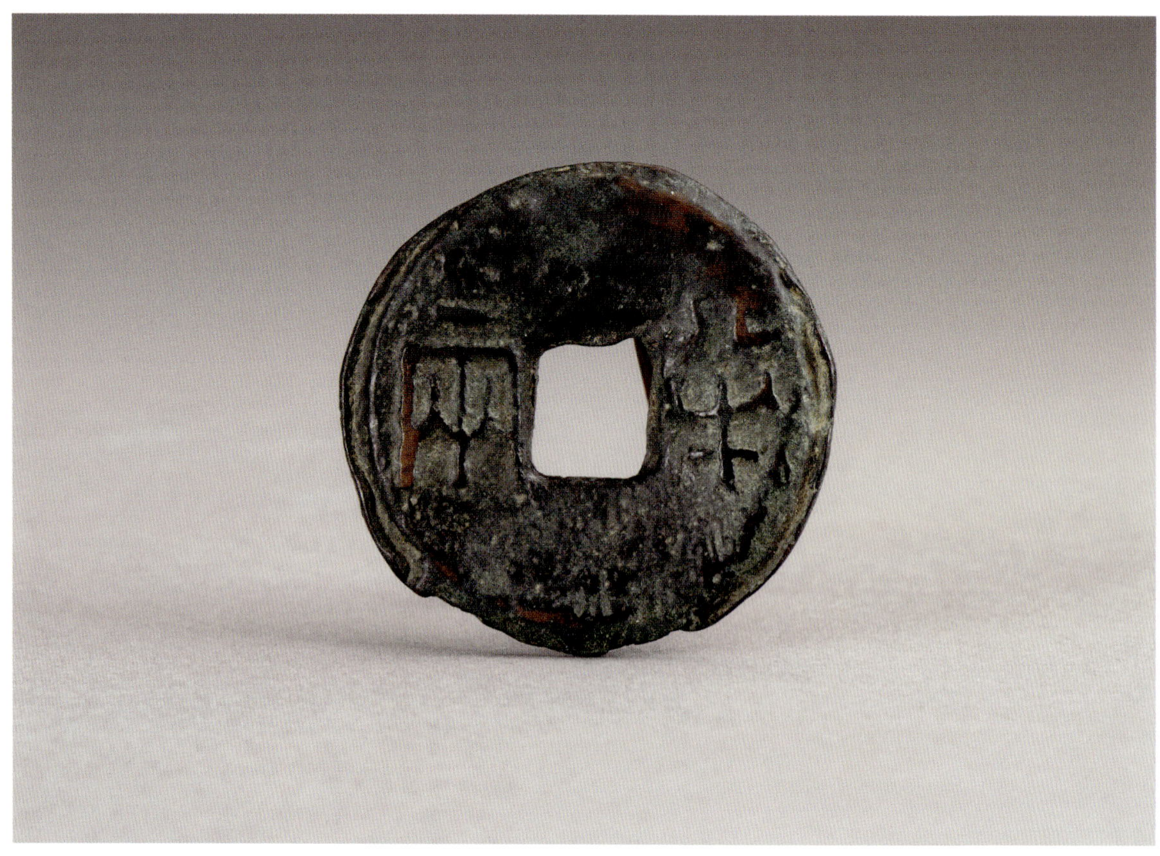

90. Money of the Seven States: Qin state coin
秦半两 / 秦半兩

Qin dynasty (221–206 BCE)
Bronze, diameter 3.5cm
Collected by the Suide County Museum
Yulin Institute of Cultural Heritage Conservation, 钱*001*

Before Qin unified the Seven Warring States, each state issued its own currency. Shovel-shaped, knife-shaped or ring-shaped, the coins could be used only in a particular state. Qin abolished all of these currencies and issued the *banliang* 半兩 (half-ounce coin) – China's first single, unified currency.

Some scholars say that its form – round, with a square hole in the middle – symbolised the emperor's pivotal role as conduit between Heaven, believed to be round, and Earth, thought to be square. It was also practical, as the hole in the middle allowed coins to be strung together and easily carried.

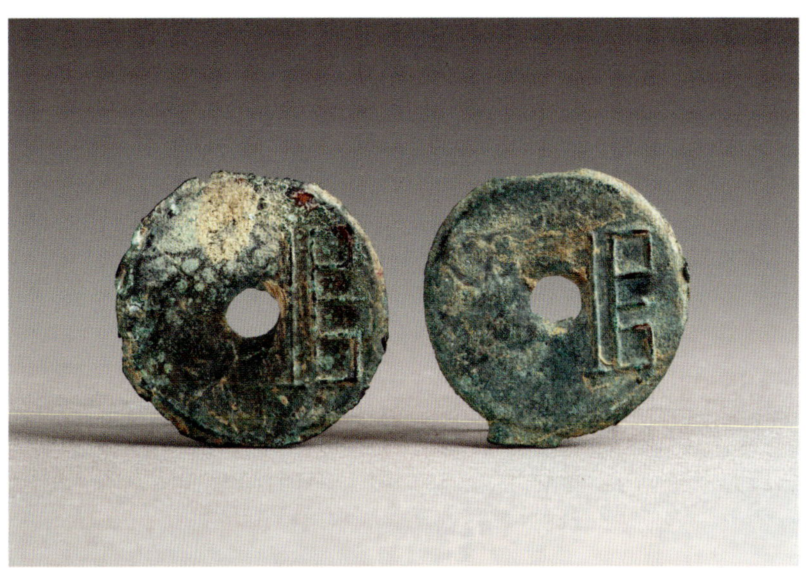

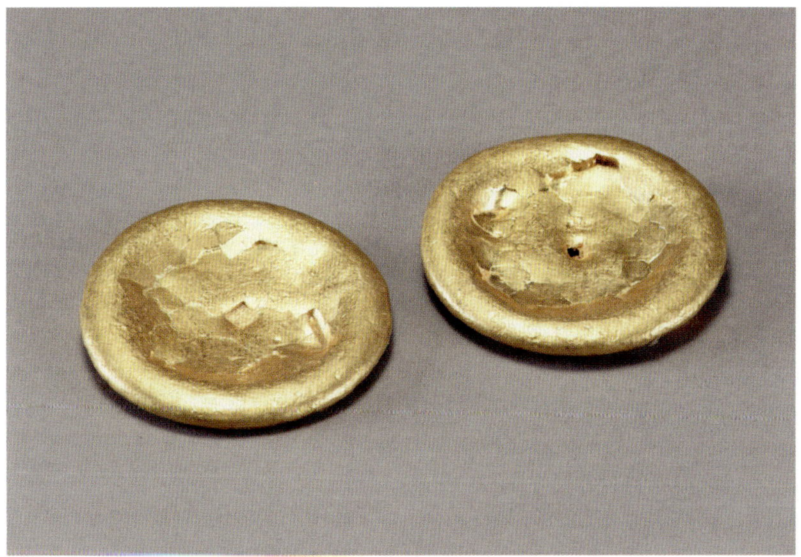

92. **Disc-shaped ingot**
金饼 / 金餅

Han dynasty (206 BCE–220 CE)

Gold, diameter 6cm

Excavated at Shilipu village, East Tanjiaxiang, Weiyang, Xi'an, 1991

Shaanxi History Museum, ZT492; ZT495

The use of gold as currency dates back to the Warring States period. Following the standardisation of coins during the Qin dynasty, gold was increasingly used as an upscale currency. Disc-shaped ingots such as these were widely used during the Han dynasty for efficient, indirect exchange and the storage of wealth.

91. **Coin with inscription**
「垣」字钱 / 「垣」字錢

Qin dynasty (221–206 BCE)

Bronze, diameter 4cm

Collected in 1998

Yulin Institute of Cultural Heritage Conservation, 钱146

秦始皇陵

The First Emperor's tomb complex

The legend of the First Emperor's tomb was immortalised in a description written by Sima Qian in his *Records of the Grand Historian*. He wrote:

> As soon as the First Emperor became King of Qin excavations and building had started at Mt Li [the location of the tomb], while after he won the empire more than 700,000 conscripts from all parts of the country worked there ... they dug through three subterranean streams and poured molten copper and bronze to make the outer coffin, and the tomb was filled with models of palaces, pavilions and offices as well as fine vessels, precious stones and rarities. Artisans were ordered to fix up crossbows so that any thief breaking in would be shot. All the country's rivers, the Yellow River and the Yangtze were reproduced in quicksilver and by some mechanical means made to flow into a miniature ocean. The heavenly constellations were shown above and the regions of the Earth below. The candles were made of whale oil to ensure their burning forever.

While the tomb itself has not yet been excavated, it has been reported that high levels of mercury recorded there might serve to confirm Sima's description. However, Sima did not record the existence of the First Emperor's Terracotta Army, which lay untouched for almost two thousand years until its discovery by peasant farmers in 1974.

THE FIRST EMPEROR'S ARMY

opposite page **Unarmoured soldiers from Pit 1 of Qin Shihuang's tomb complex.**

The Qin Terracotta Army occupies four large pits located 1.5 kilometres east of the Emperor's burial mound (see map on page 16). It is estimated that there are 8000 soldiers in total, with approximately 3000 having been excavated to date. The life-size, life-like soldiers, each weighing 100–300 kilograms and standing about 180 centimetres high, continue to fascinate people around the globe.

Pit 1, the largest, contained an army of foot soldiers, armoured officers and wooden carriages, with each carriage drawn by four horses. Pit 2 housed the cavalry, with armoured cavalrymen, war chariots drawn by four horses, archers and foot soldiers. Pit 3 is much smaller, and contained only one chariot, sixty-eight high-ranking officers and foot soldiers. To date, this is the only pit that has been excavated in its entirety.

Scholars continue to debate the function of the First Emperor's Army. Some think that, due to the fact the soldiers face east, they were intended to protect the First Emperor in the spirit world from possible attack by those he had slaughtered during his conquest of China. Others question the soldiers' readiness for battle, as they are not fully armoured. Further questions are raised by the chariot in Pit 3, which stands empty, awaiting its commander into eternity.

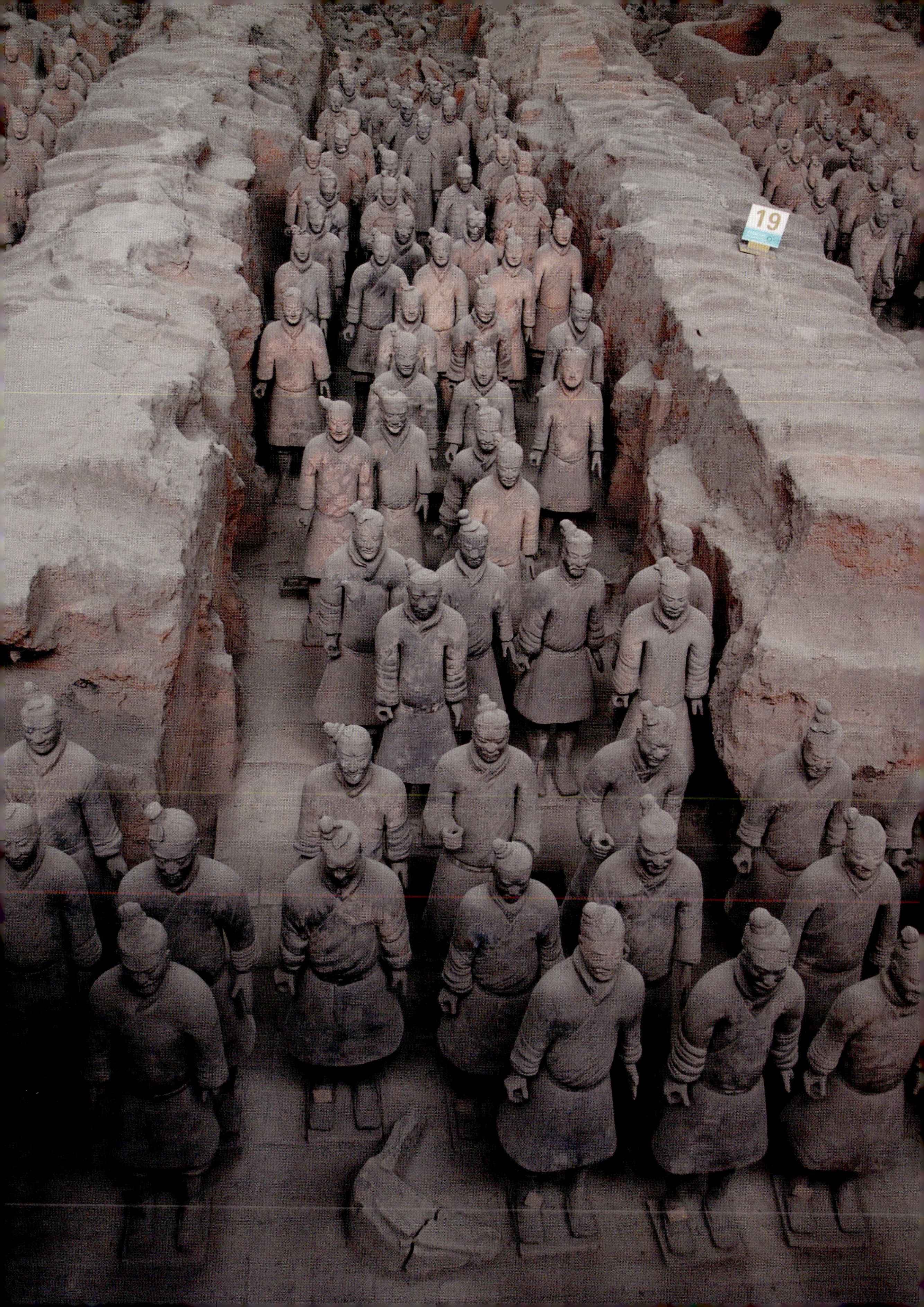
19

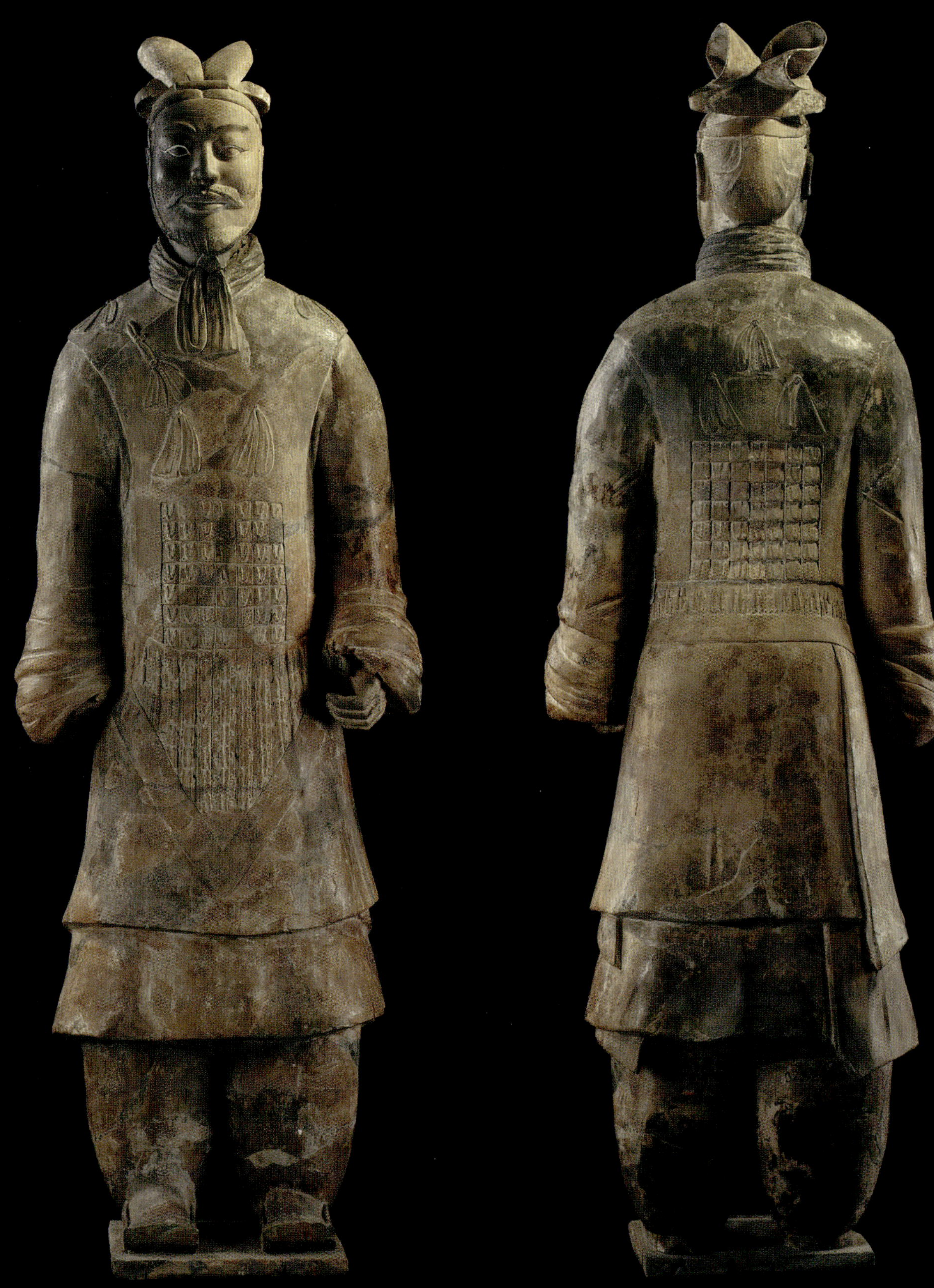

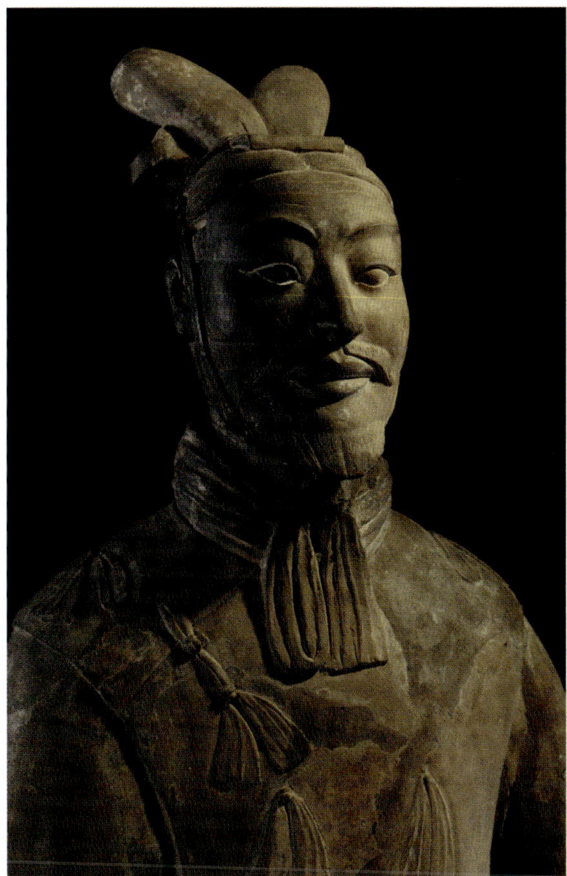

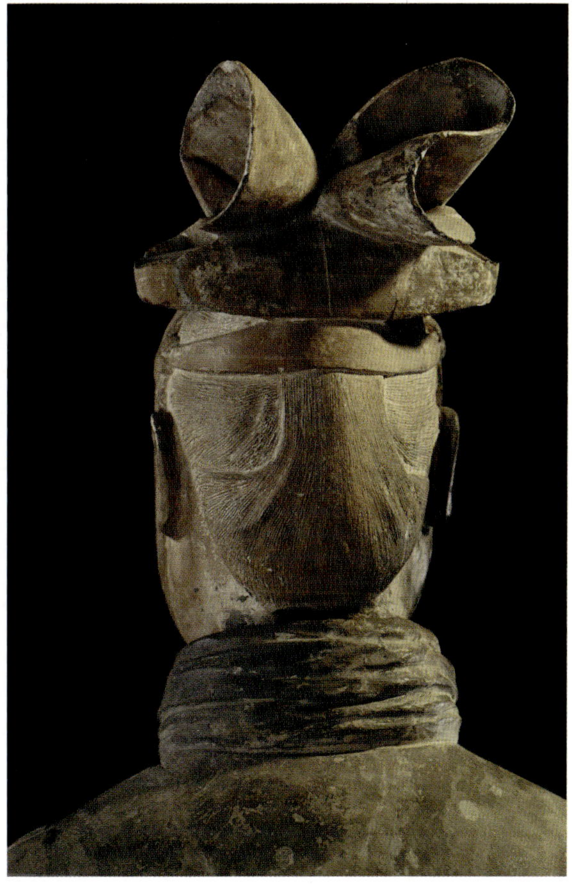

93. Armoured general
铠甲将军俑 / 鎧甲將軍俑

Qin dynasty (221–206 BCE)

Pottery, height 196cm

Excavated from Pit 1, Qin Shihuang tomb complex, 1977

Emperor Qin Shihuang's Mausoleum Site Museum, 002524

The general is the most impressive of the terracotta figures. Standing at nearly 2 metres in height, his imposing stature and poise indicate his status within the army. The general's armour extends below his waist and ends in a triangle; his head-dress is distinctive, consisting of a flat, rectangular front, split into two peaks – referred to as a 'pheasant-tail' cap. The bows on his chest and on the rear of his armour are thought to indicate rank.

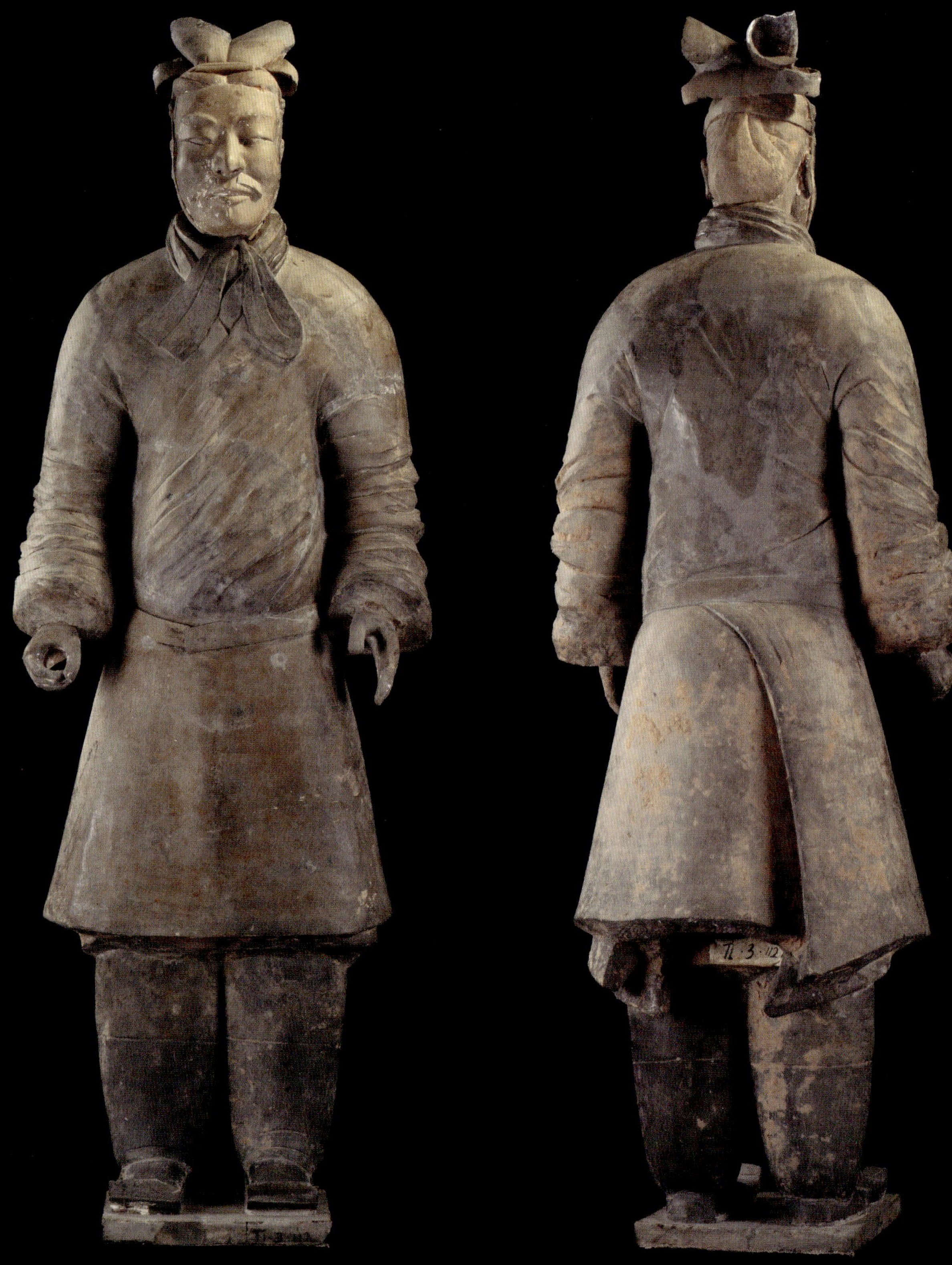

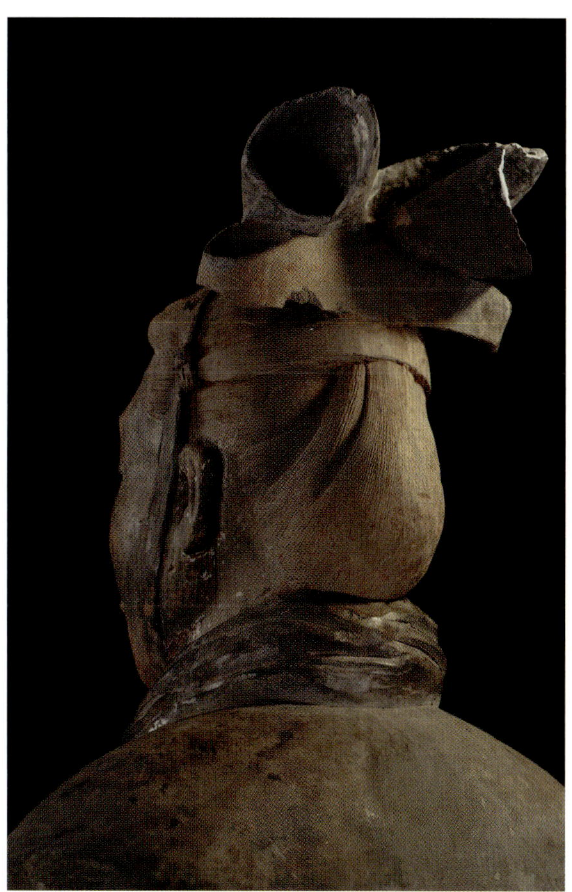

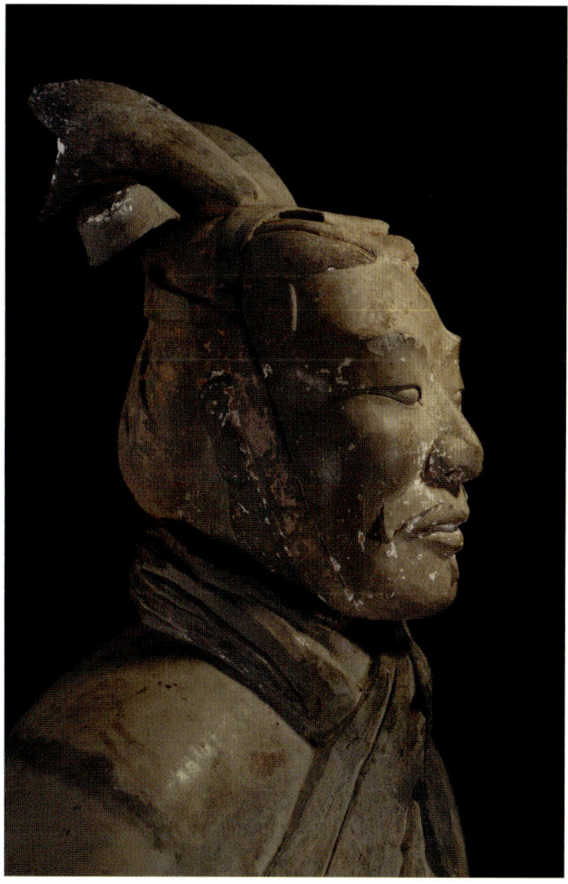

94. Unarmoured general
战袍将军俑 / 戰袍將軍俑

Qin dynasty (221–206 BCE)

Pottery, height 196cm

Excavated from Pit 1, Qin Shihuang tomb complex, 1976

Emperor Qin Shihuang's Mausoleum Site Museum, 000852

In contrast to the armoured general, the unarmoured general wears a scarf and loose robes that are secured around his waist by a belt and buckle. The folds of the cloth are carefully rendered and incised with details to suggest texture.

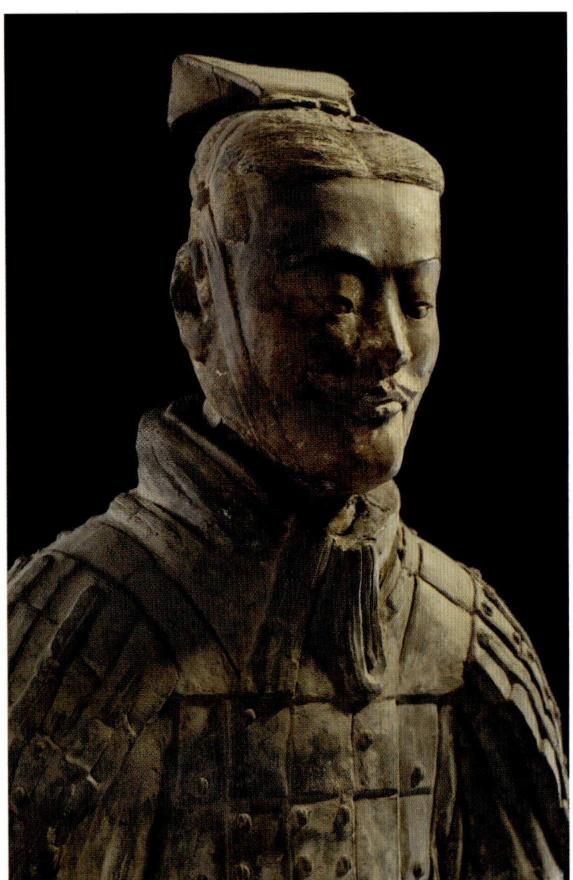

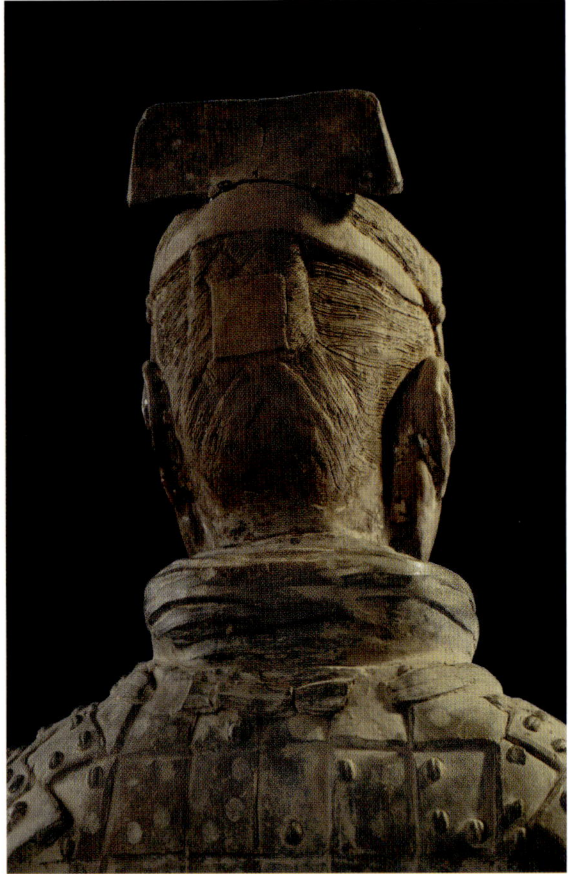

95. Armoured military officer
中级铠甲军吏俑 / 中級鎧甲軍吏俑

Qin dynasty (221–206 BCE)

Pottery, height 190cm

Excavated from Pit 1, Qin Shihuang tomb complex, 1978

Emperor Qin Shihuang's Mausoleum Site Museum, 002758

The accessories of each figure determine his rank. This figure's hat ties under his chin, identifying him as a member of the officer class. He is slightly shorter than the general, and his pose is more hesitant, suggesting he is awaiting instruction rather than delivering it.

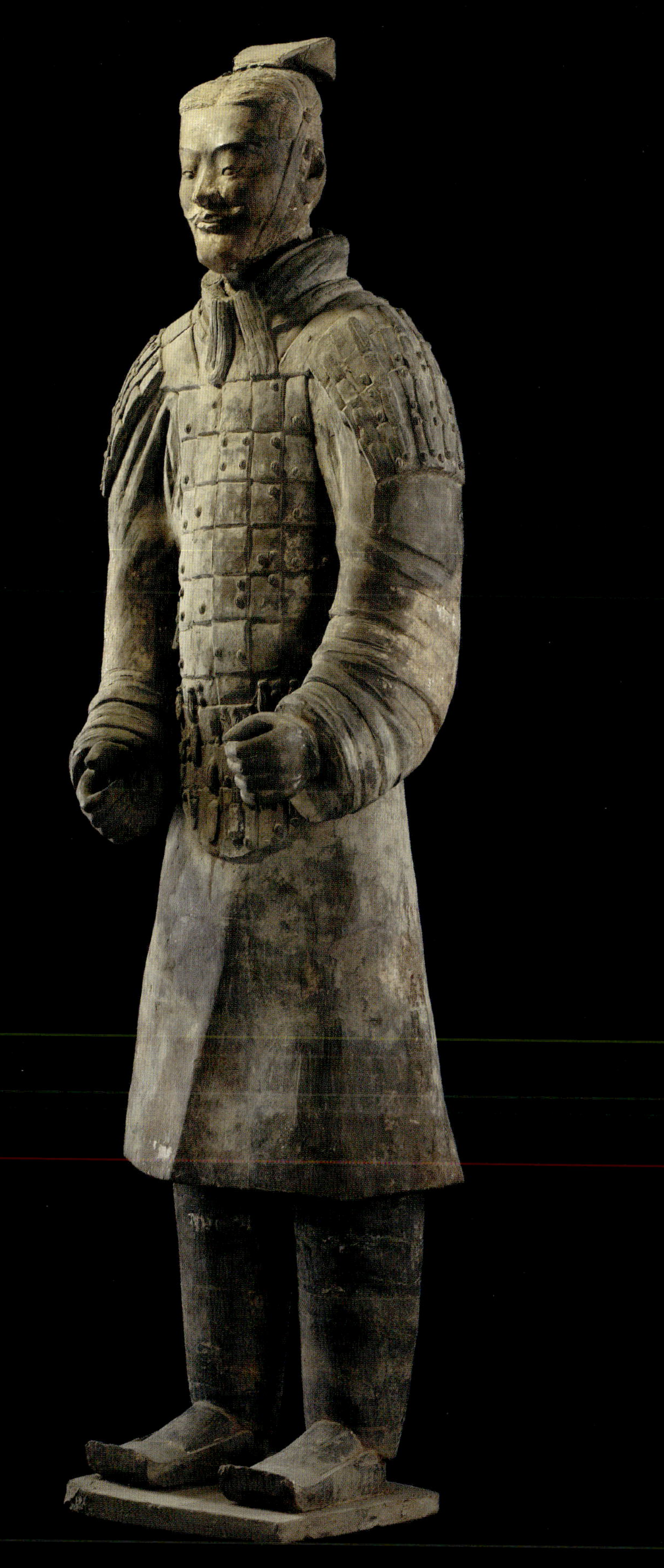

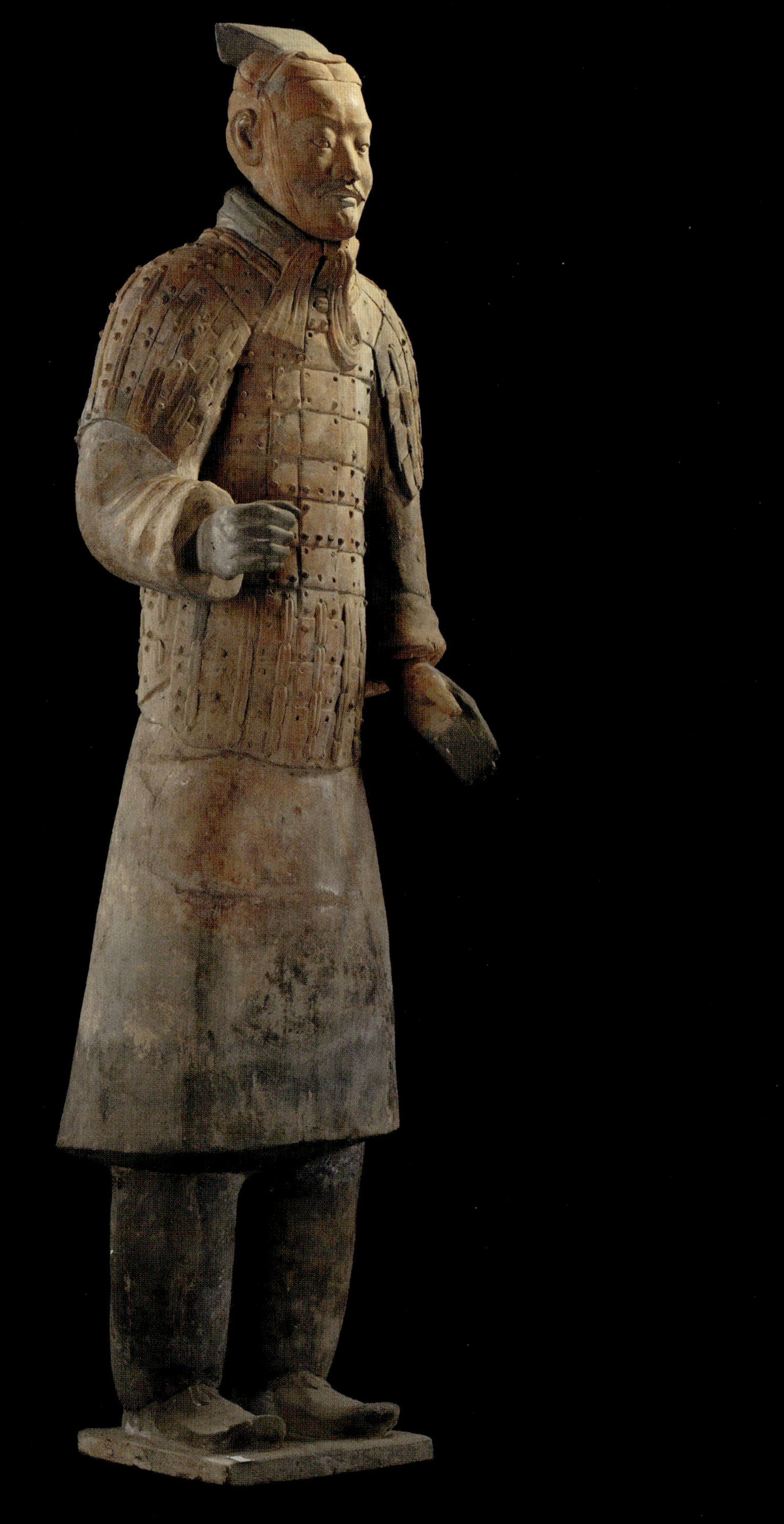

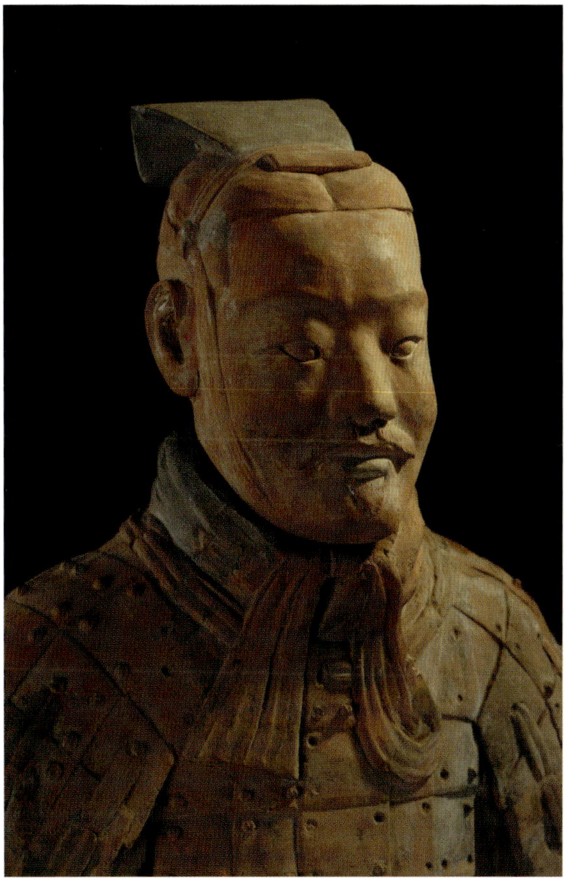

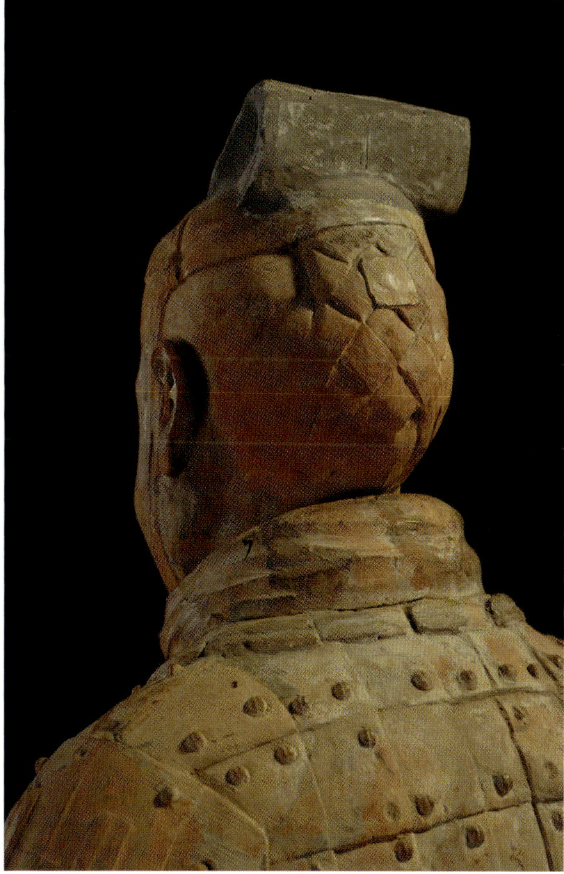

96. **Armoured military officer**
中级铠甲军吏俑 / 中級鎧甲軍吏俑

Qin dynasty (221–206 BCE)

Pottery, height 191cm

Excavated from Pit 1, Qin Shihuang tomb complex, 1976

Emperor Qin Shihuang's Mausoleum Site Museum, 002526

Originally, it was thought that the terracotta warriors were made from mass-produced moulded components assembled into different combinations and finished with detailed sculpting. However, recent research has shown that the variation in figures exceeds the possibilities of combination that a set number of parts would have enabled.

Instead, each figure was made from the feet up, with each successive body part being made from thick coils of clay. The head was made and fired separately, then joined to the body with soft clay. Sculptural detail was added by hand to the basic human form, including, for example, the remarkably individualised facial features and hair, and the plated armour and folded scarf of this officer. The figures were then dried in the shade and fired in large kilns at temperatures between 950°C and 1050°C before being painted.

The warriors bear the stamps or carved names of their makers. While this could be read as a mark of authorship, it may also have acted as a means for administrative leaders to monitor progress and to assess the work of individual makers.

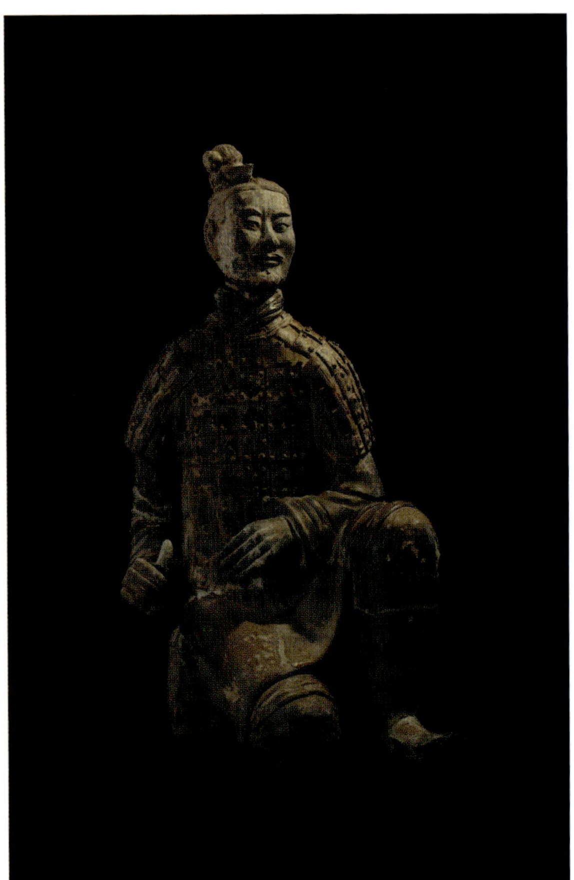

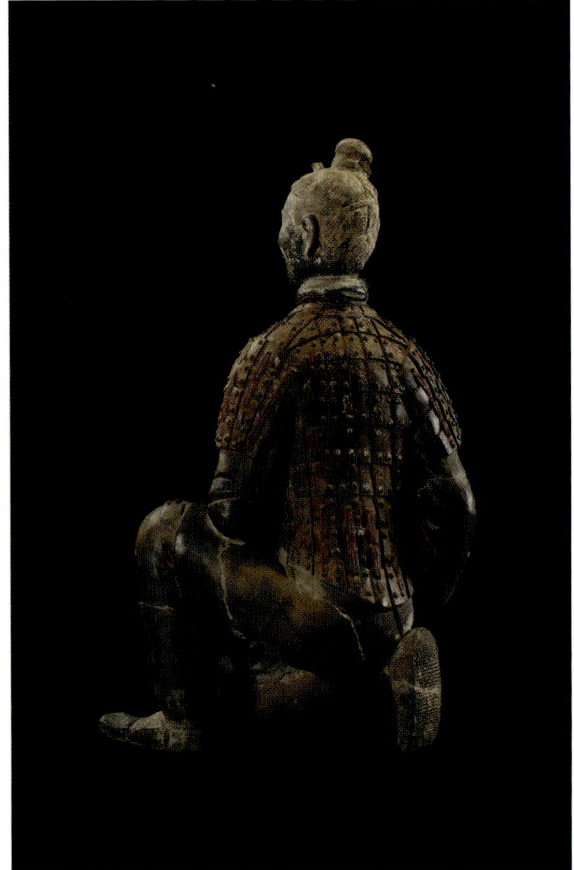

97. Kneeling archer
彩绘跪射俑 / 彩繪跪射俑

Qin dynasty (221–206 BCE)
Pottery, height 120cm
Excavated from Pit 2, Qin Shihuang tomb complex, 1999
Emperor Qin Shihuang's Mausoleum Site Museum, 002812

The kneeling and standing archers come exclusively from Pit 2. Positioned at the forefront of the force, they were the primary defence line, intended to protect the cavalry forces and chariots. The kneeling archer is equipped with body and shoulder armour, and would have held a crossbow in his hands. The degree of detail extends to the tread on his shoe, the ribbons holding his armour together and a unique plaited hairstyle.

The kneeling archers also have much surviving pigment, indicating that they, like all of the warriors, were originally painted in vivid colours. Their faces and hands were painted to approximate flesh, and their robes and armour were enlivened by colouring with mineral pigments such as cinnabar (red), azurite (blue), malachite (green), bone white, and a colour known as 'Han purple', produced from barium copper silicate.

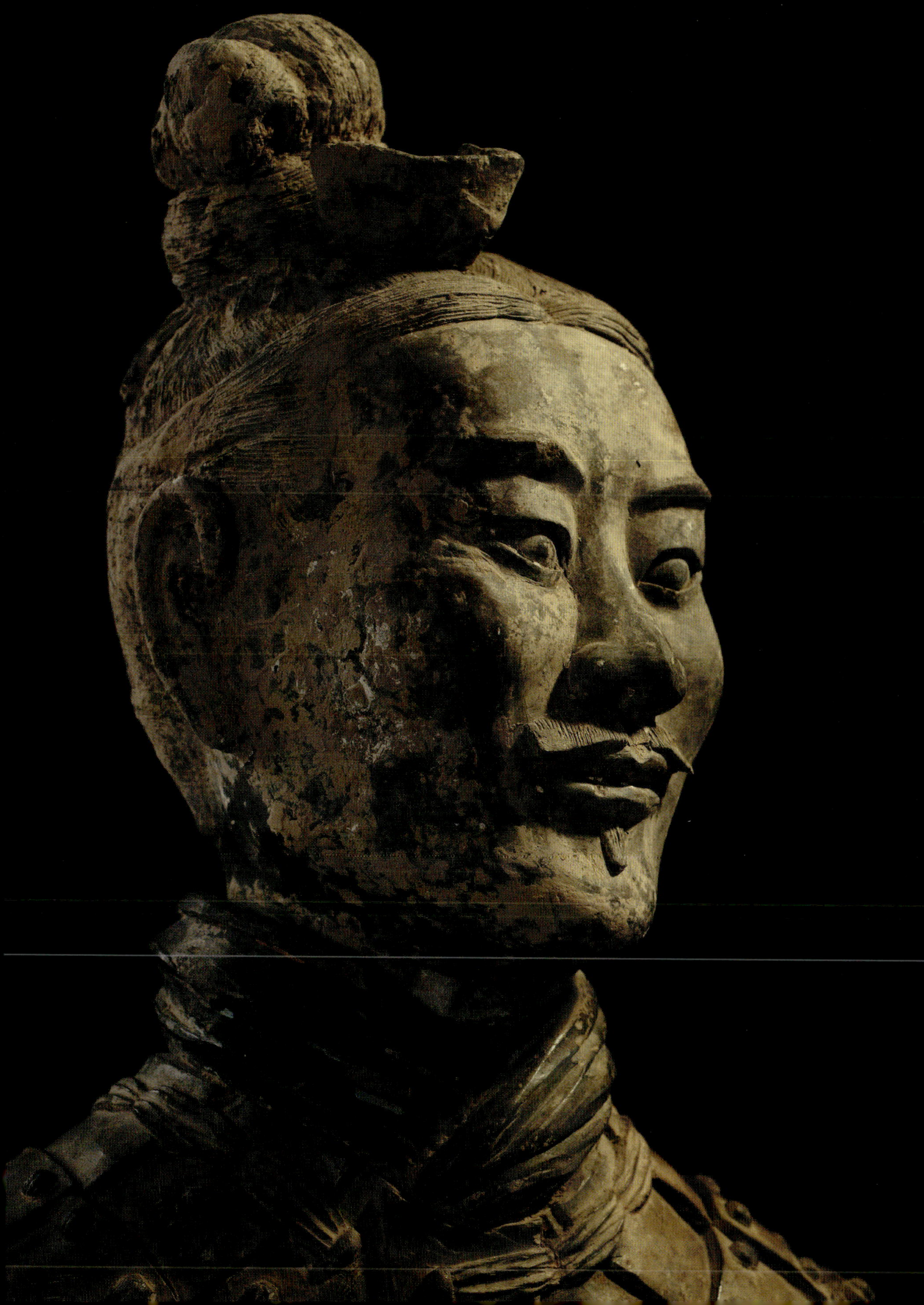

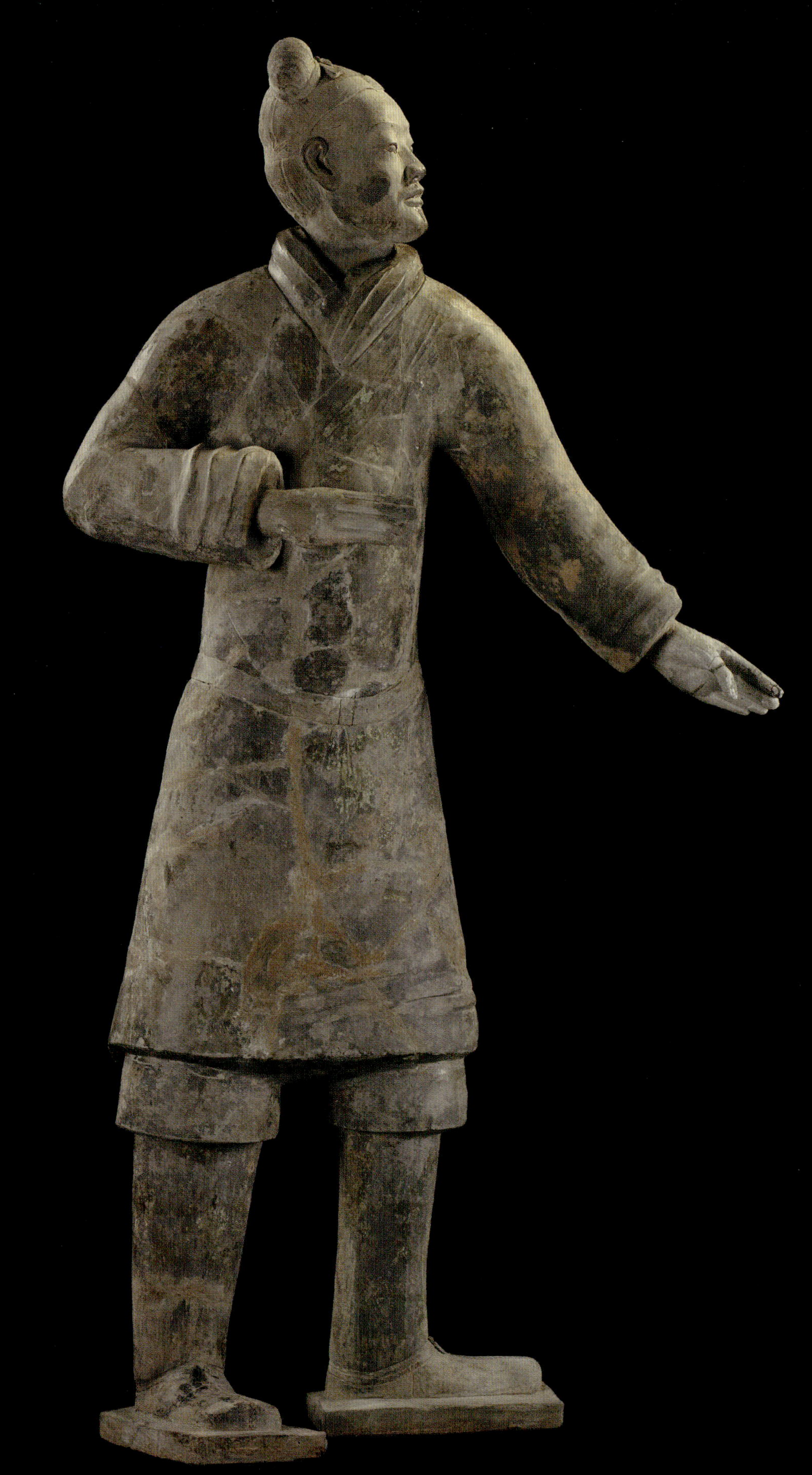

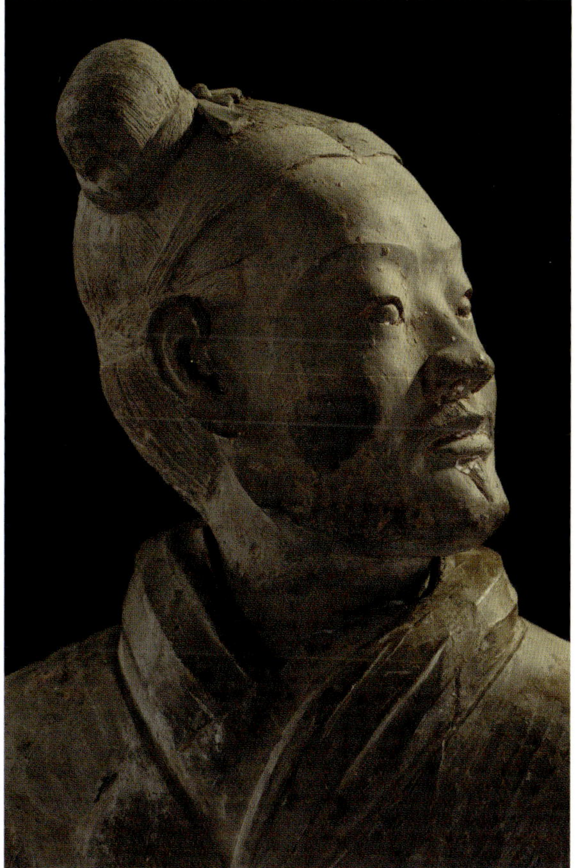

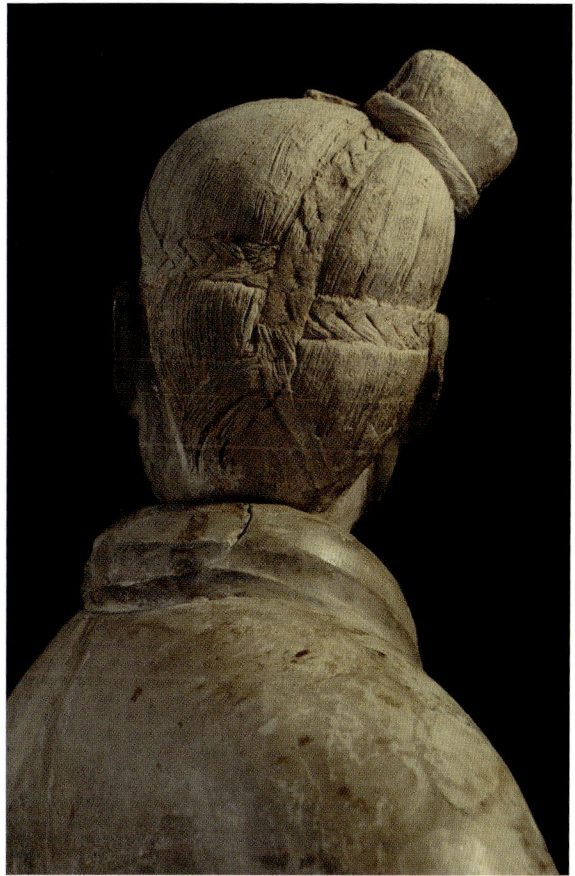

98. Standing archer
立射俑 / 立射俑

Qin dynasty (221–206 BCE)

Pottery, height 184cm

Excavated from Pit 2, Qin Shihuang tomb complex, 1978

Emperor Qin Shihuang's Mausoleum Site Museum, 002816

The standing archer is the most dynamic of the warrior figures. Like the kneeling archer, the standing archers were positioned around the outer perimeters of Pit 2 as a defensive force. This figure is lightly dressed in loose robes to allow for freedom of movement, enabling him to fire his crossbow and reload with speed and agility.

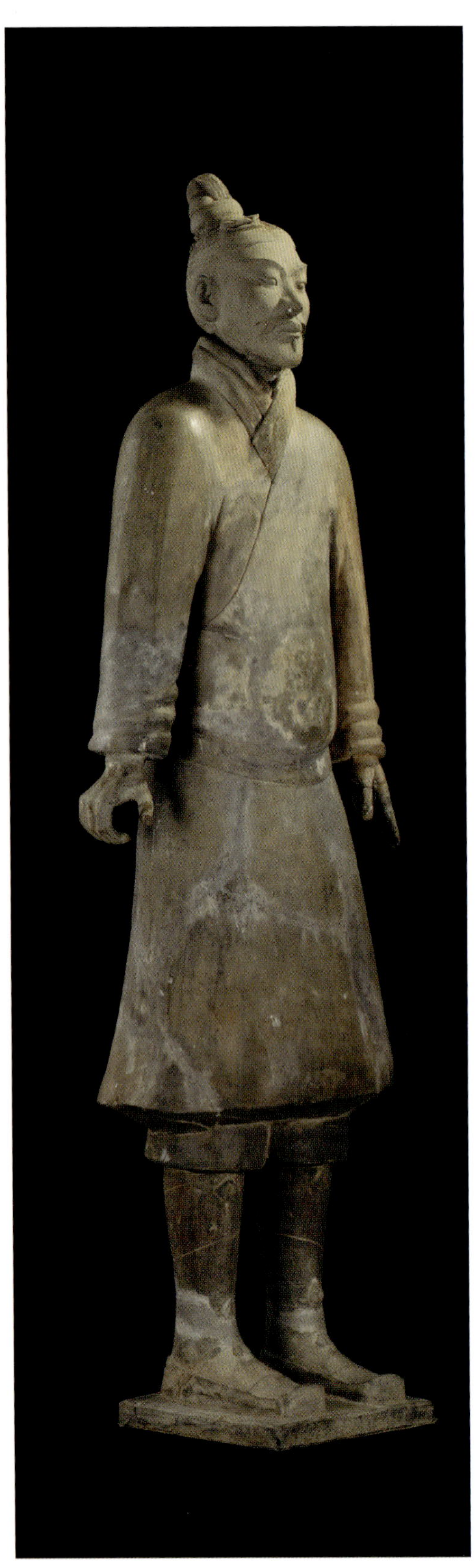

99. Unarmoured infantryman
战袍武士俑 / 戰袍武士俑

Qin dynasty (221–206 BCE)

Pottery, height 189cm

Excavated from Pit 2, Qin Shihuang tomb complex, 1977

Emperor Qin Shihuang's Mausoleum Site Museum, 002759

There are an estimated 6000 infantrymen in the Terracotta Army, some of whom are armoured, and others, such as this figure, who are not. His right hand would originally have held a weapon such as a bronze lance or sword. His simple head-dress, consisting of only a scarf, indicates his lowly rank, and his hair is tied in a bun.

100. Civil official
文官俑

Qin dynasty (221–206 BCE)

Pottery, height 188cm

Excavated from the Civil Official Pit, Qin Shihuang tomb complex, 2000

Emperor Qin Shihuang's Mausoleum Site Museum, 006488

In 2000, a pit in the southwest corner of the tomb mound was found to contain twelve figures, including eight wearing official robes, and equipped with a knife and a grindstone, implements used to write on bamboo strips. They are thought to be civil officials, workers in one of Qin Shihuang's government departments. A gap under the official's left arm may originally have held a bamboo document, perhaps for the First Emperor's inspection.

In planning for his afterlife, it seems the First Emperor not only prepared an army to protect him, but also included terracotta bureaucrats to help him rule the universe over which he assumed he would govern for eternity.

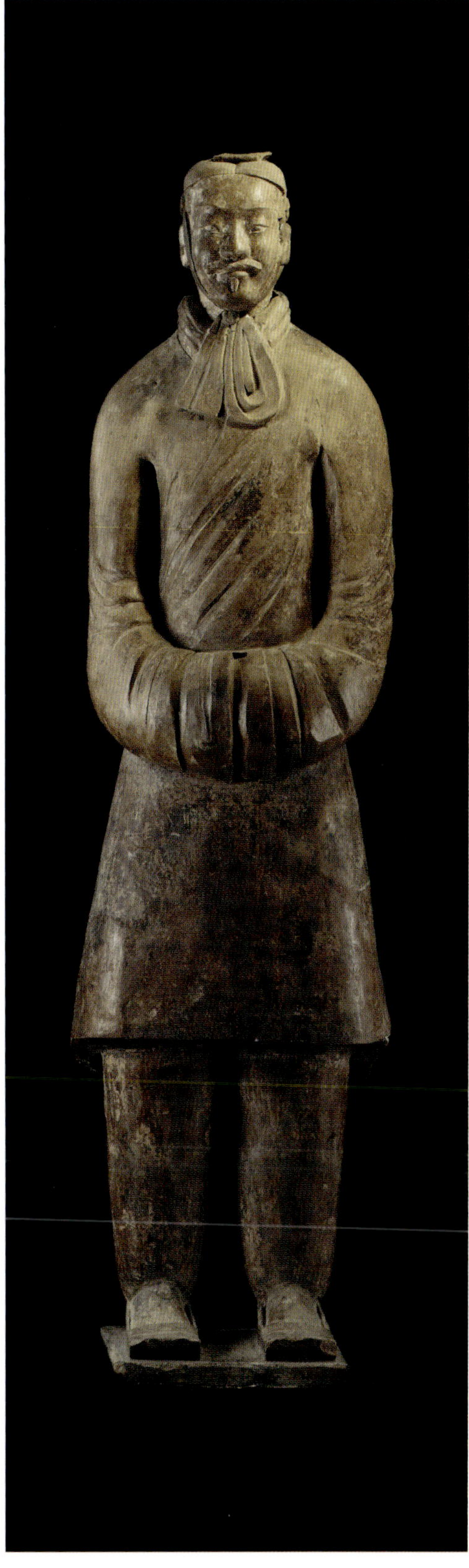

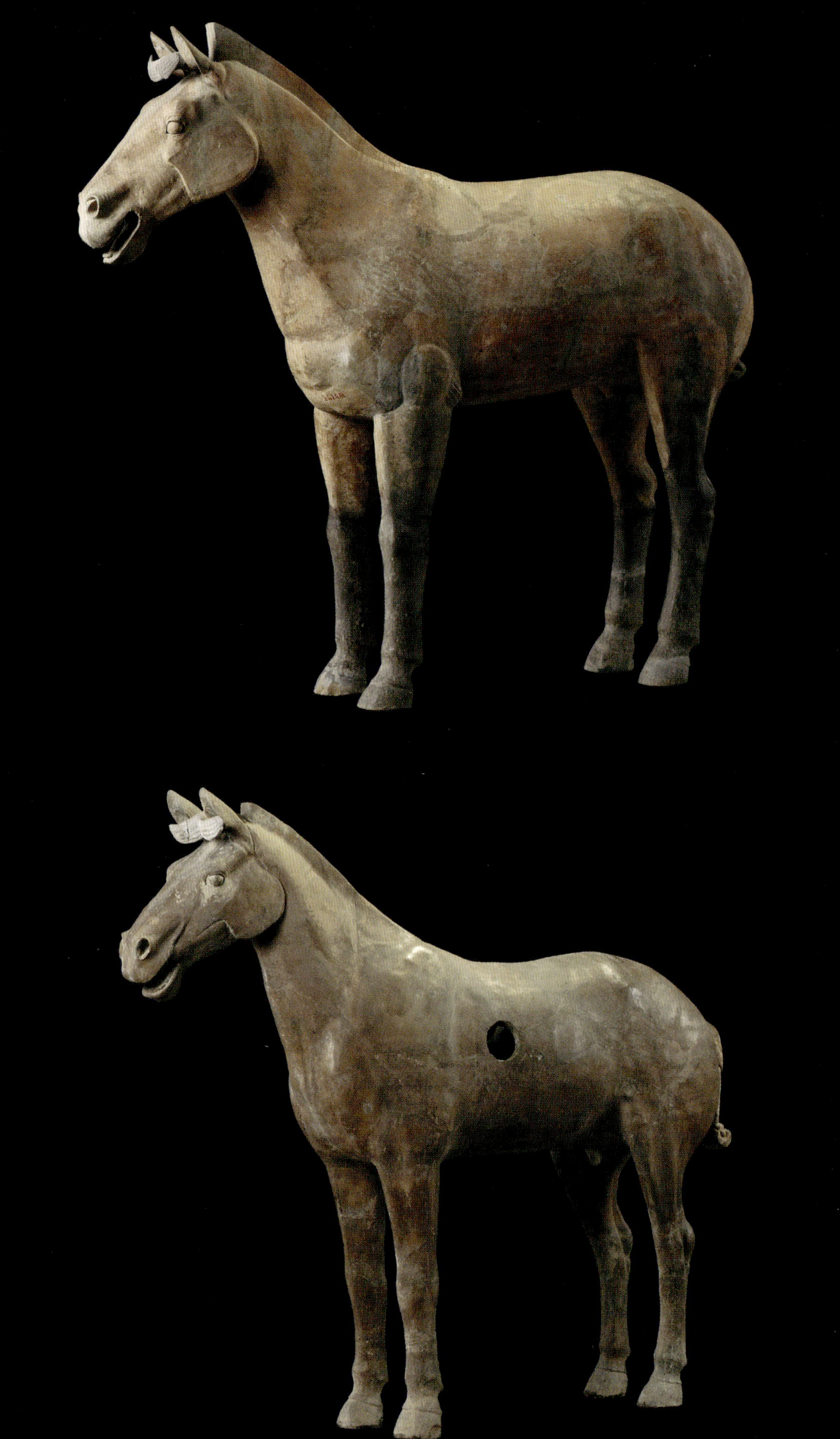

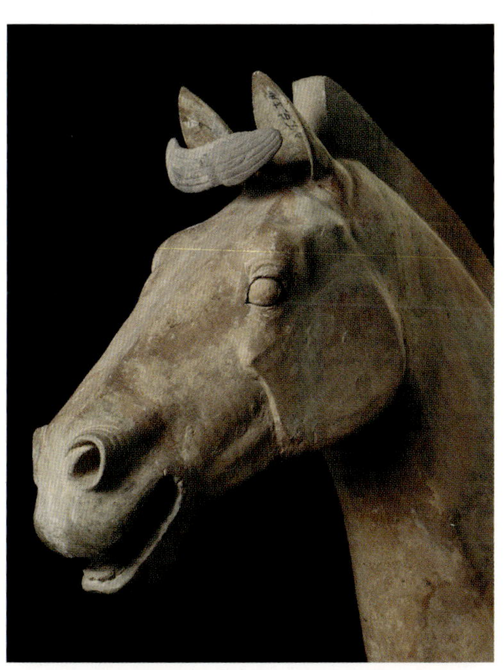

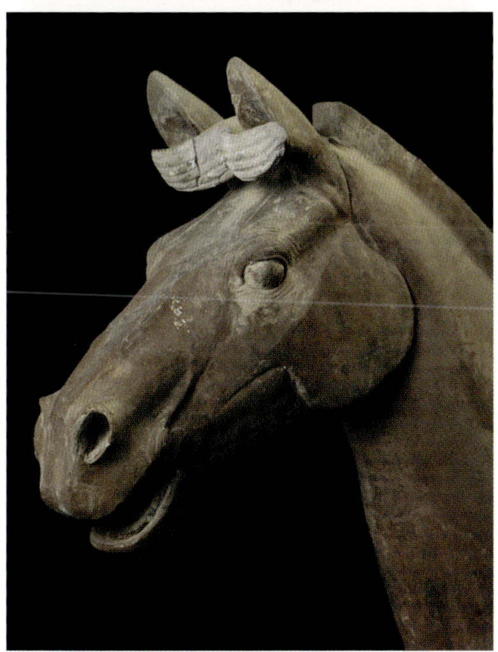

101. Chariot horse
车马 / 車馬

Qin dynasty (221–206 BCE)
Pottery, 171 x 217cm
Excavated from Pit 2, Qin Shihuang tomb complex, 1977
Emperor Qin Shihuang's Mausoleum Site Museum, 002767

102. Chariot horse
车马 / 車馬

Qin dynasty (221–206 BCE)
Pottery, 166 x 193cm
Excavated from Pit 1, Qin Shihuang tomb complex, 1977
Emperor Qin Shihuang's Mausoleum Site Museum, 002548

Both real and terracotta horses accompanied the First Emperor into the afterlife. Although these terracotta horses are from two different pits, they are both chariot horses, and would have been hitched, four across, to chariots by wooden yokes fixed to a crossbar. The chariots and fittings, being made from wood, have long since disintegrated, with only traces and occasionally impressions of them still remaining.

The horses' tails are carefully plaited and tied up to keep them free of the harnessing, and their mouths are open to accommodate the bit. The hole in the side of the horse is an air vent to ensure even firing of the interior and exterior, and to prevent cracking of the hollow body.

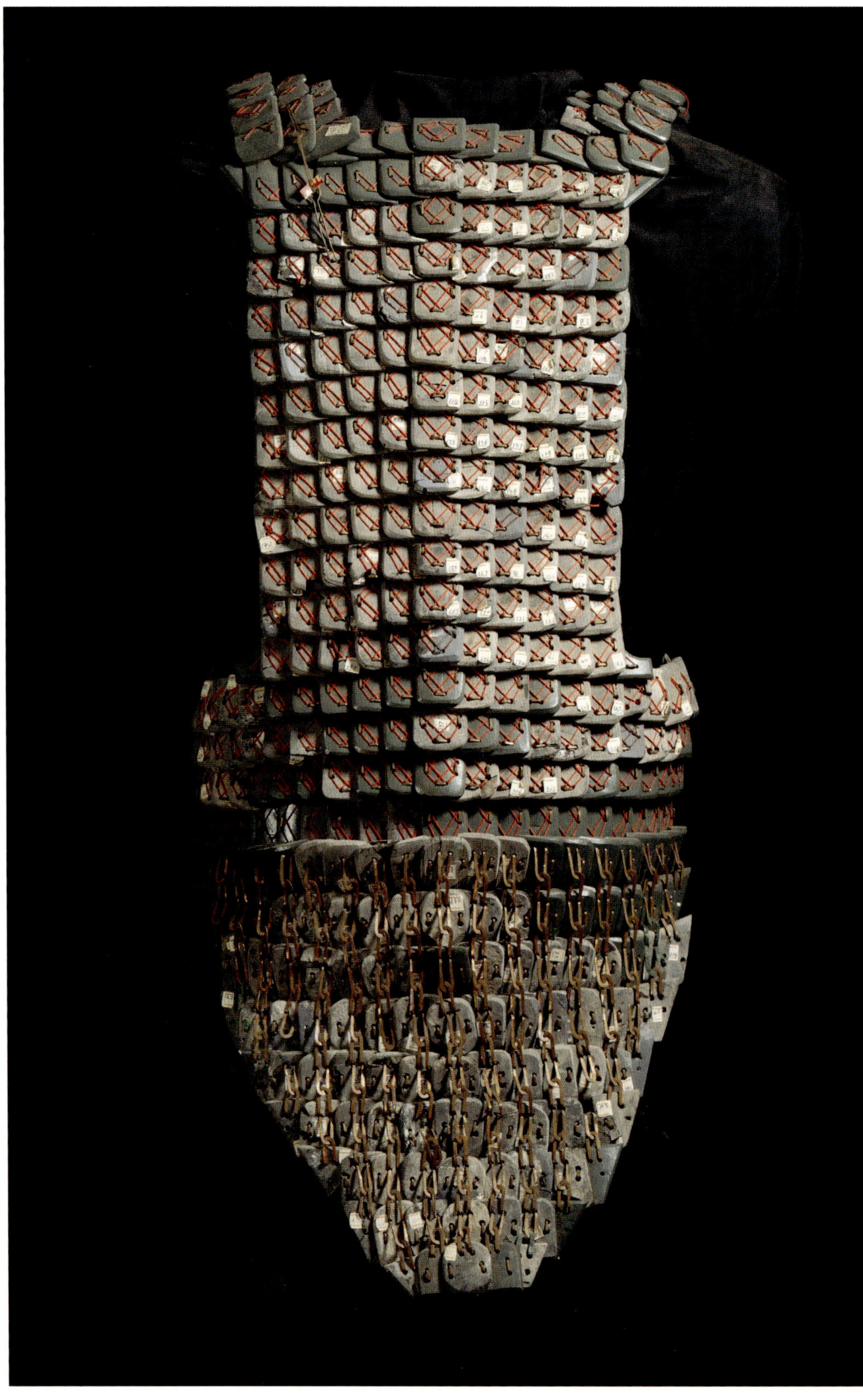

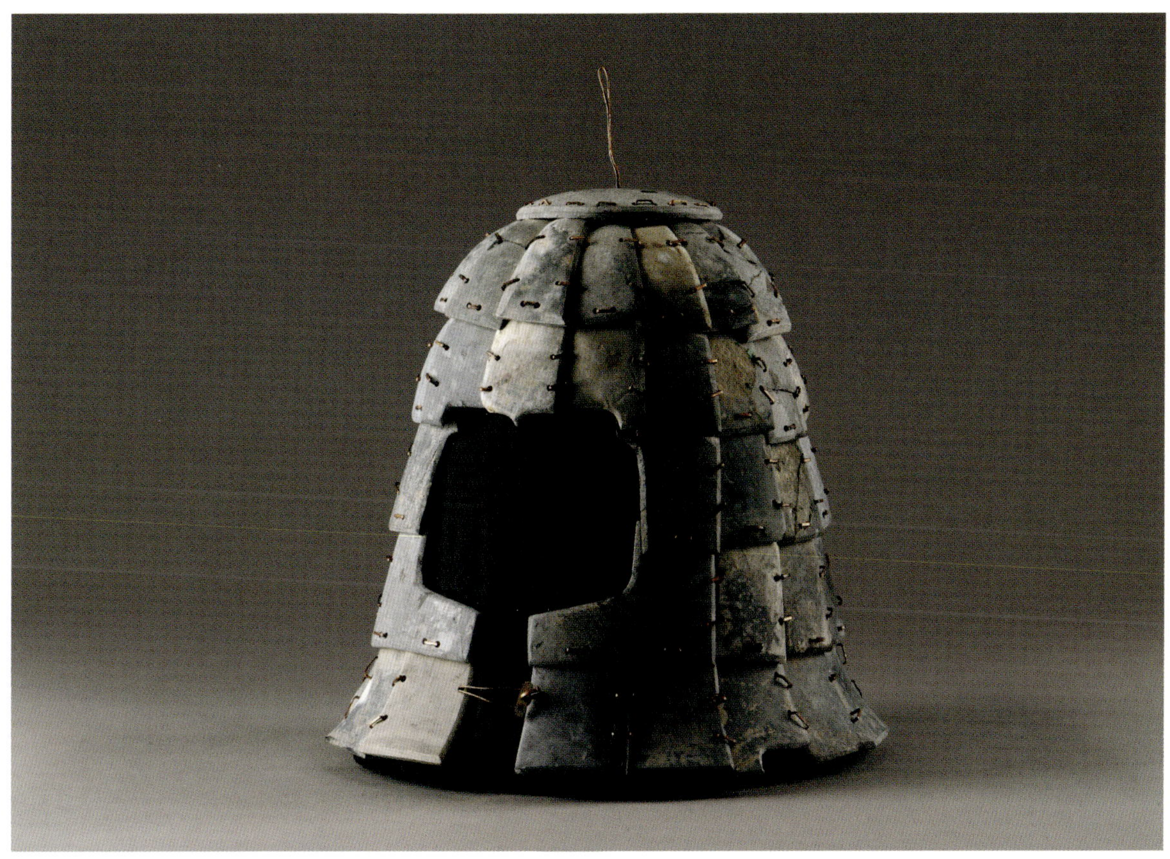

103. Model armour
石铠甲 / 石鎧甲

Qin dynasty (221–206 BCE)

Stone, 105 x 54cm

Excavated from Pit K9801, Qin Shihuang tomb complex, 1998

Shaanxi Provincial Institute of Archaeology, 001175

104. Model helmet
石胄

Qin dynasty (221–206 BCE)

Stone, 34 x 34cm

Excavated from Pit K9801, Qin Shihuang tomb complex, 1998

Shaanxi Provincial Institute of Archaeology, 007089

An 'armoury for the afterlife' was discovered in 1998 when a pit at the southeastern corner of the First Emperor's burial mound was excavated (see map on page 16). It is estimated that the pit contains fifty helmets, 150 suits of armour, and one set of horse armour. Each suit of armour weighs 18 kilograms and is composed of over 600 limestone plaques that were originally laced together with copper wire.

The armour emulates that used by Qin warriors, which would have been made from lacquered leather. However, the sheer weight of these stone suits means they could never have been worn, and were instead produced for burial purposes. The use of stone rather than iron suggests that the armour was intended to provide protection against supernatural forces in the afterlife.

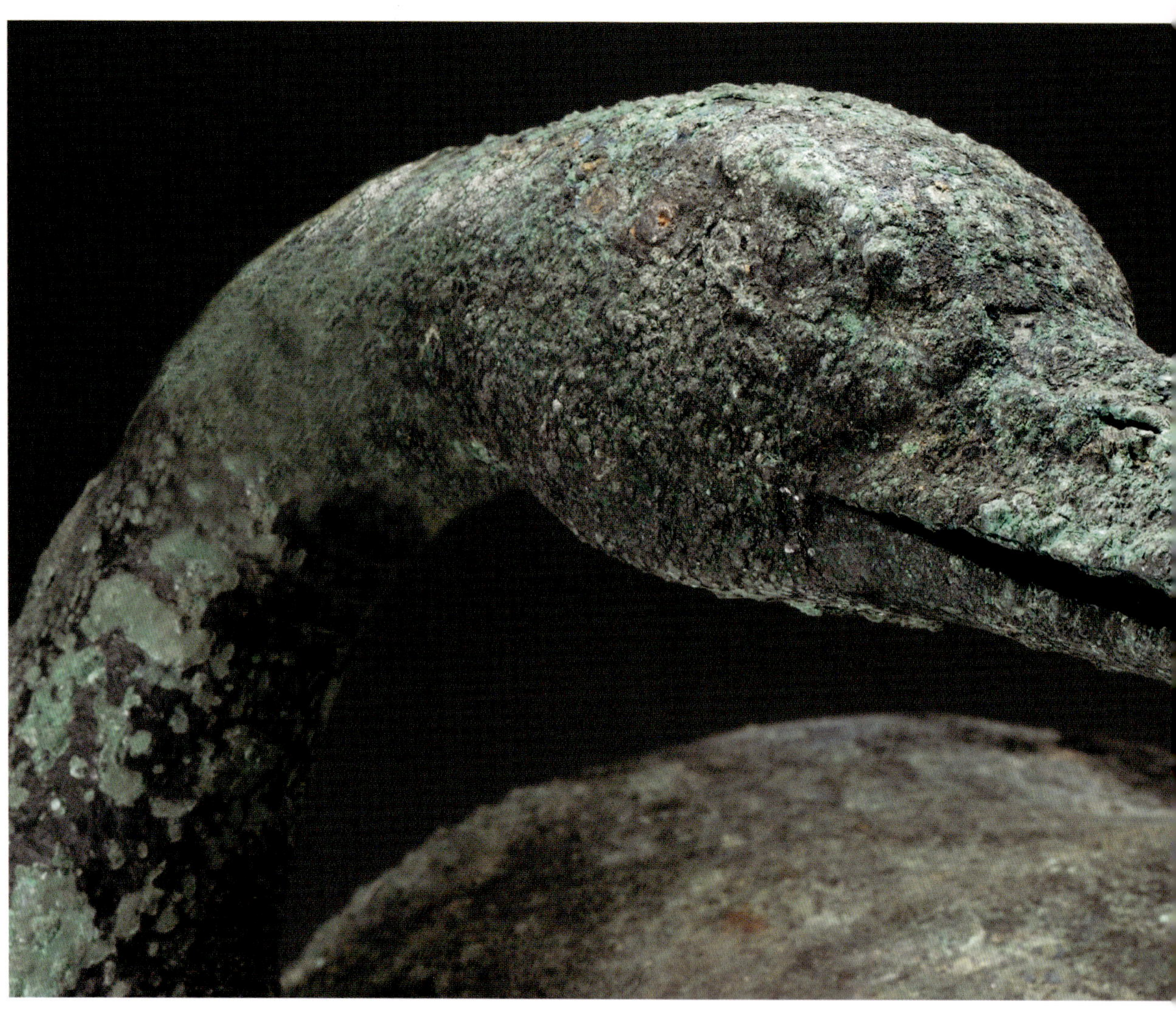

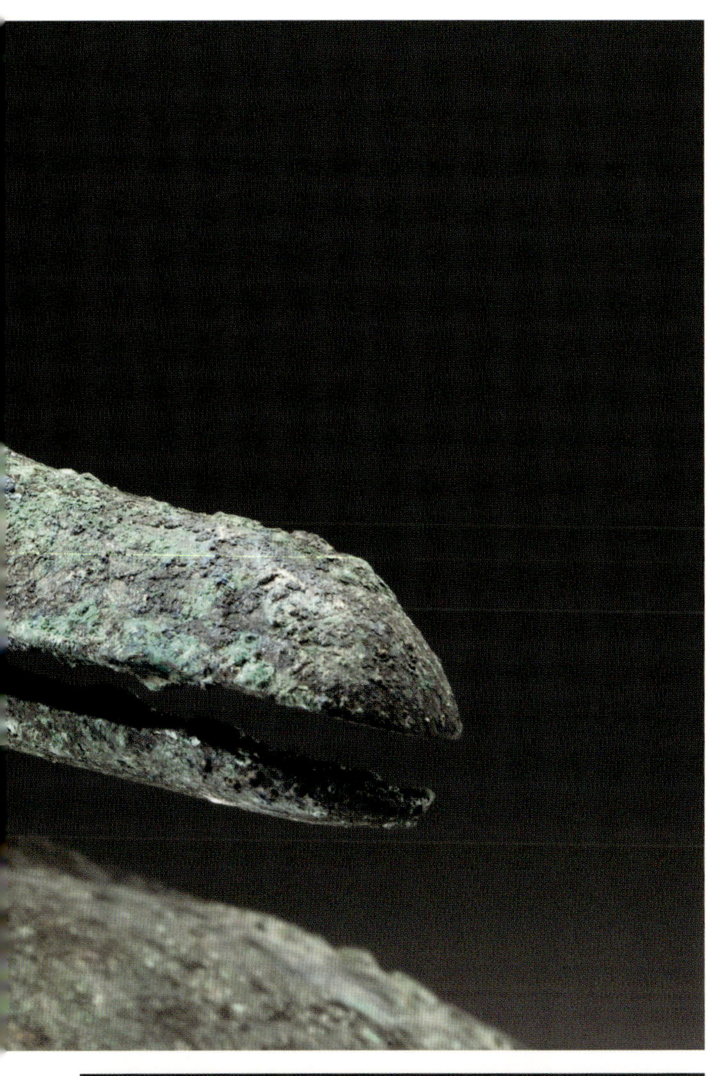

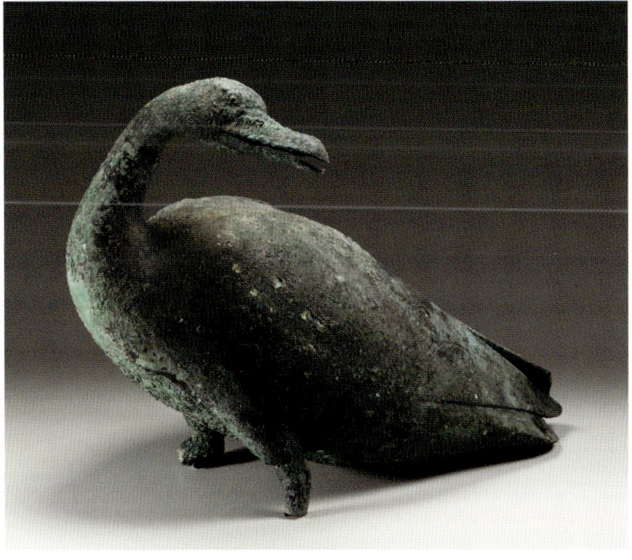

105. Goose
铜雁 / 銅雁

Qin dynasty (221–206 BCE)

Bronze, 26.5 x 50.5cm

Excavated from Pit K0007, Qin Shihuang tomb complex, 2001–2003

Shaanxi Provincial Institute of Archaeology, K007T3:49

Within the burial complex, provisions were also made to ensure there was entertainment for the First Emperor in his afterlife. In 2001, a pit containing fifteen seated terracotta musicians and forty-six bronze waterbirds arranged along an artificial waterway was discovered to the northeast of the burial mound (see map on page 16). It is thought that the birds were trained to perform to music. Each bird is unique – this bronze goose is modelled after a specific type of wild goose, with short legs and thick, webbed feet.

106. **Chariot model no. 1**
1号铜车马（复制品）/
1 號銅車馬（複製品）

Modern replica in bronze, 152 x 225cm
Emperor Qin Shihuang's Mausoleum Site Museum, MMYL007

107. **Chariot model no. 2**
2号铜车马（复制品）/
2 號銅車馬（複製品）

Modern replica in bronze, 106 x 317cm
Emperor Qin Shihuang's Mausoleum Site Museum, MMYL008

In 1980, two half-life-sized bronze chariots were found in a pit to the west of the First Emperor's burial mound (see map on page 16): exactly scaled replicas of the wooden chariots used during his reign. The first is a war chariot, and the second a 'comfortable' chariot, both driven by four white horses. The latter is most likely a replica of the kind of carriage used by the First Emperor on his regular inspection tours around his empire.

Each chariot is crafted in bronze with extraordinary detail, and adorned with silver and gold ornaments. They are decorated with rich and elaborate designs, depicting clouds and dragons, as well as abstract patterns. Even more than the Terracotta Army, these chariots demonstrate the aesthetic and technological sophistication of artisans in the Qin period. They represent a high-point of verisimilitude in the history of Chinese art.

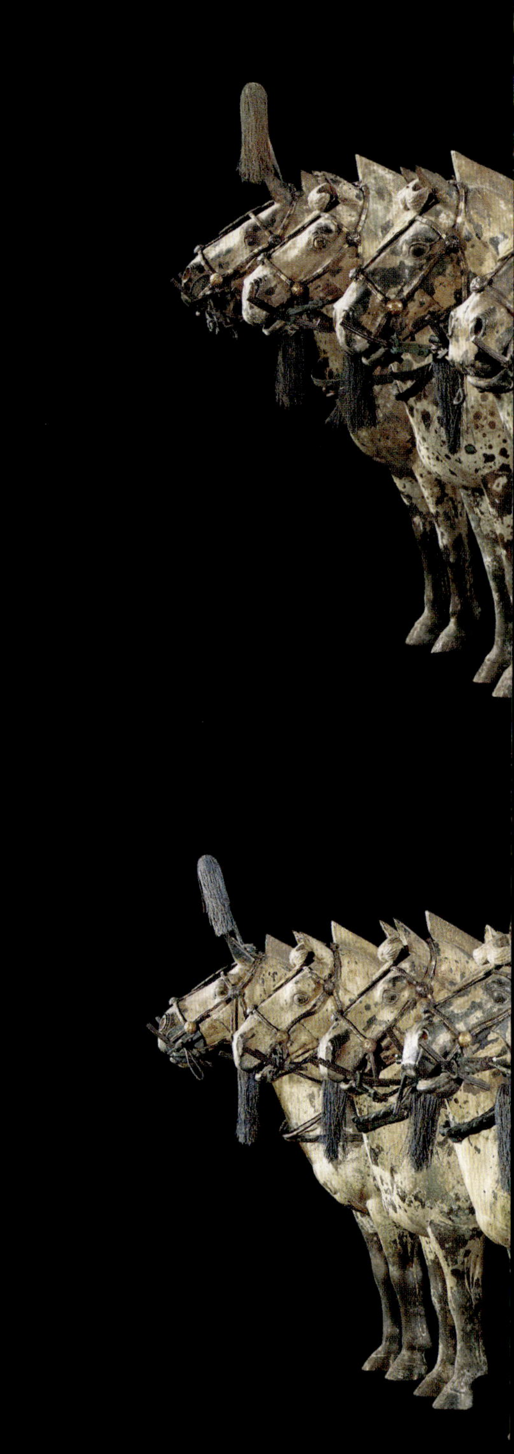

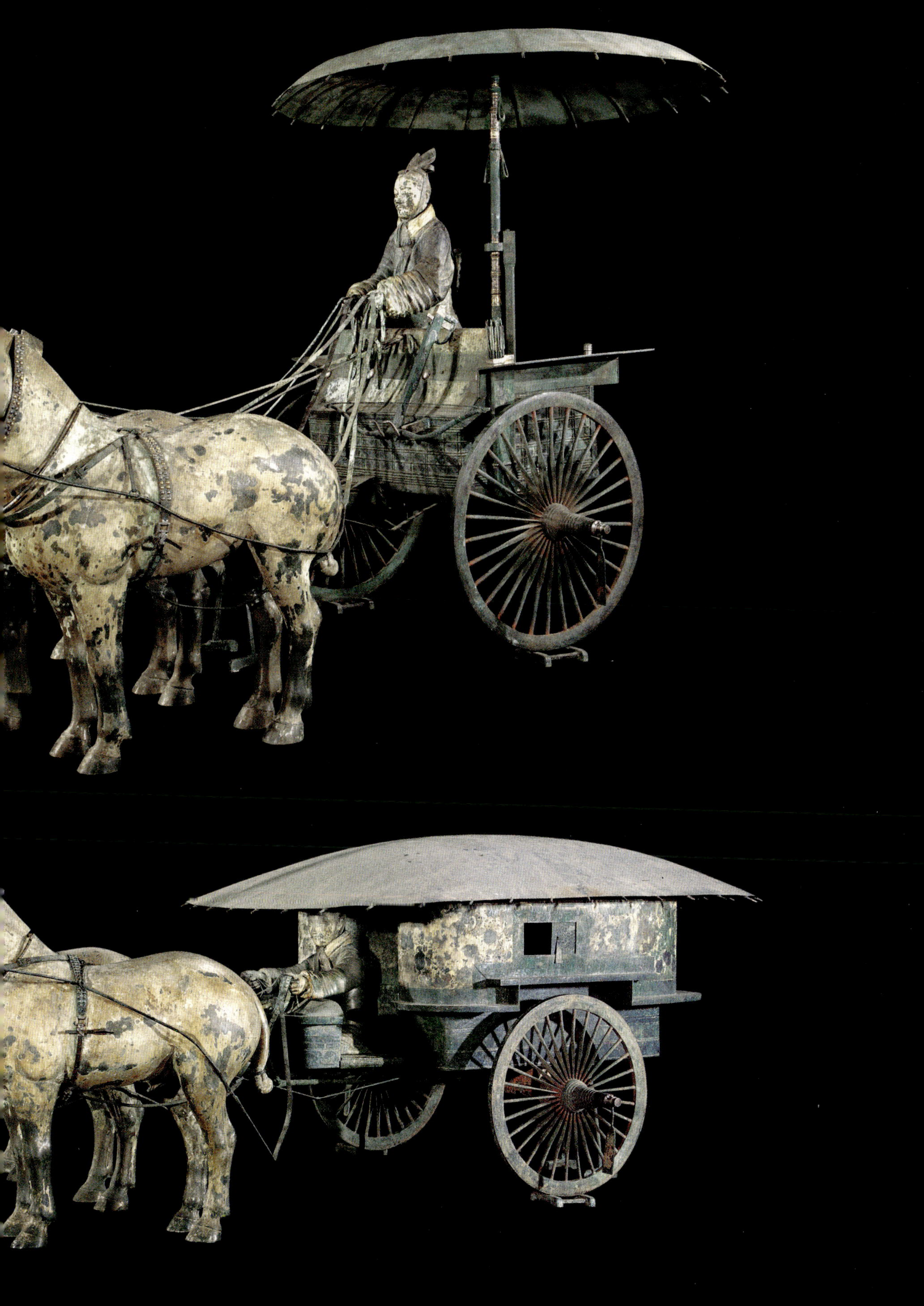

漢代

The Han dynasty

Following the First Emperor's death in 210 BCE, the Qin dynasty went into immediate decline, and bitter civil warfare ensued. By 206 BCE Liu Bang established himself as emperor of the new Han dynasty, which lasted for nearly 400 years. The first half (206 BCE–9 CE), ruled from the capital at Chang'an, is known as the Western Han dynasty. After a brief interregnum under Wang Mang (9–23 CE), the Han dynasty re-established itself further east at Luoyang. This second period (25–220 CE) is known as the Eastern Han dynasty.

The Han dynasty is considered the golden age of ancient China. While the Han inherited the First Emperor's unified empire, they rejected many of the principles of his rule. And while his tomb was considered by Sima Qian to be decadent, a symbol of a despotic, tyrannical ruler, Han emperors continued to invest in large-scale mausoleums. These reflected an understanding of the afterlife as a continuation of this world, and provided emperors with an environment that would fulfil their practical and spiritual needs.

HAN YANGLING MAUSOLEUM

EMPEROR JING OF HAN (157–141 BCE)

opposite page **Partially excavated soldiers from Han Yangling Mausoleum.**

The burial site of Emperor Jing, the fourth Han emperor, who reigned from 157 BCE to 141 BCE, was uncovered at Han Yangling during the construction of an airport expressway. His mausoleum consists of a central pyramid-shaped burial mound, surrounded by eighty-one tomb passages of varying lengths.

To date, eleven of the passages have been excavated, revealing thousands of terracotta figures and animals, as well as weapons, horse and chariot fittings, terracotta storage vessels and official seals.

During his reign, Emperor Jing was successful in suppressing the rebellion of the Seven States in the east, thereby securing the centralisation and authority of the Han government.

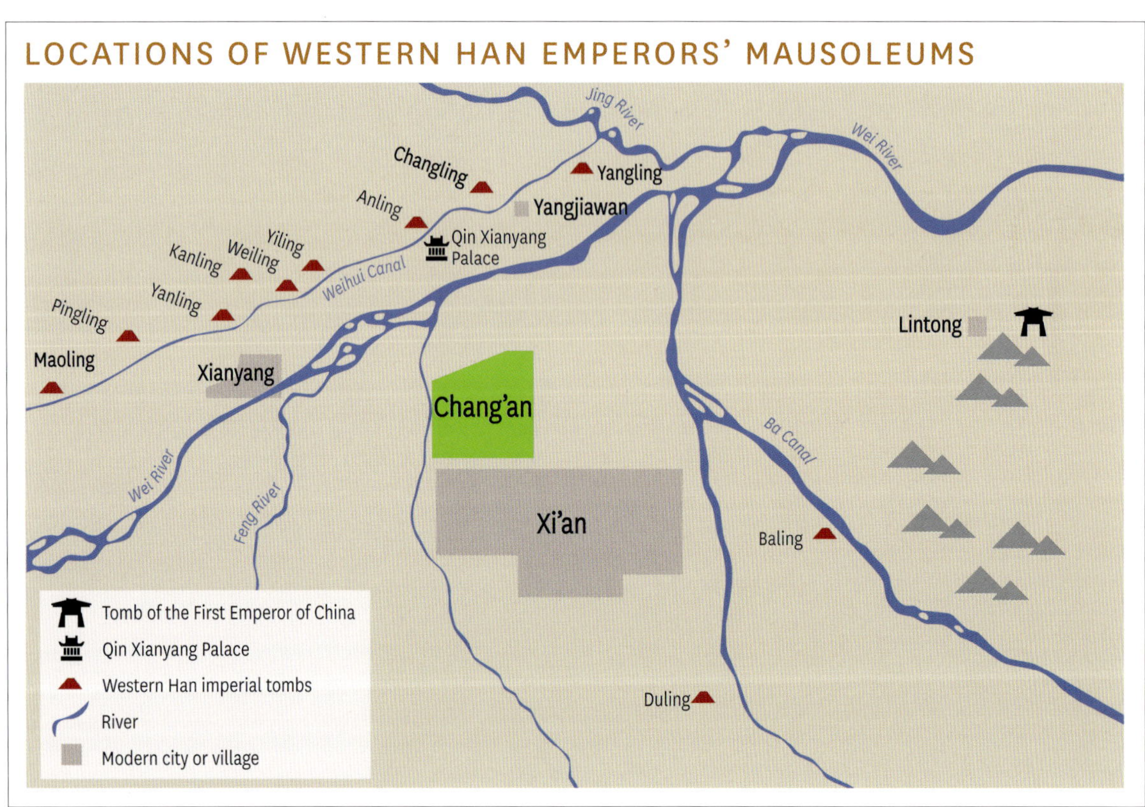

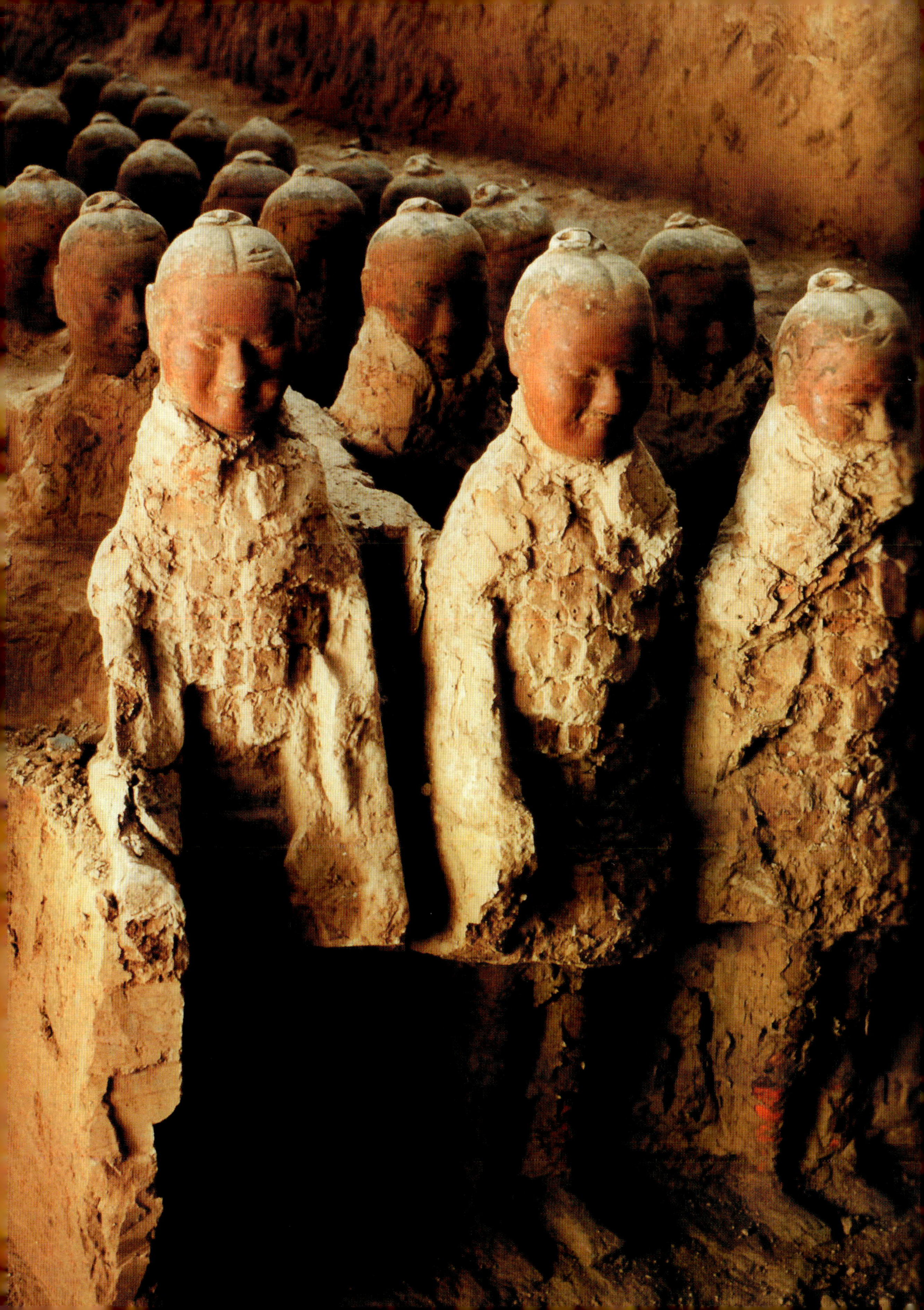

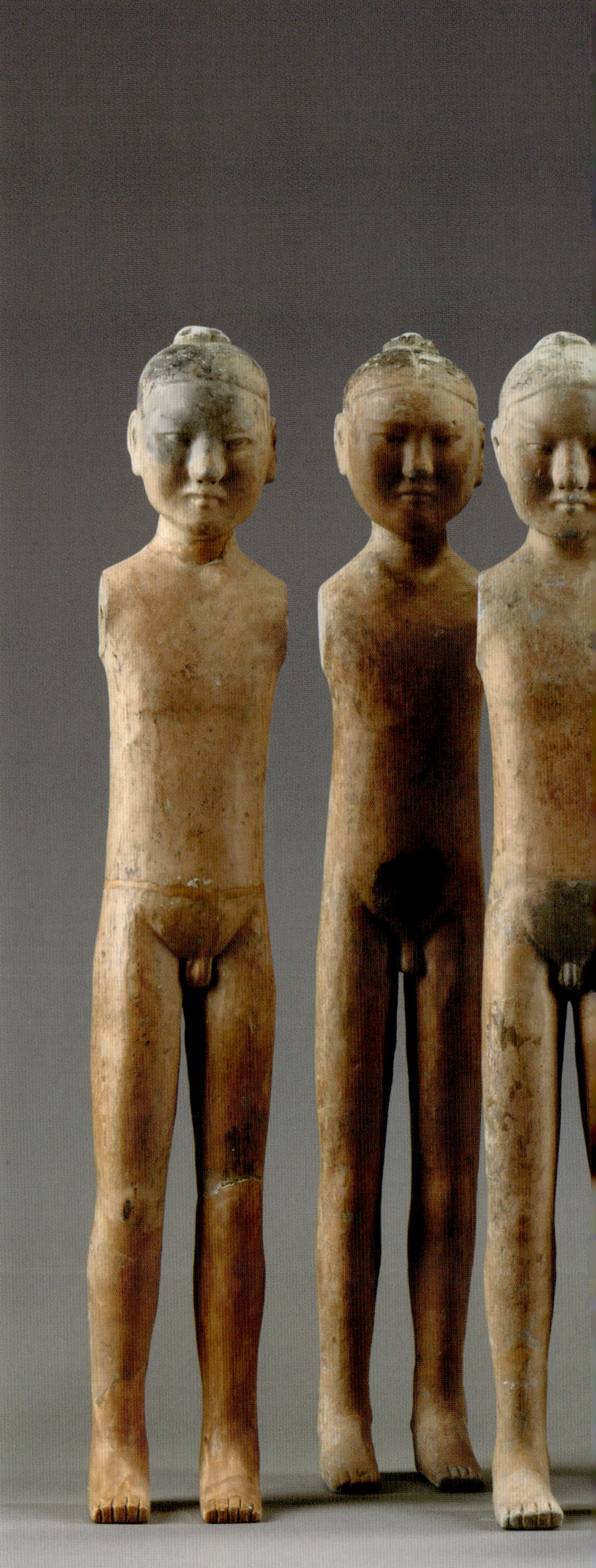

108. Ten soldiers from Han Yangling Mausoleum
着衣式男武士俑

Western Han dynasty (206 BCE–9 CE)

Painted pottery, average height 57cm

Excavated from the Southern Burial Pit, Han Yangling, Xianyang, 1992

Han Yangling Museum, YG2074; YG2075; YG2141; YG2142; YG2145; YG2144; YG2138; YG2081; YG2085; YG 2100

In contrast to the First Emperor's army, the figures at Han Yangling are smaller in scale, less than half-size, and more simply executed. They measure approximately 60 centimetres high, and were originally made with movable wooden limbs, and were dressed in silk clothing. The cloth and wood have since decayed, leaving behind the terracotta bodies, with their individualised facial features. As with the First Emperor's army, these troops were intended to protect Emperor Jing in his afterlife.

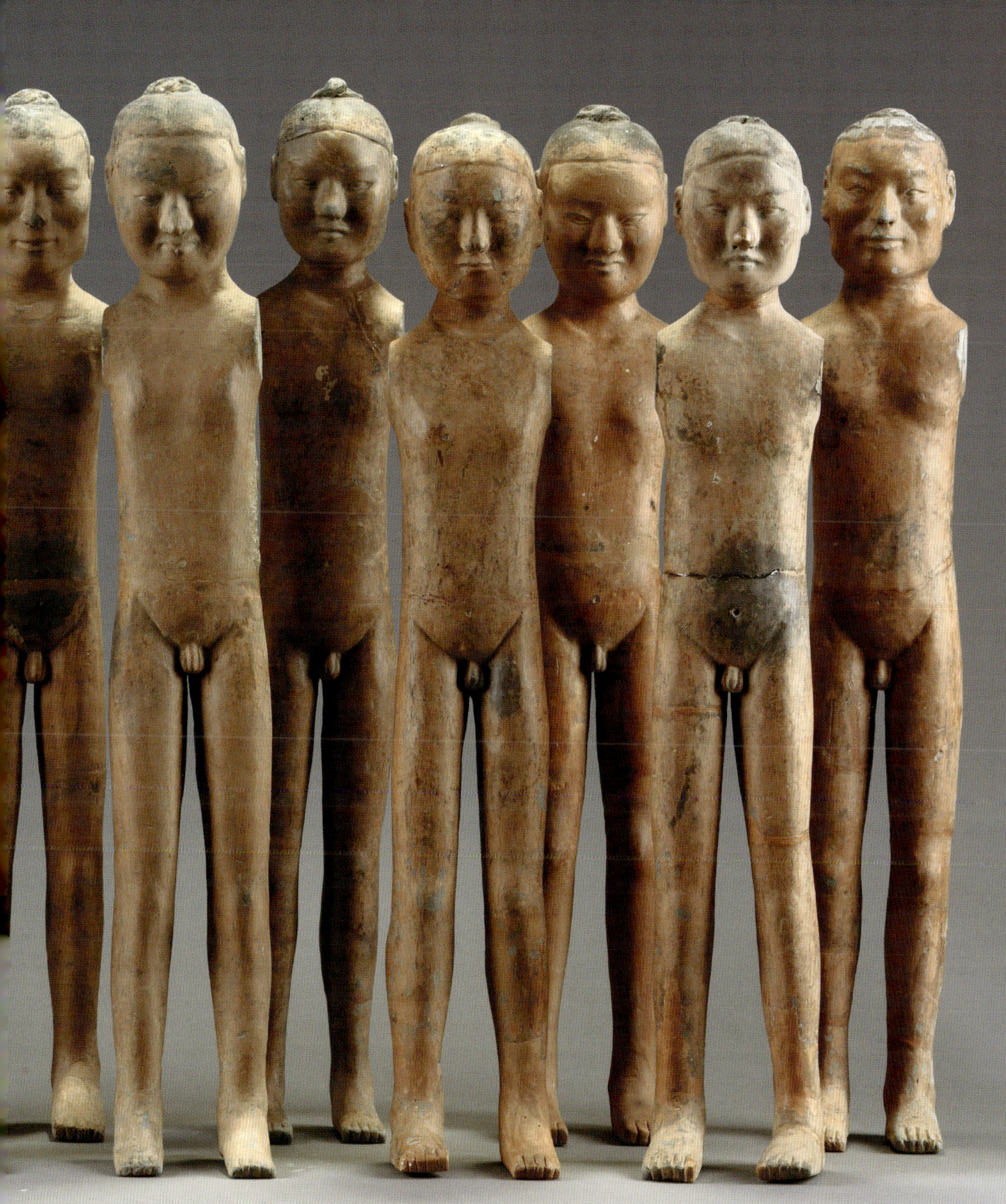

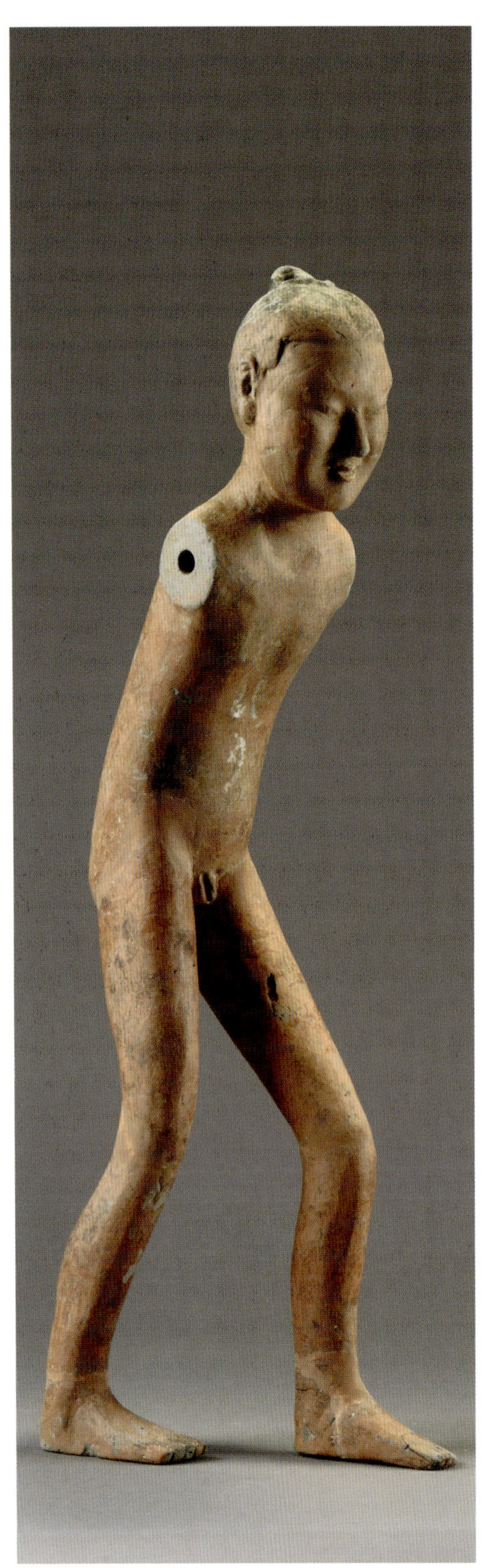

109. Walking soldier from Han Yangling Mausoleum
着衣行走武士俑

Western Han dynasty (206 BCE–9 CE)

Painted pottery, 54 x 9cm

Excavated from the Southern Burial Pit, Han Yangling, Xianyang, 1990

Han Yangling Museum, YG2229

110. Bitch and dog from Han Yangling Mausoleum
陶狼犬; 陶家犬

Western Han dynasty (206 BCE–9 CE)

Painted pottery, 21 x 31.5cm; 21 x 30cm

Excavated from the Outer Burial Pit, Diling, Han Yangling, Xianyang, 1998; 1992

Han Yangling Museum, YG1491; YG1540

Hundreds of charming pottery animals have been excavated from pits to the east of Emperor Jing's tomb. They are all domesticated species – pigs, cows, goats, dogs, chickens and horses – and males and females of each animal are present. All are rendered in pottery, and are painted to accentuate their realistic features. Unlike the waterbirds in the First Emperor's tomb, they were not included for entertainment, but for more pragmatic reasons: to provide Emperor Jing with food supplies in the afterlife.

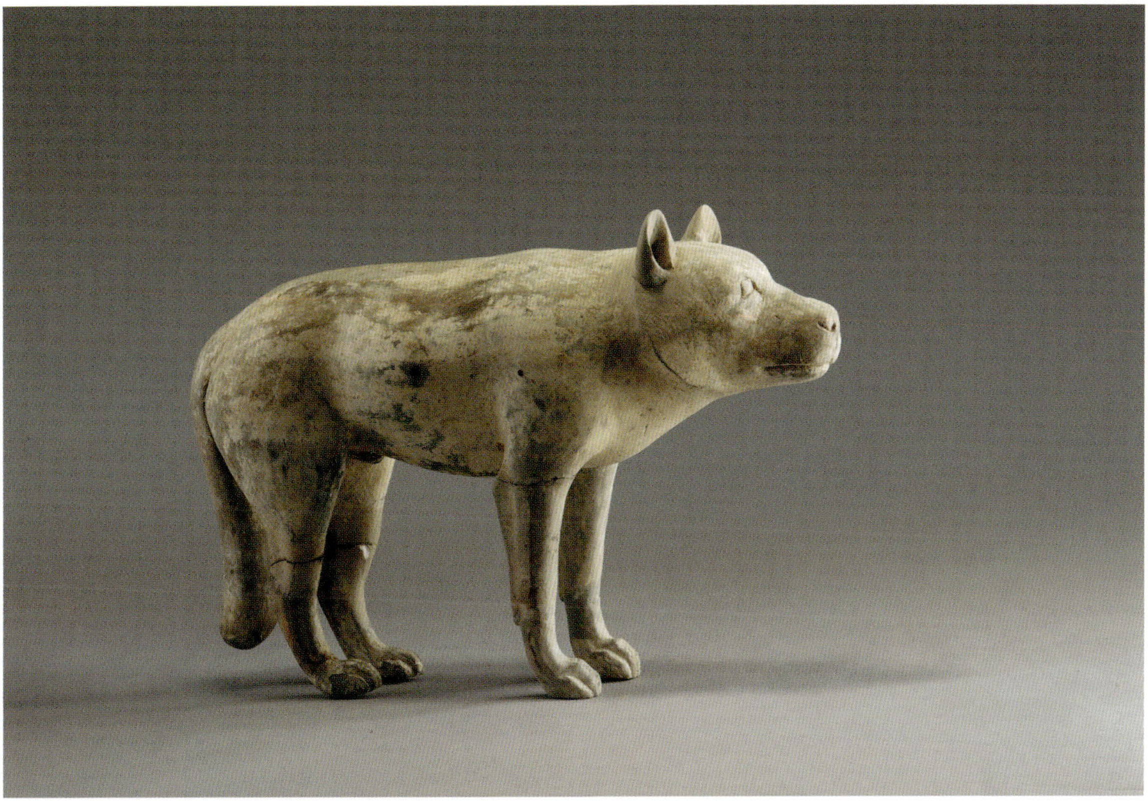

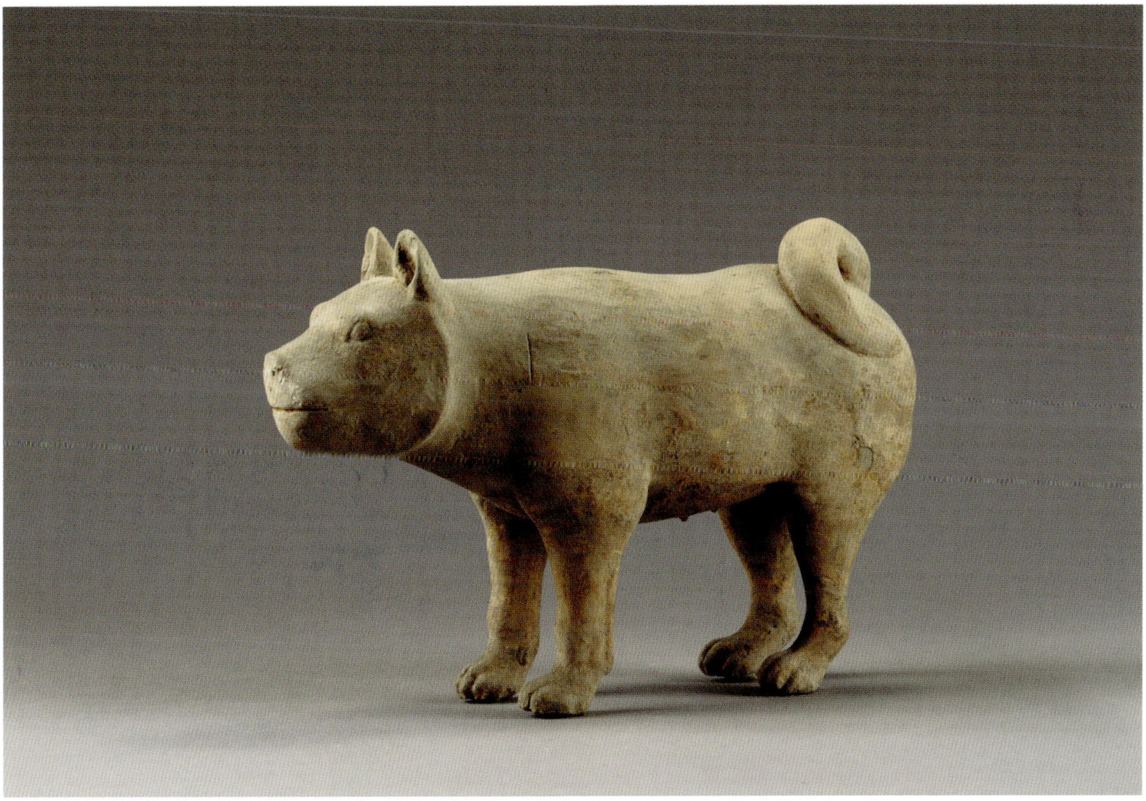

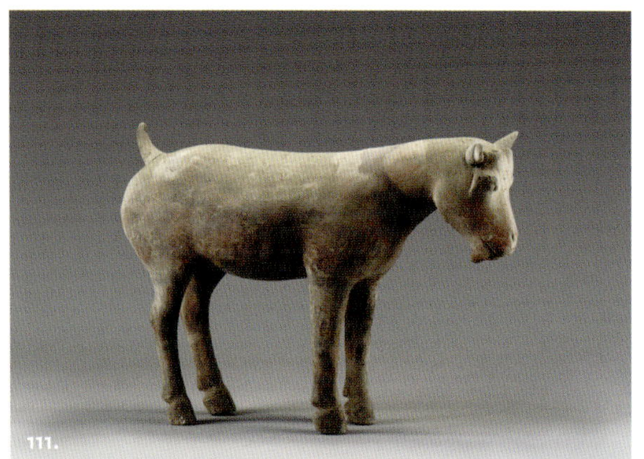

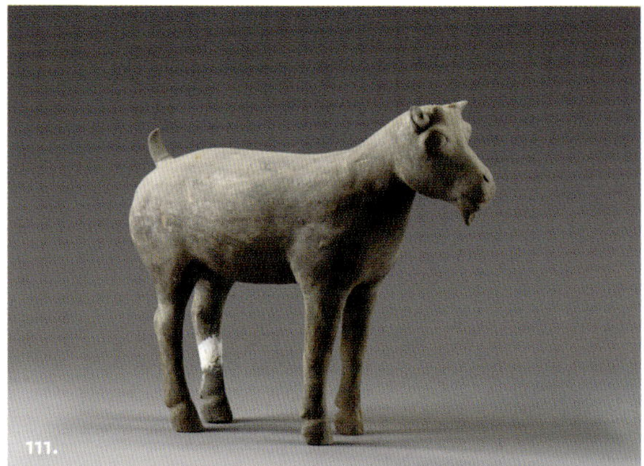

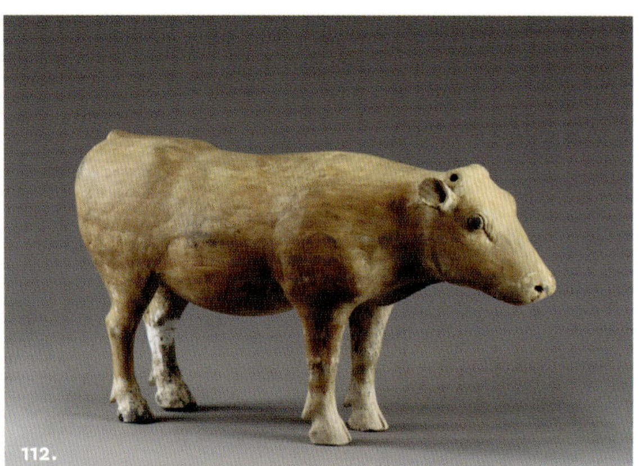

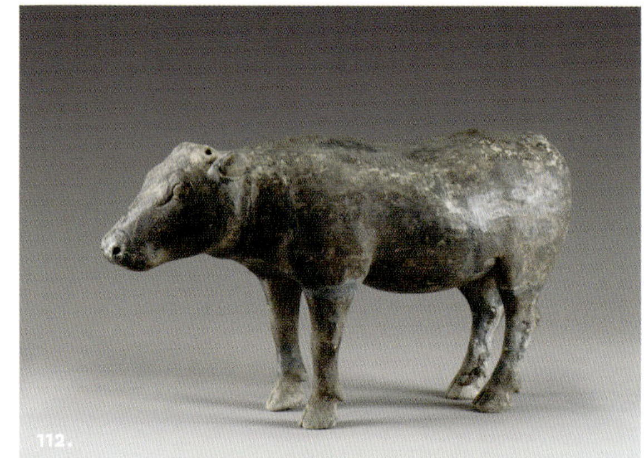

111. **Pair of goats from Han Yangling Mausoleum**
陶山羊

Western Han dynasty (206 BCE–9 CE)

Painted pottery, 26.3 x 38.5cm; 30 x 37.7cm

Excavated from the Outer Burial Pit to the east of Diling, Han Yangling, Xianyang, 2003

Han Yangling Museum, YG1866; YG1930

112. **Pair of cattle from Han Yangling Mausoleum**
陶牛

Western Han dynasty (206 BCE–9 CE)

Painted pottery, 38 x 70cm

Excavated from the garden of the Accompanying Burial Grave, Han Yangling, Xianyang, 1998

Han Yangling Museum, YG1972; YG1973

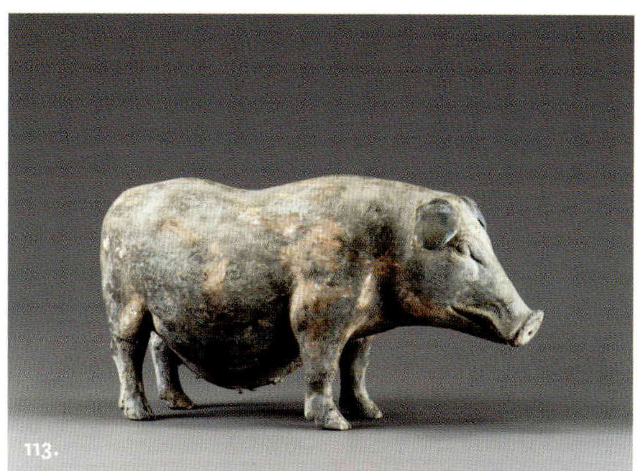

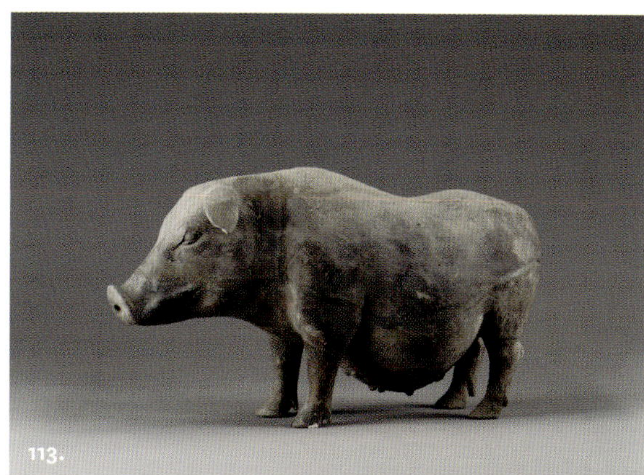

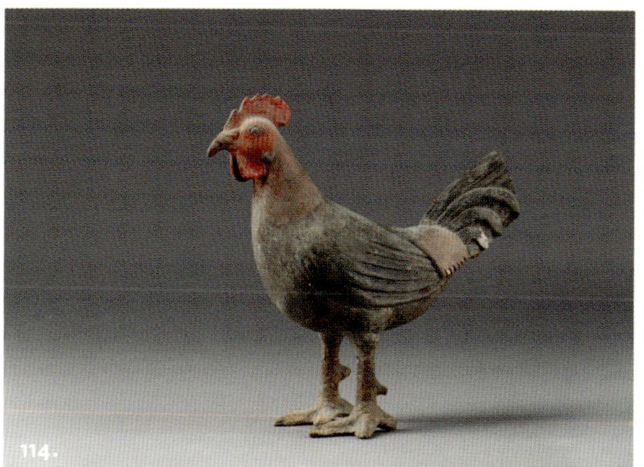

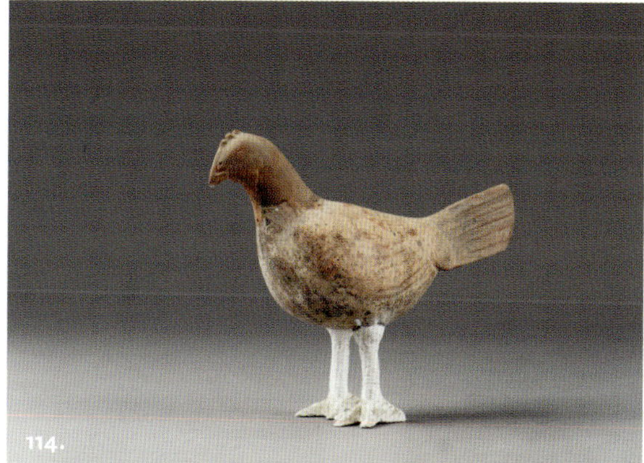

113. Pair of sows from Han Yangling Mausoleum
陶母猪 / 陶母豬

Western Han dynasty (206 BCE–9 CE)

Painted pottery, 23 x 45cm; 24 x 40cm

Excavated from the Burial Pit, Diling, Han Yangling, Xianyang, 2000; 1999

Han Yangling Museum, YG0916; Shaanxi Provincial Institute of Archaeology, K21:017

114. Cock and hen from Han Yangling Mausoleum
陶公鸡; 陶母鸡 / 陶公雞; 陶母雞

Western Han dynasty (206 BCE–9 CE)

Painted pottery, 16 x 16cm; 12.5 x 15.5cm

Excavated from the Burial Pit, Han Yangling, Xianyang, 2003

Shaanxi Provincial Institute of Archaeology, K19:13; K19:12

A HAN GENERAL'S TOMB

In 1965, more than 3000 items, including a vast army of pottery soldiers, were discovered in pits near a satellite tomb in the village of Yanjiawan, near the burial complex of the first Han dynasty emperor, Gaozu, at Changling. Due to the high proportion of military paraphernalia present in the pits, it is believed that they belonged to Zhou Bo (d. 169 BCE) or his son Zhou Yafu (d. 143 BCE), the latter being the general who helped Emperor Jing defeat the Seven States.

In total, 1965 warriors, 583 cavalrymen and 410 shields have been excavated. The figures demonstrate a high degree of realism, but differ in style from those at Han Yangling or the First Emperor's tomb. Detail is incised and painted onto the figures, rather than being moulded and sculpted as with the First Emperor's Terracotta Army, or accessorised with real cloth, as at Han Yangling.

The dramatically reduced scale of the figures was associated with decreased costs invested in production and transportation, perhaps a direct response to the criticism levelled at the First Emperor's decadence. Nonetheless, the efforts made to represent the worlds of the Han elite in miniature for the afterlife were no less ambitious than those of the First Emperor.

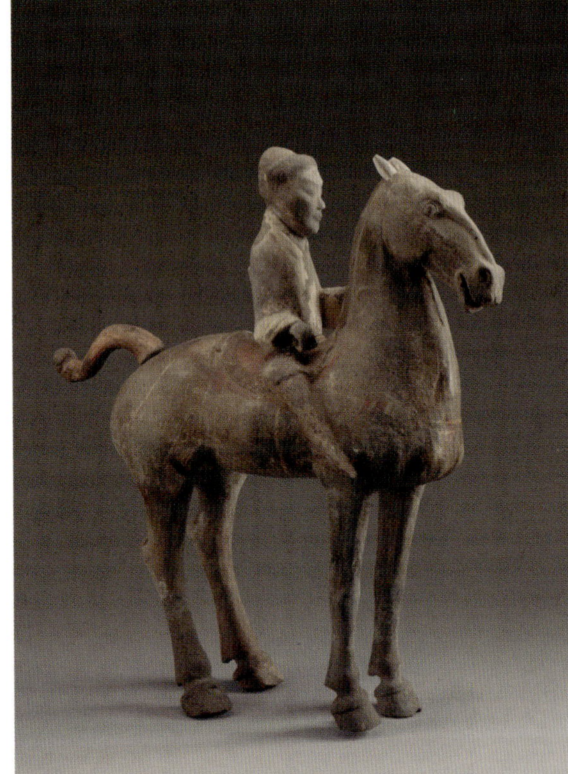

115. Five medium cavalrymen from the Han general's tomb at Yangjiawan
彩绘小骑马俑 / 彩繪小騎馬俑

Western Han dynasty (206 BCE–9 CE)
Painted pottery, average height 58cm
Excavated at Yangjiawan, Xianyang, 1965
Xianyang Museum, YLX0004; YLX0005; YLX0006; YLX0007; YLX0008

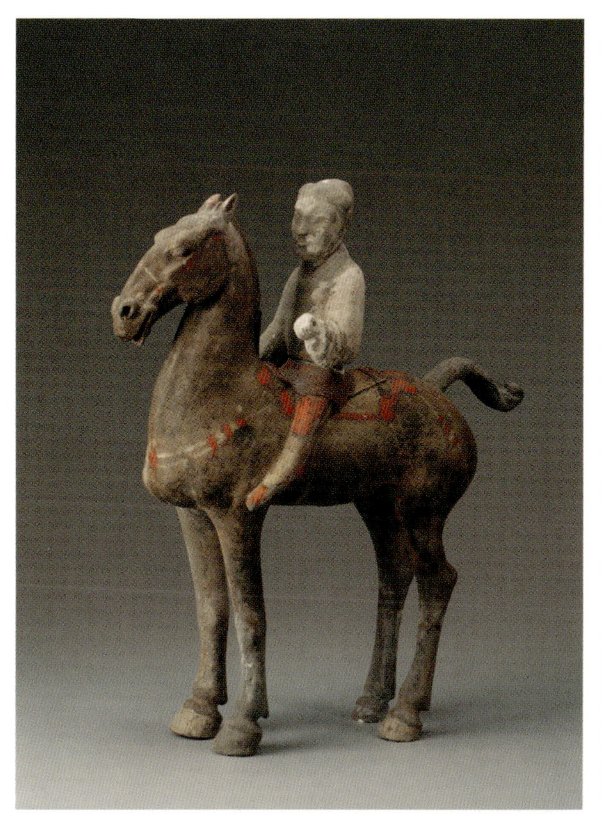
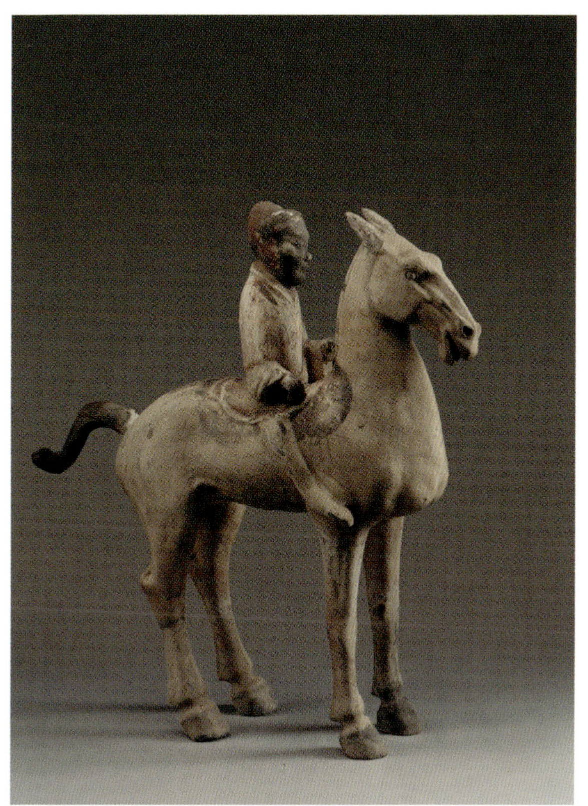
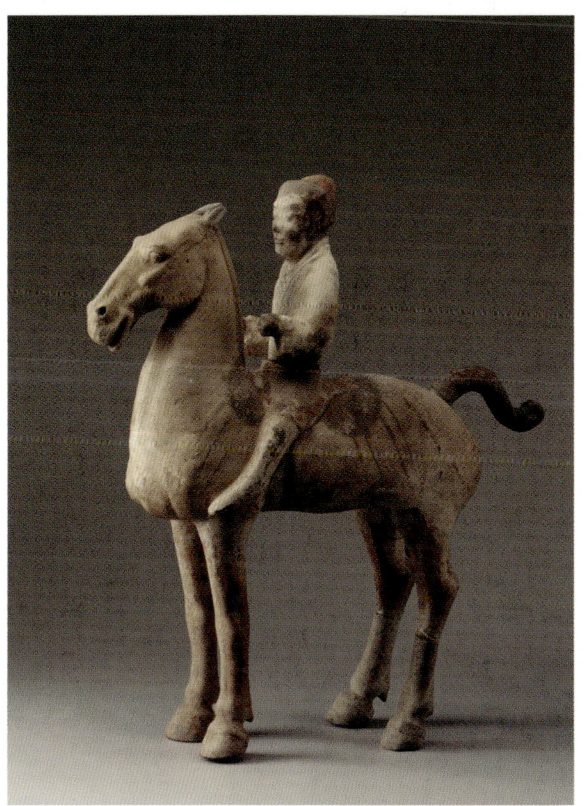
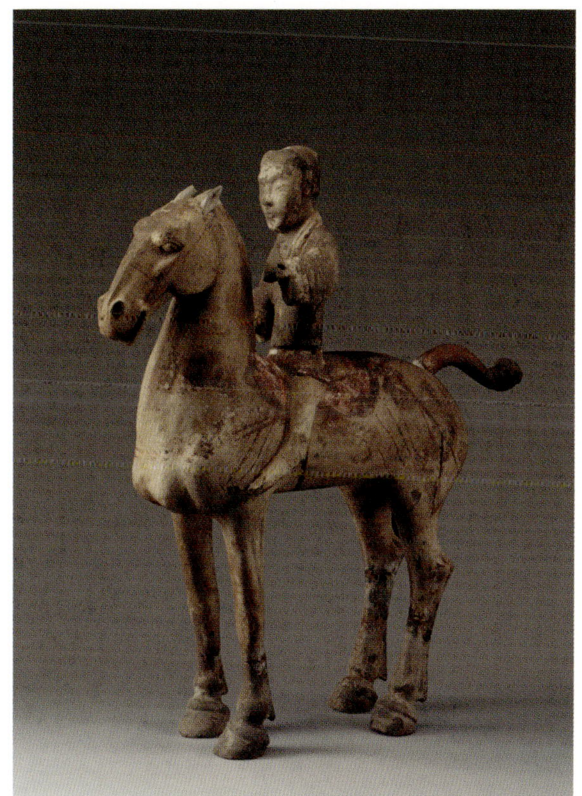

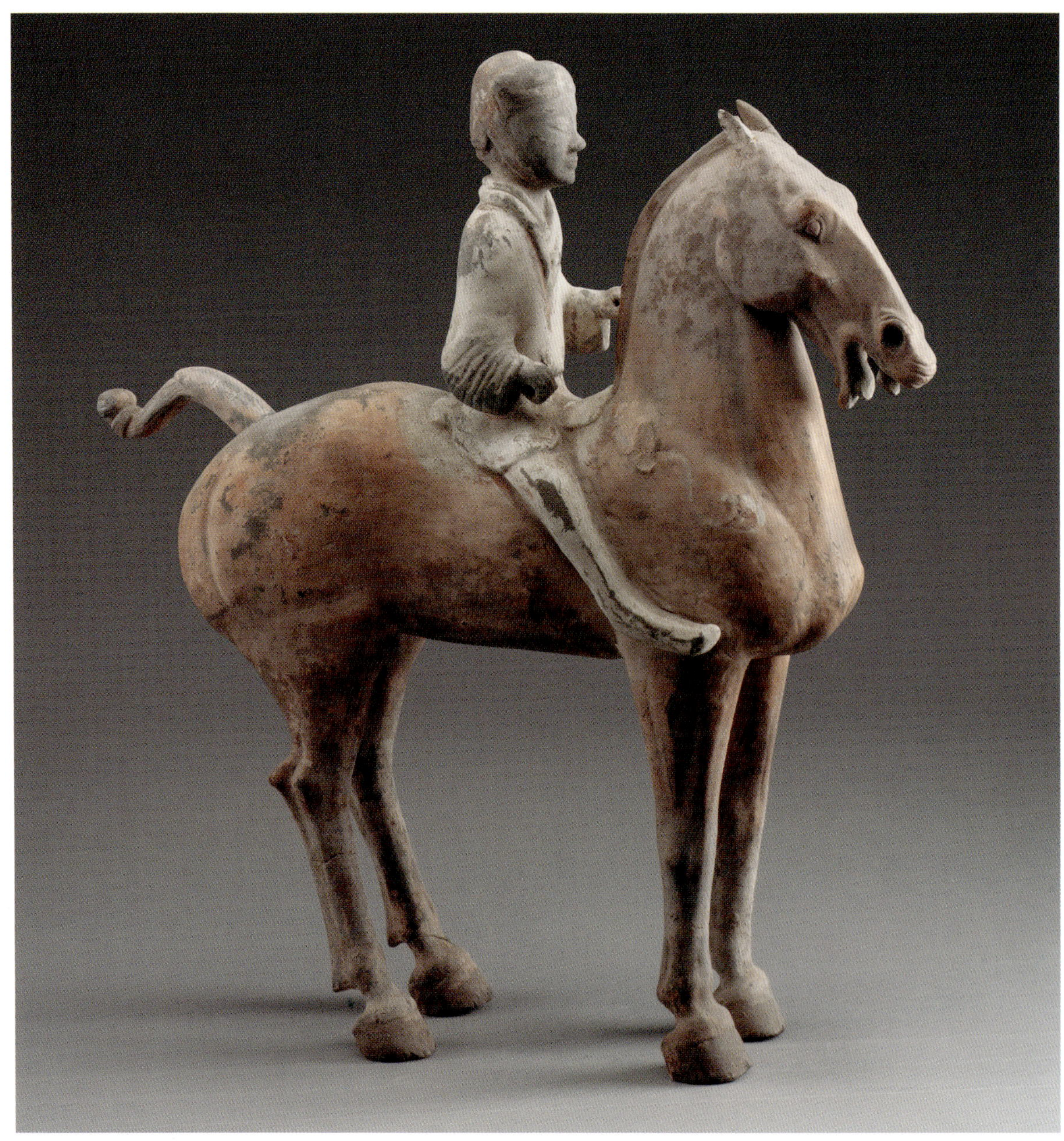

116. Five large soldiers on horseback from the Han general's tomb at Yangjiawan
彩绘大骑兵俑 / 彩繪大騎馬俑

Western Han dynasty (206 BCE–9 CE)
Painted pottery, average height 68cm
Excavated at Yangjiawan, Xianyang, 1965
Xiangyang Museum, yqd005; yqd013; yqd014; yqd017; yqd015

The marked presence of cavalrymen at Yangjiawan suggests that soldiers on horseback were more widely used in Han military battle than chariots.

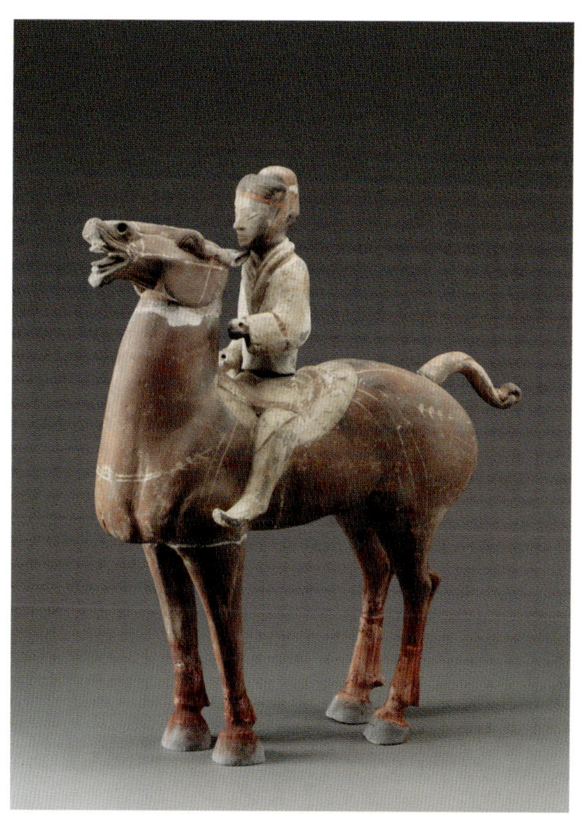
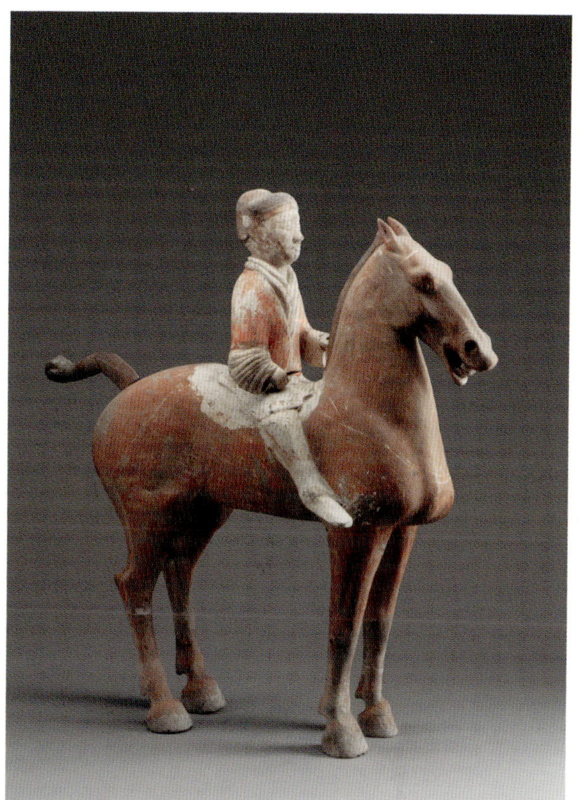
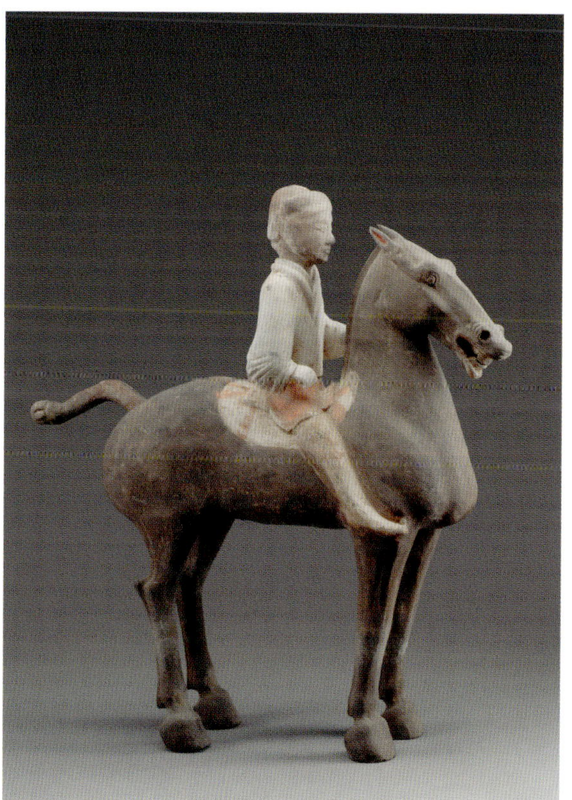
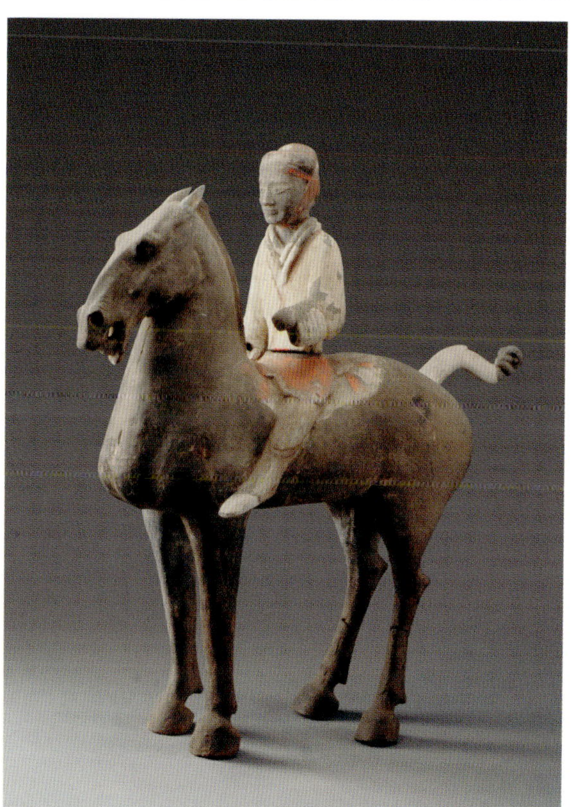

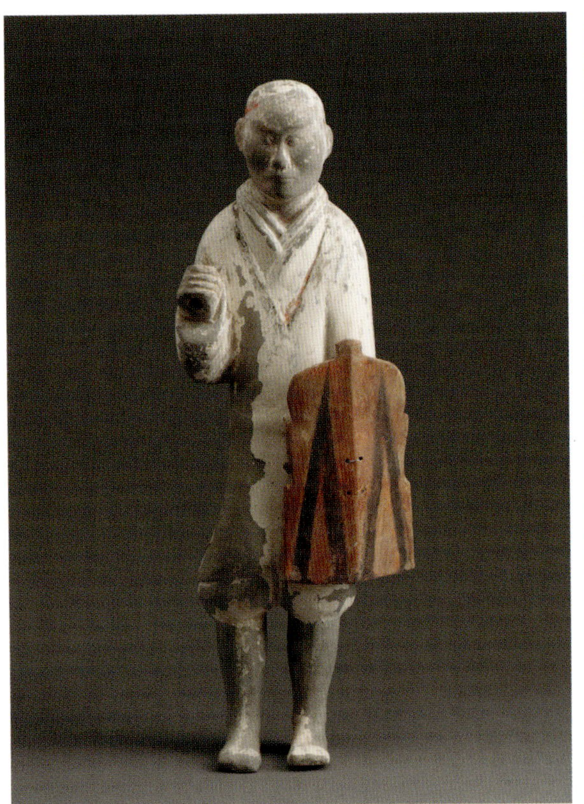

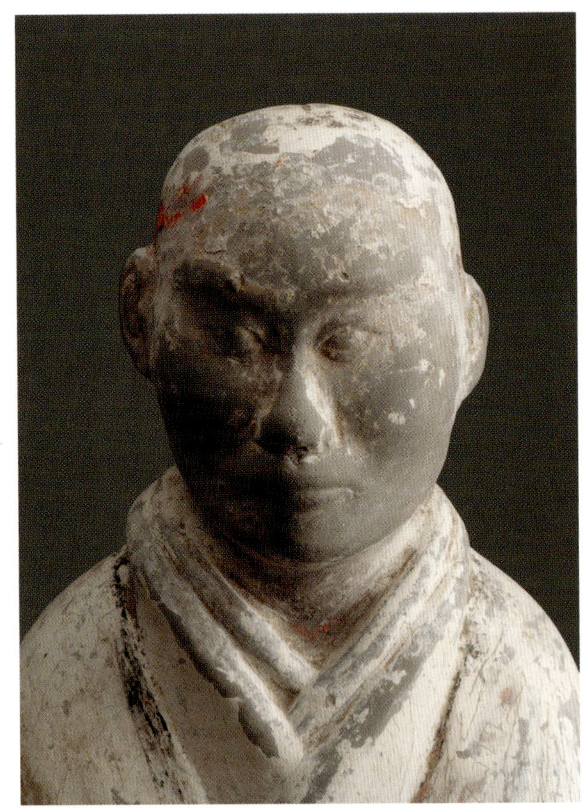

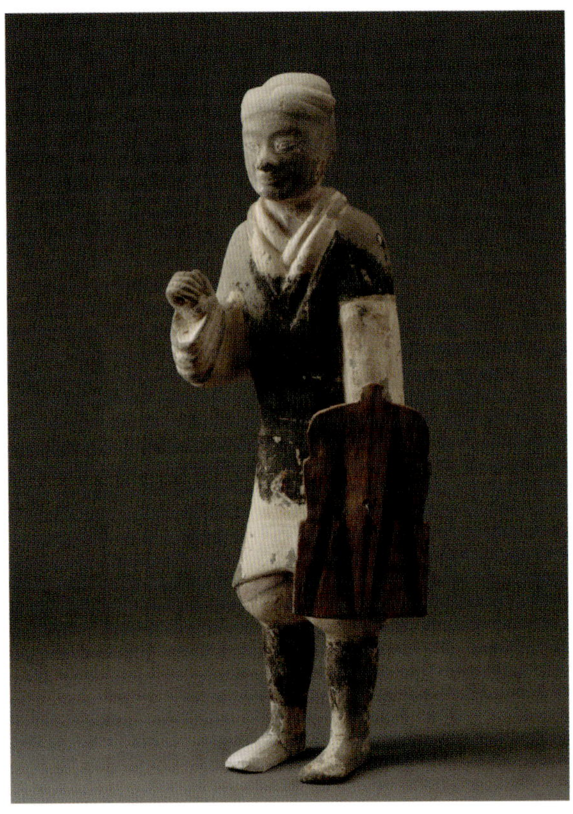

117. Five standing soldiers from the Han general's tomb at Yangjiawan
彩绘步兵俑 / 彩繪步兵俑

Western Han dynasty (206 BCE–9 CE)
Painted pottery, average height 49.5cm
Excavated at Yangjiawan, Xianyang, 1965
Xianyang Museum, 杨-0008; 杨-0010; 杨-1897; 杨-1898; 杨-1901

The infantry soldiers stand erect, and are painted in bright colours. In one hand they each hold a shield, which is decorated with geometric patterns, and originally held a long weapon in the other. The facial features vary from soldier to soldier, and it is suggested that they represent different ethnic groups, including troops from the western regions of the Empire (modern-day Sichuan), who were known for their military aptitude.

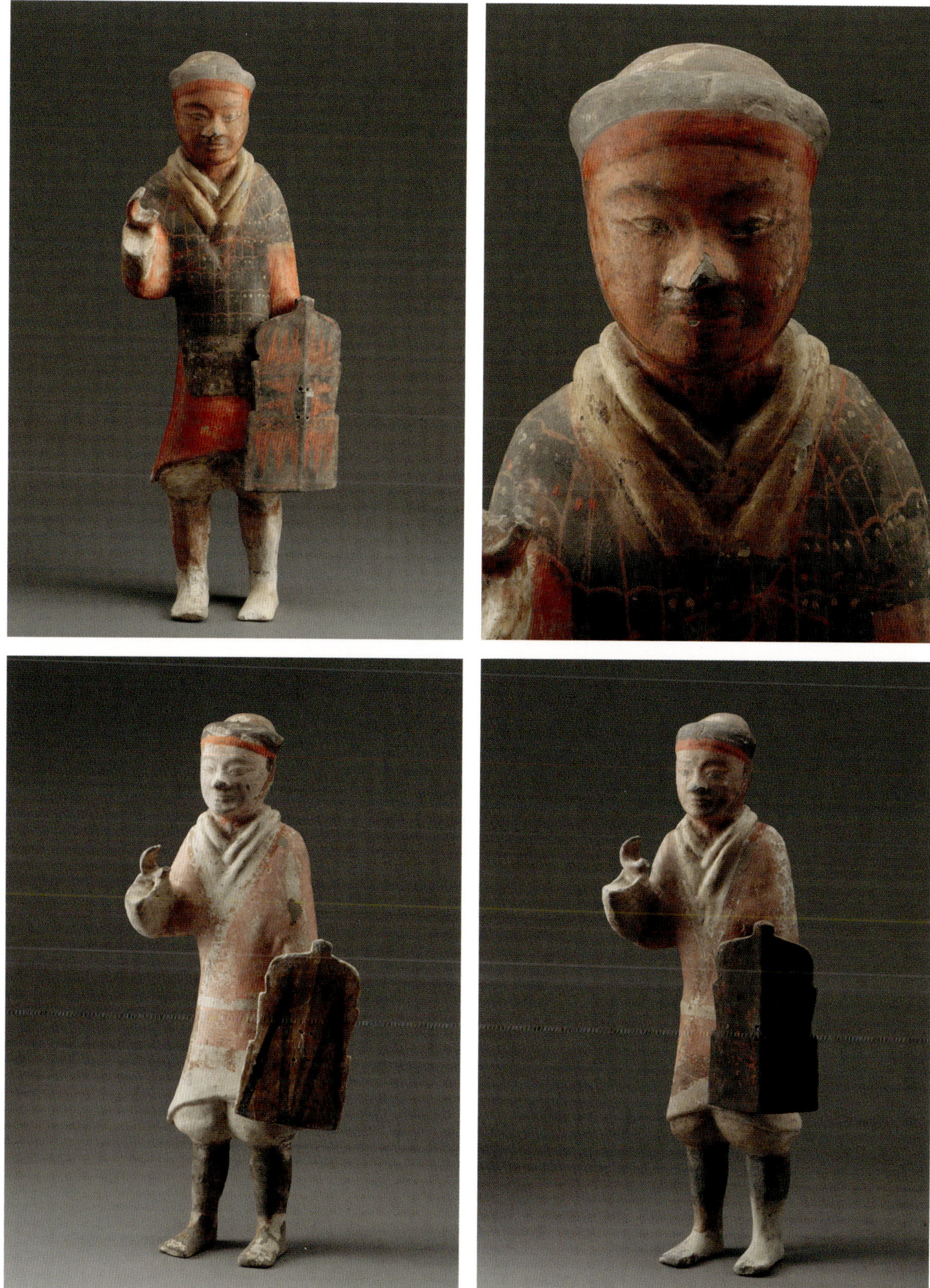

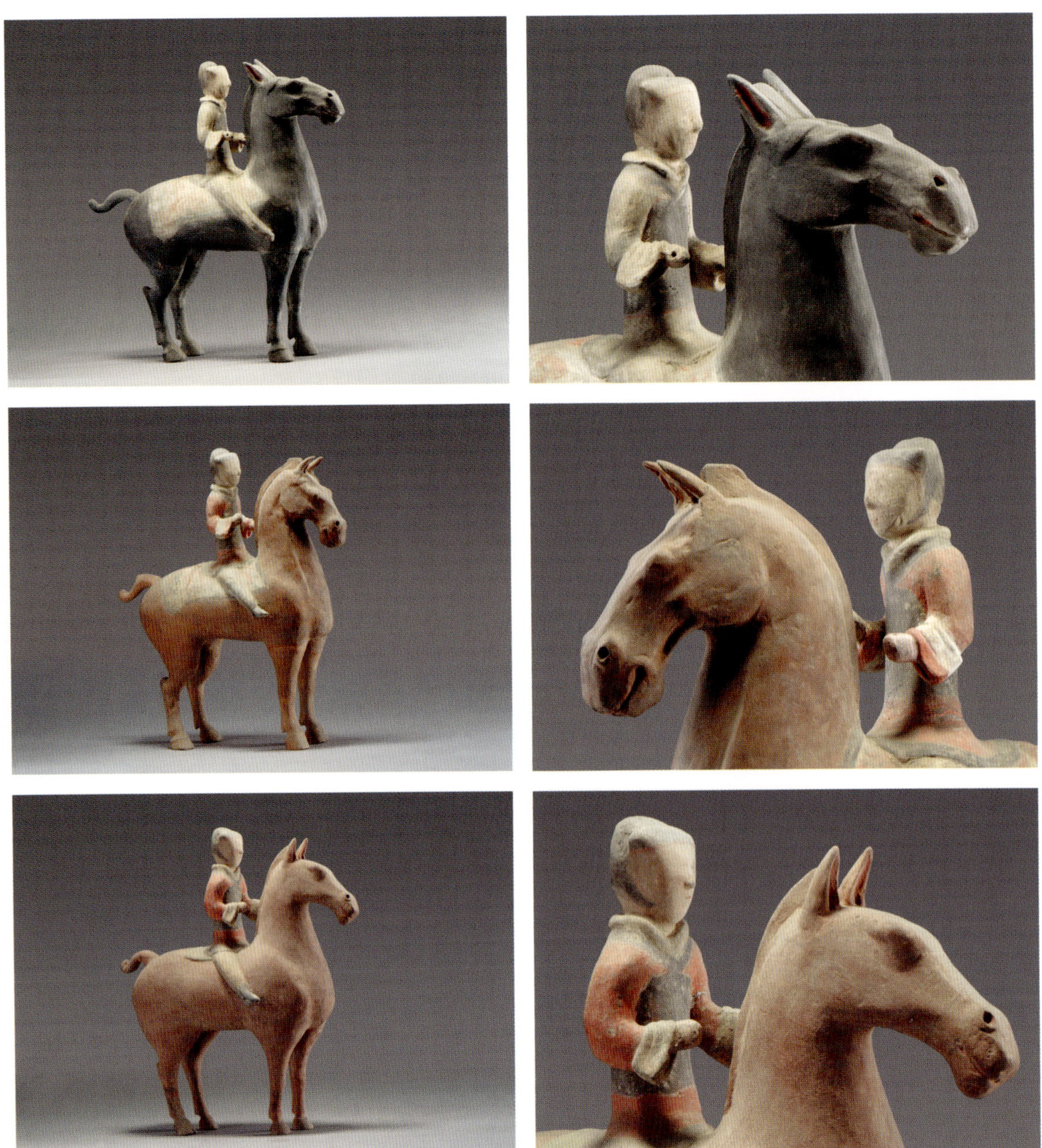

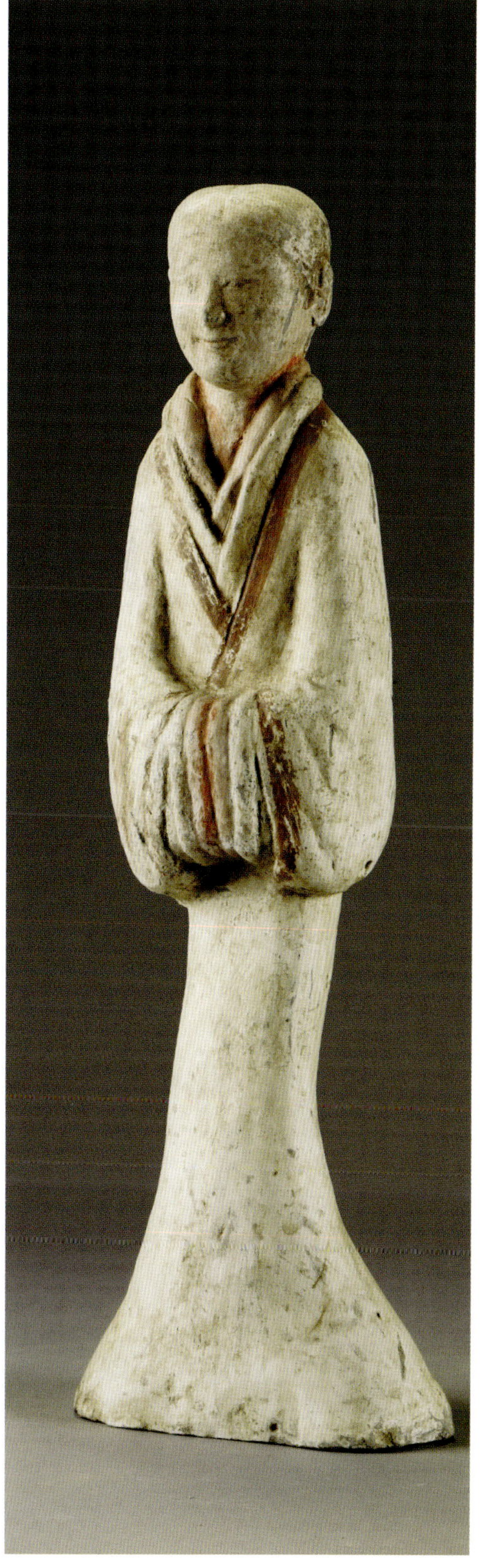

118. Three cavalrymen
彩绘骑马俑 / 彩繪騎馬俑

Western Han dynasty (206 BCE–9 CE)
Painted pottery, heights 37.6cm; 37.2cm; 30.8cm
Excavated from the Accompanying Burial Grave, Changling, Xianyang, 2003
Han Yangling Museum, YG1293; YG1294; YG1297

The exact origin of these three cavalrymen is unclear, but it is thought that they were excavated from a tomb near the first Han emperor's tomb at Changling. They are now in the collection of Han Yangling Museum.

119. Painted maid from Changling Mausoleum
粉彩女俑

Western Han dynasty (206 BCE–9 CE)
Painted pottery, 47 x 15.5cm
Excavated from the Accompanying Burial Grave, Changling, Xianyang, 2007
Han Yangling Museum, M193:25

This painted maid was excavated from an accompanying tomb of a noble, near Emperor Jing's burial complex. She is wearing full-length, layered robes, with long, wide sleeves trimmed with bands of bright colours, and appears alert, as if waiting to attend to her master or mistress. It is suggested that servants were not just present to provide for the comfort of the deceased, but also to make sure that meals and ceremonies would be correctly prepared for seasonal rites and rituals.

MAOLING MAUSOLEUM

EMPEROR WU OF HAN

Emperor Wu is considered one of the greatest emperors in Chinese history. As the fifth Han emperor, he further expanded the realm of China and ruled from a strong, centralised state. His reign lasted a remarkable fifty-four years, from 141 BCE to 87 BCE.

Like his predecessors, Emperor Wu was fascinated with immortality. He carried out ceremonies to worship the gods of Heaven and seek immortality, and built lofty towers to entice immortals down to Earth so that he might meet them.

Construction of Emperor Wu's tomb began in the second year of his reign, and continued for fifty-three years. He was buried at Maoling, in the largest of all tombs built during the Han dynasty. These architectural elements come from the site of Maoling Mausoleum, and offer an indication of the splendour of Emperor Wu's ambitions.

120. Gate ring holder (*Pushou*) with beast pattern
兽面纹玉铺首 / 獸面紋玉鋪首

Western Han dynasty (206 BCE–9 CE)
Jade, 35.6 x 34.2cm
Excavated at the southeast of Maoling, Xingping, 1975
Maoling Museum, 0640

Intended to hold a pendant ring, this majestic jade door-knocker would have been secured on the outer door of a palace. Its size suggests the palace was of a grand scale. The zoomorphic visage with bulging eyes was intended to ward off evil spirits. It also contains representations of the four cardinal emblems, although they are not arranged directionally.

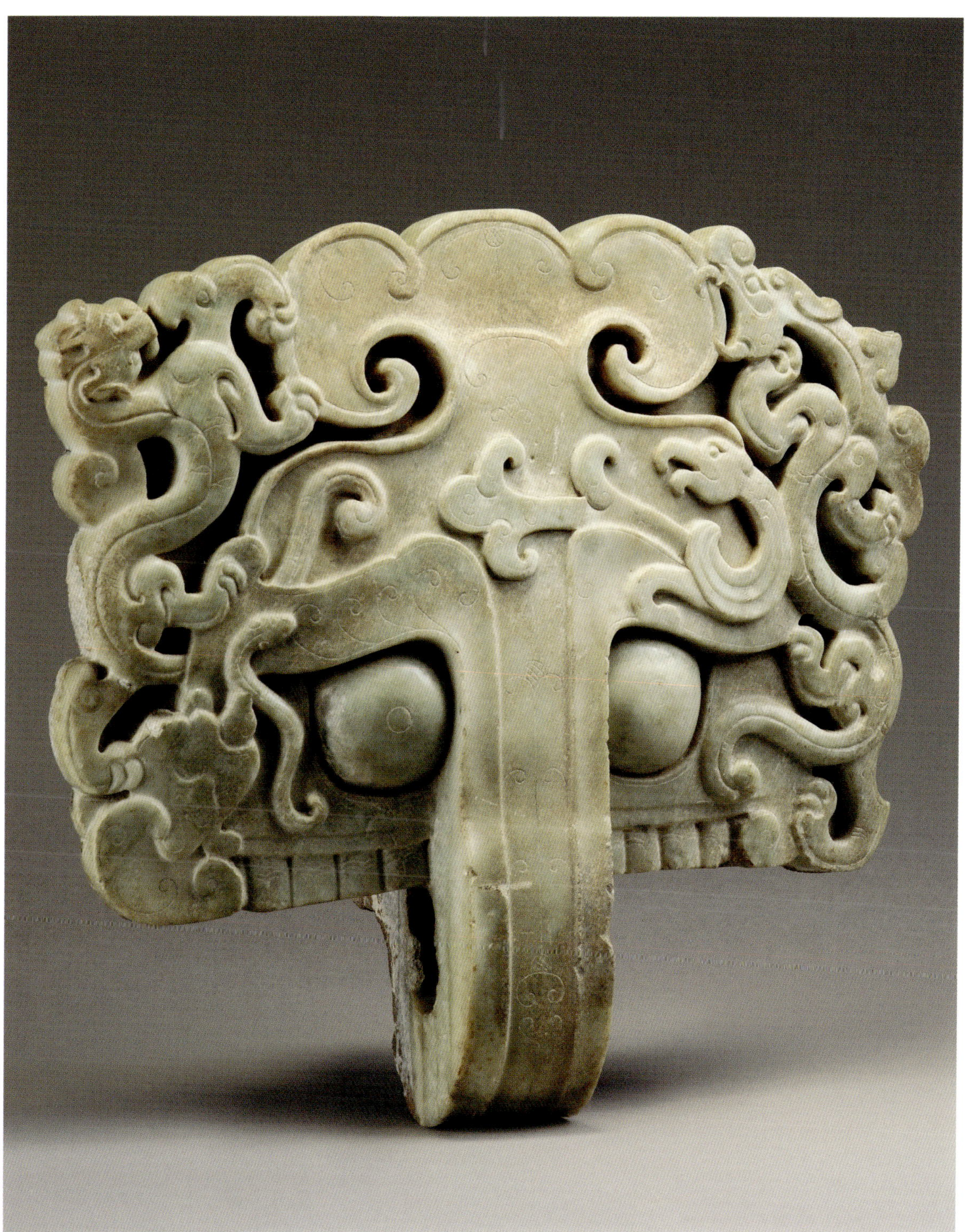

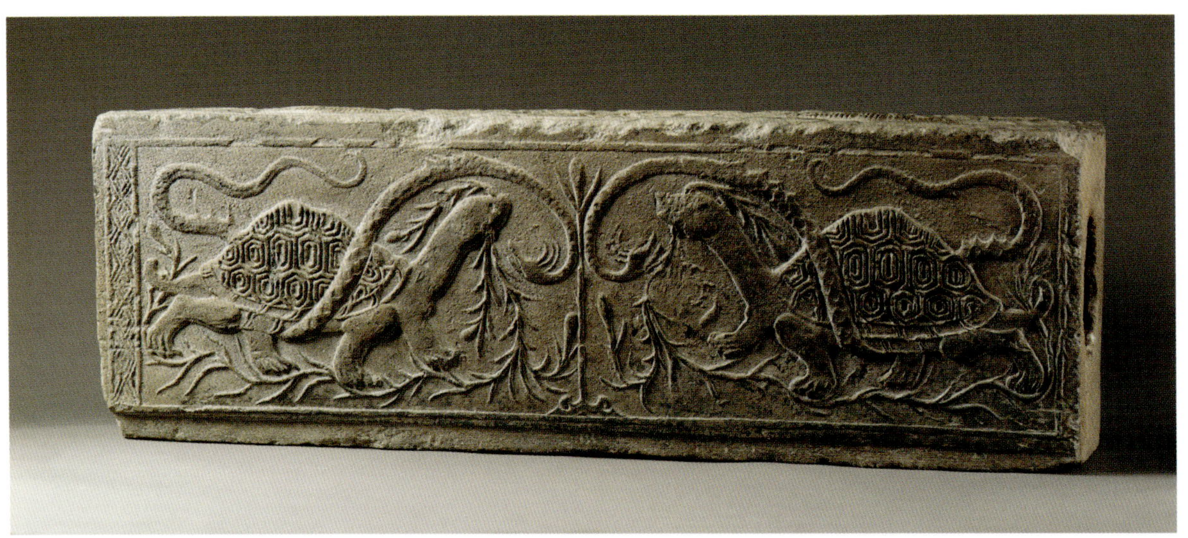

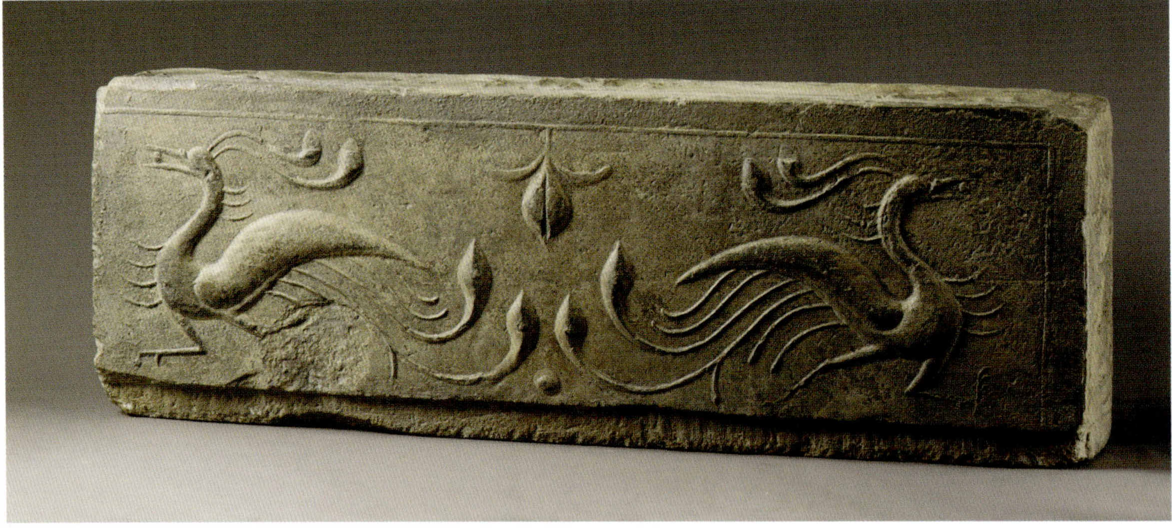

121. **Hollow brick with tortoise and snake pattern**
玄武纹空心砖 / 玄武紋空心磚

Western Han dynasty (206 BCE–9 CE)

Pottery, 37.5 x 117.5cm

Excavated at Daochang village, Nanweixiang, Xingping, 1974. Donated by the villager Zhang Wanping

Maoling Museum, 0644

122. **Hollow brick with vermilion bird pattern**
朱雀纹空心砖 / 朱雀紋空心磚

Western Han dynasty (206 BCE–9 CE)

Pottery, 40.5 x 116.5cm

Donated by Nan Shengzhe and others, Bei village, Nanweizhen, Xingping, 1975

Maoling Museum, 0432

These decorated bricks represent the four cardinal emblems, mythological creatures derived from Chinese constellations. Each creature was associated with a direction and a season: the black tortoise of the north (catalogue number 121); the vermilion bird of the south (catalogue number 122); the white tiger of the west (catalogue number 123); and the azure dragon of the east (catalogue number 124).

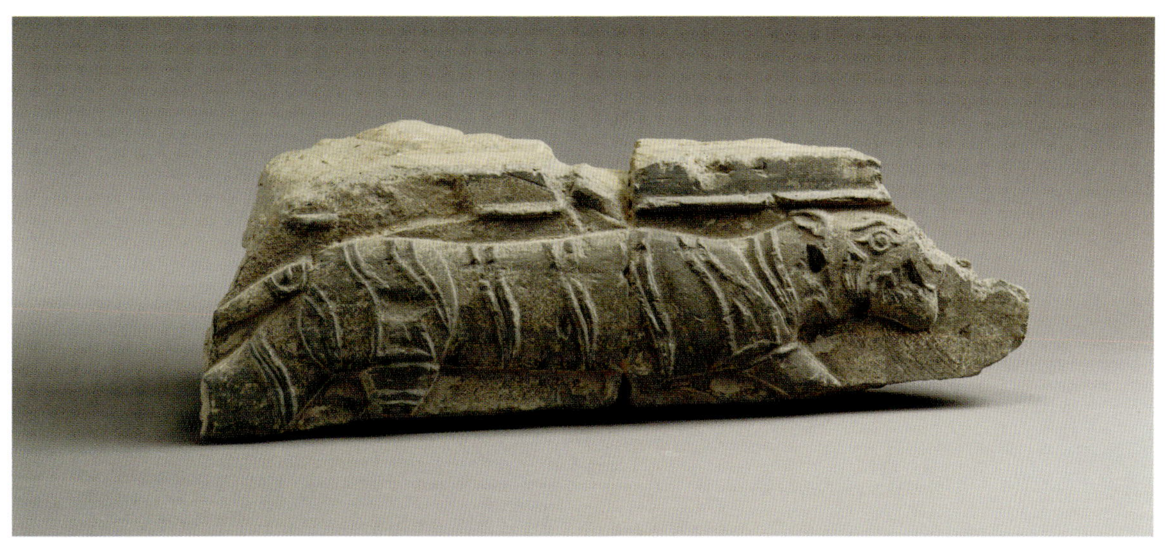

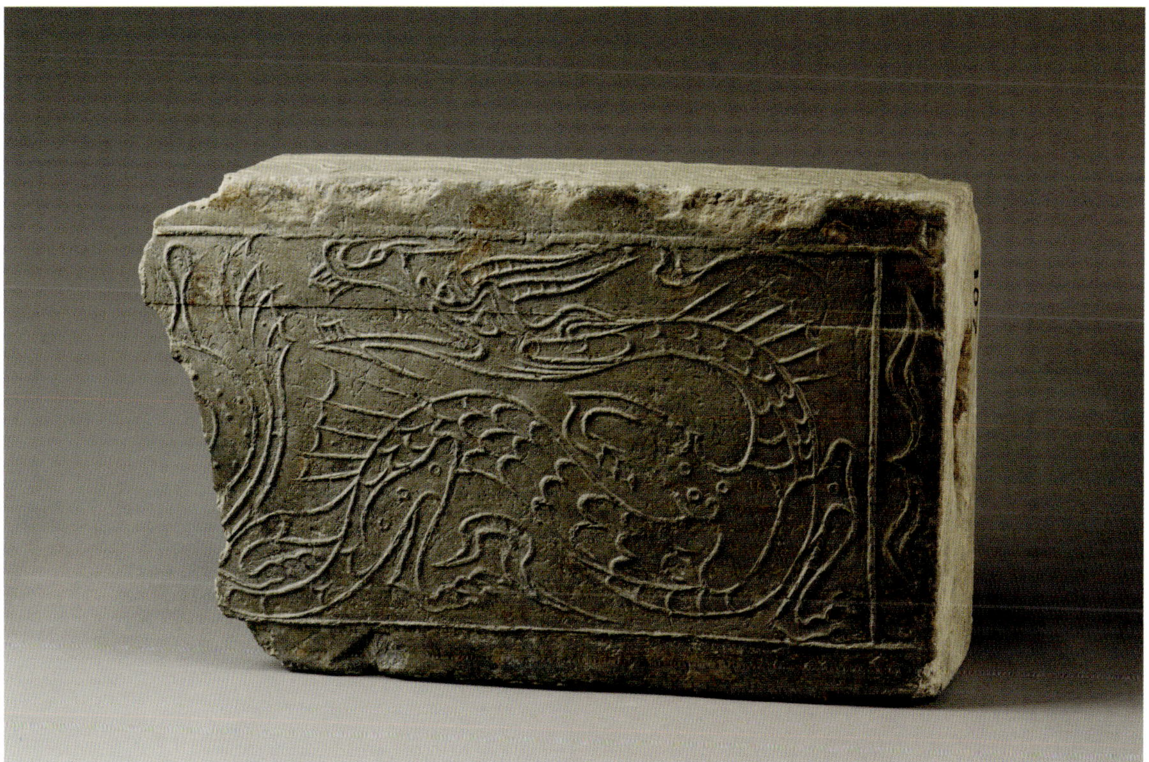

123. Hollow brick with tiger pattern
虎纹空心砖 / 虎紋空心磚

Western Han dynasty (206 BCE–9 CE)

Pottery, 13.8 x 45.5cm

Excavated at Daochang village, Nanweixiang, Xingping, 1974. Donated by the villager Zhang Wanping

Maoling Museum, 0643

124. Hollow brick with dragon pattern
龙纹空心砖 / 龍紋空心磚

Western Han dynasty (206 BCE–9 CE)

Pottery, 38.1 x 64.7cm

Excavated at Beiwu village, Xiwuxiang, Xingping, 1969. Donated by the villager Duan Zhi

Maoling Museum, 0107

EASTERN HAN DYNASTY

Following the dissolution of the Western Han empire, China flourished again under the Eastern Han dynasty (25–220 CE). The capital moved further east, to Luoyang in present-day Henan. During this period, trade with foreigners expanded, and the arts and learning thrived, perhaps stimulated by new influences and knowledge.

125. Mythical stone creatures
石神兽天禄; 石神兽天禄 /
石神獸天祿; 石神獸天祿

Eastern Han dynasty (25–220 CE)
Stone, lengths 216cm
Excavated at Shenjiaqiao, Xianyang, 1960
Xi'an Beilin Museum, 六0—169; 六0—170

These two mythological creatures may have been stone lion guardians, placed in front of a noble's tomb. The female (above) restrains a playful cub under her paw, representing nurture, while the male (below) rests his on a ball, representing supremacy. Such figures assumed popularity during the Han dynasty. Together, they would protect their owner into eternity.

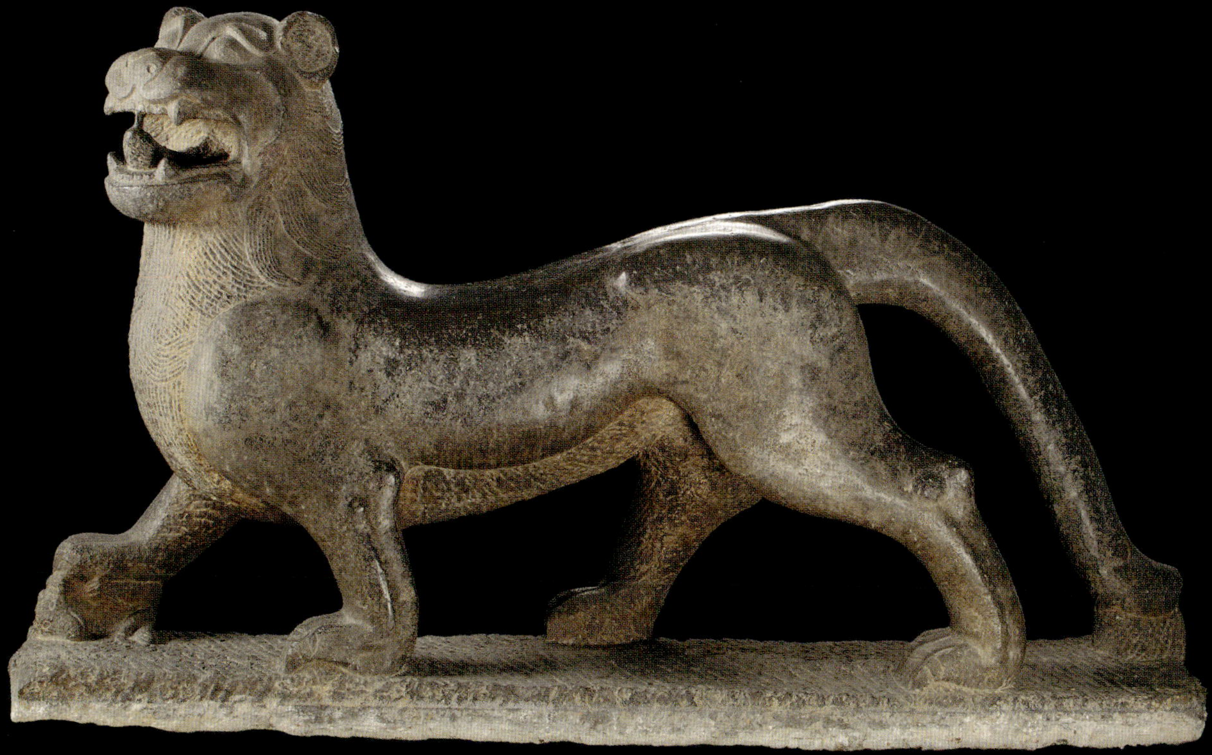

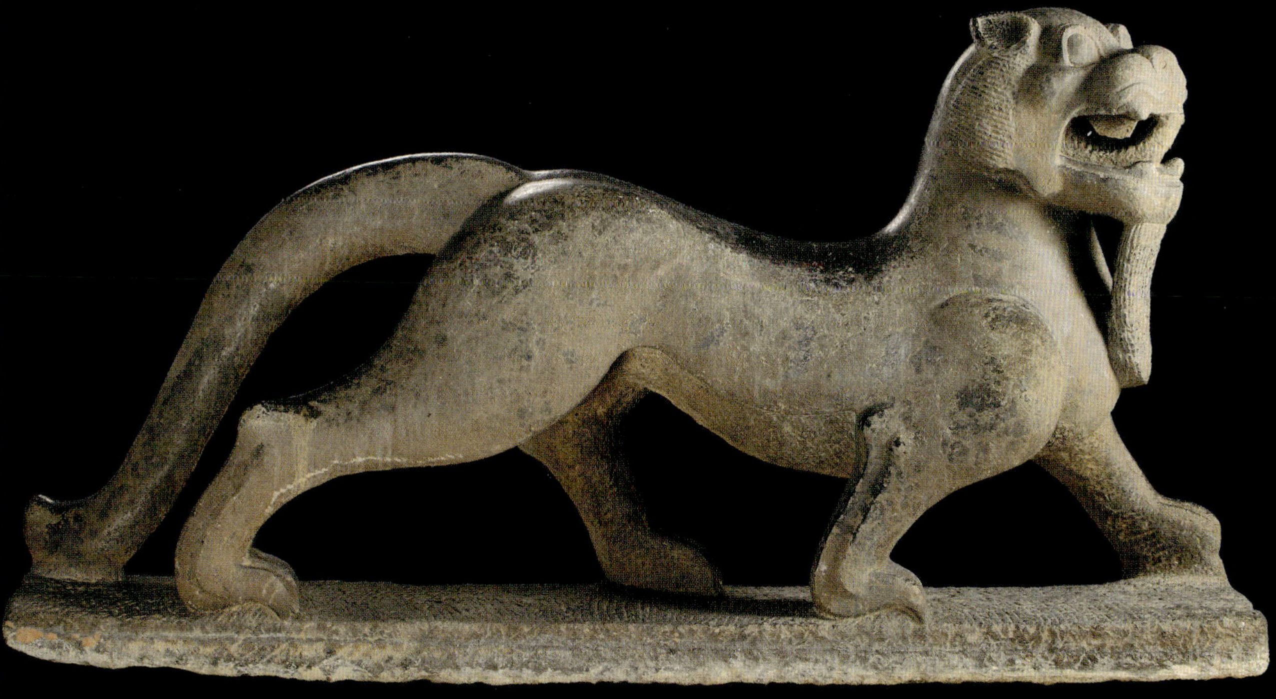

126. Tomb gate
画像石 / 畫像石

Eastern Han dynasty (25–220 CE)
Carved and painted stone, approx. 170 x 288cm
Excavated at Baijiashan village, Suide, Yulin, 1998
Suide County Museum, 270; 271; 272; 274; 275

Tomb gates such as this, constructed from five slabs of carved and painted stone, were doorways between Heaven and Earth. Their iconography hints at the celestial journey the deceased would need to take after death to reach Heaven. On the two outer slabs, immortals are climbing swirling tendrils of clouds and mushrooms of immortality, while the inner two depict vertical towers, suggesting an alternative route to paradise.

The horizontal lintel appears to represent a battle scene, perhaps indicating the challenges the deceased would face on their journey. The action reads from right to left, and increases in intensity, climaxing with a group of riders on horseback, trampling over a decapitated soldier towards a mound defended by crouching figures armed with crossbows. Beyond the mound is a comparatively peaceful scene, presumably the desired destination, where deer are calmly grazing. These scenes both depicted and facilitated the deceased on their journey to Heaven, helping them overcome evil spirits and achieve their immortal goal.

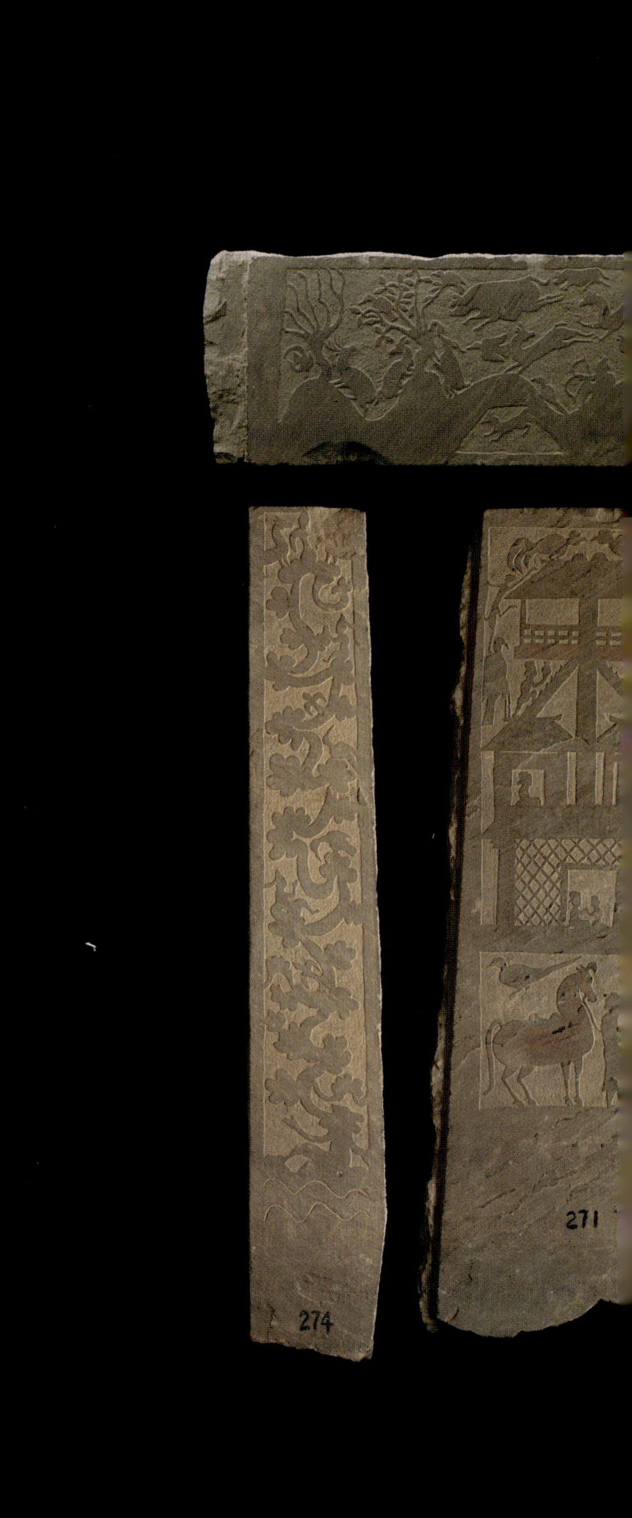

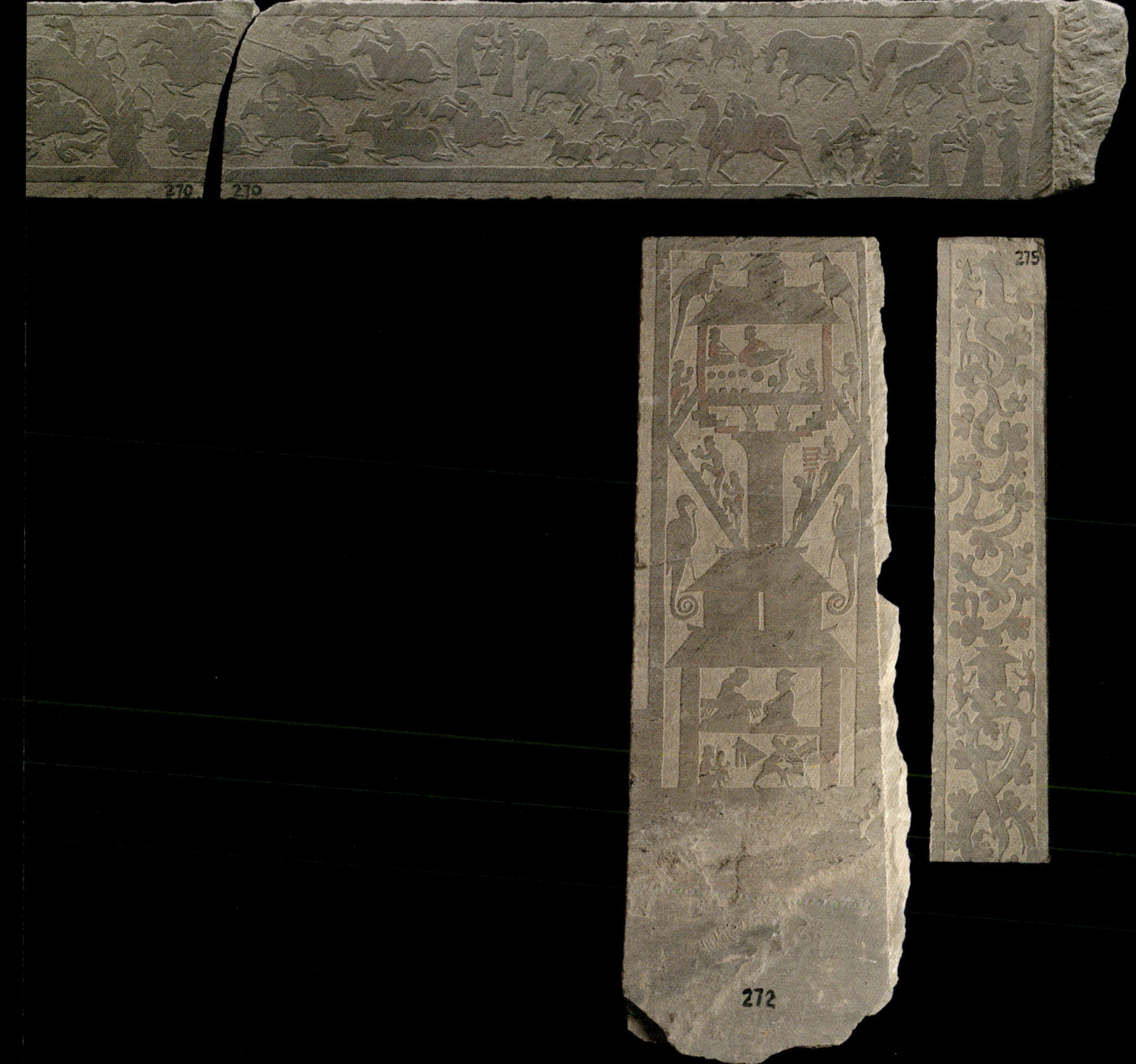

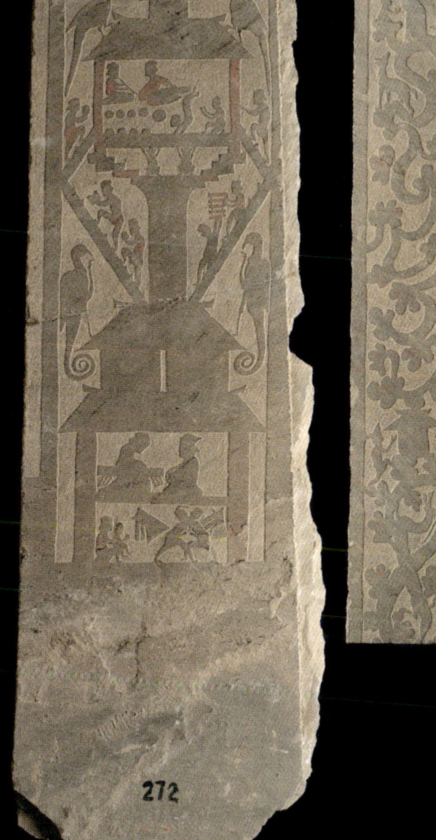
275
272

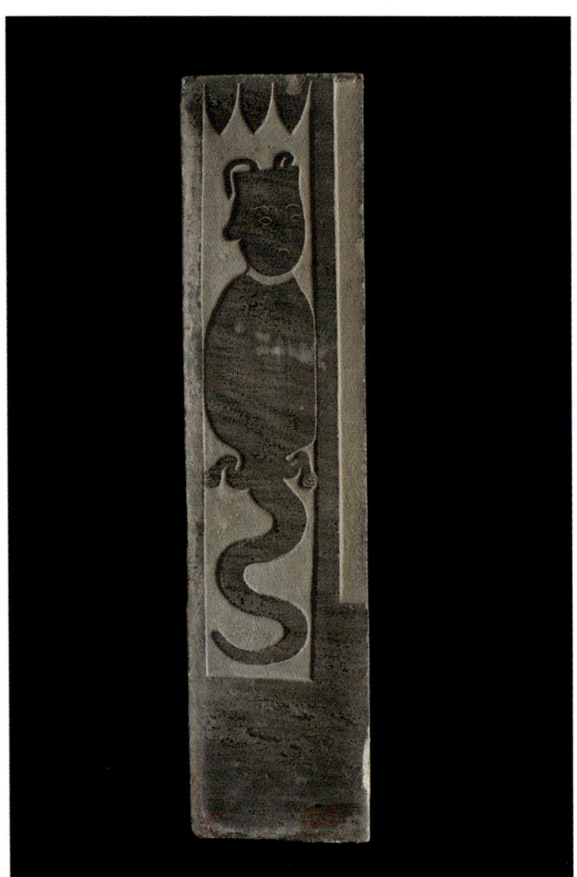

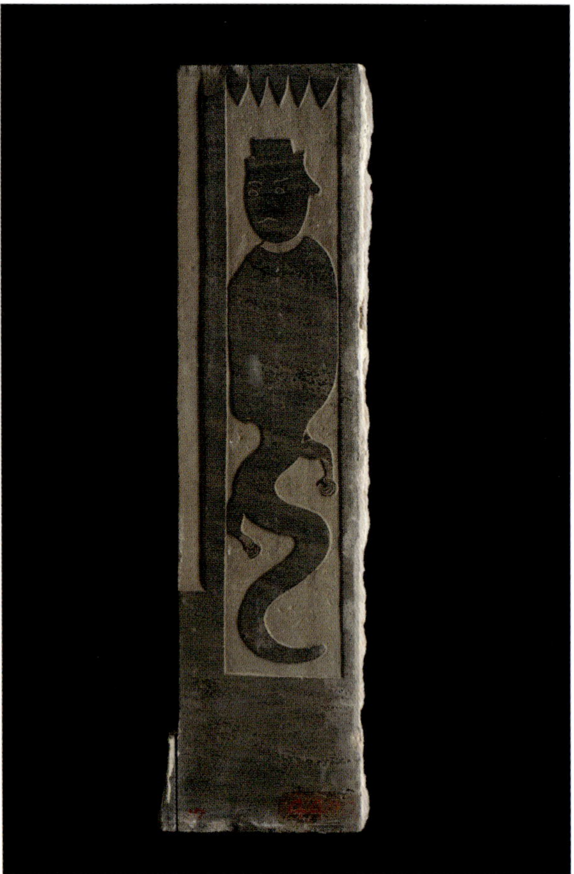

127. Tomb gate (Fuxi and Nüwa)
画像石（伏羲; 女娲）/
畫像石（伏羲; 女媧）

Eastern Han dynasty (25–220 CE)
Carved and painted stone, 123 x 31cm; 124 x 31cm
Collected at Peijiamao, Suide, Yulin, 1987
Suide County Museum, 16; 17

Fuxi and Nüwa played multiple roles in ancient Chinese history and mythology. Nüwa was a matriarchal figure central to the creation myth, while Fuxi was mythologised as a bearer of human culture. In Han art, they were a popular motif, represented as hybrids of humans and serpents. Together, they were considered a divine pair, most likely to embody the *yin* 陰 and *yang* 陽 harmony, and to emphasise their roles as deities of creation.

128. Winged immortal
铜羽人 / 銅羽人

Eastern Han dynasty (25–220 CE)
Bronze, height 15.3cm
Excavated at the archaeological site of Han Chang'an, Xi'an, 1964
Xi'an Museum, G82

In the Han period, immortals became agents between Heaven and Earth. People hoped they would help them obtain immortality and aid their ascension to Heaven. Immortal figures, occupying the liminal realm between Heaven and Earth, can be identified by their large ears and their hybrid nature: this figure has sprouted wings and feathers delicately incised on its body. This winged immortal would have supported a candle, to illuminate the pathway of the deceased's celestial journey.

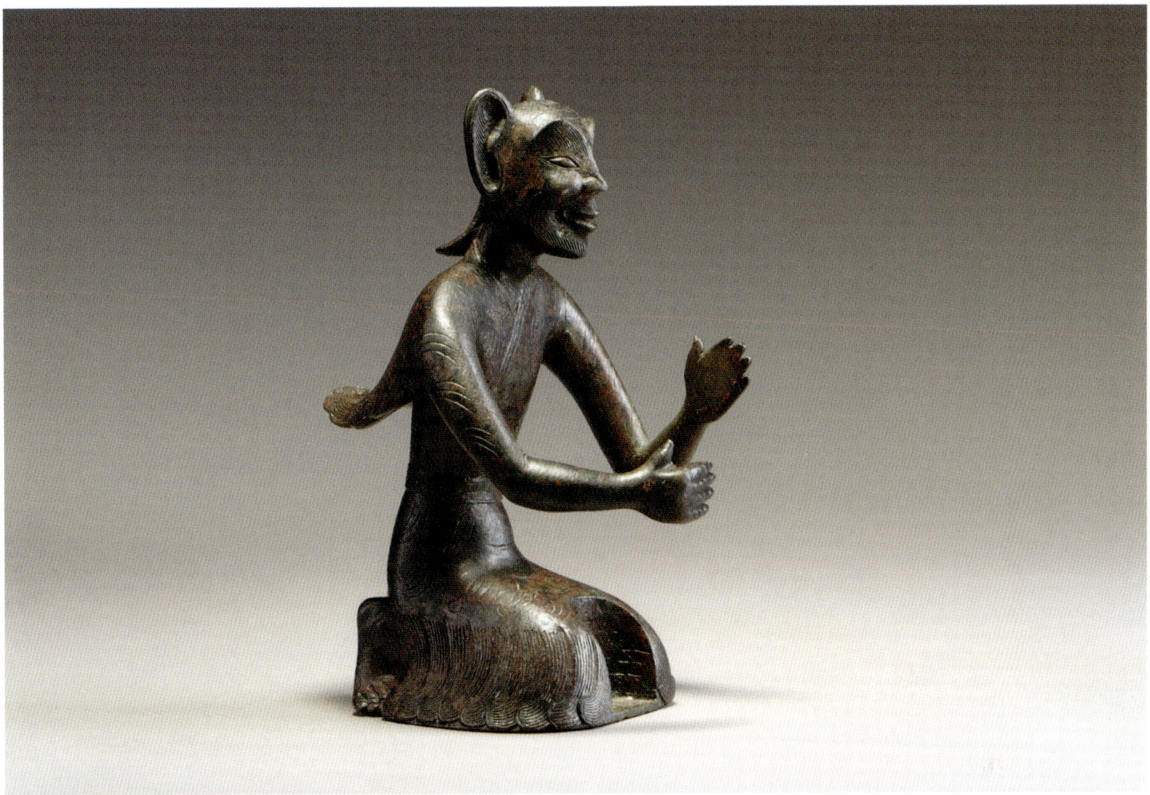

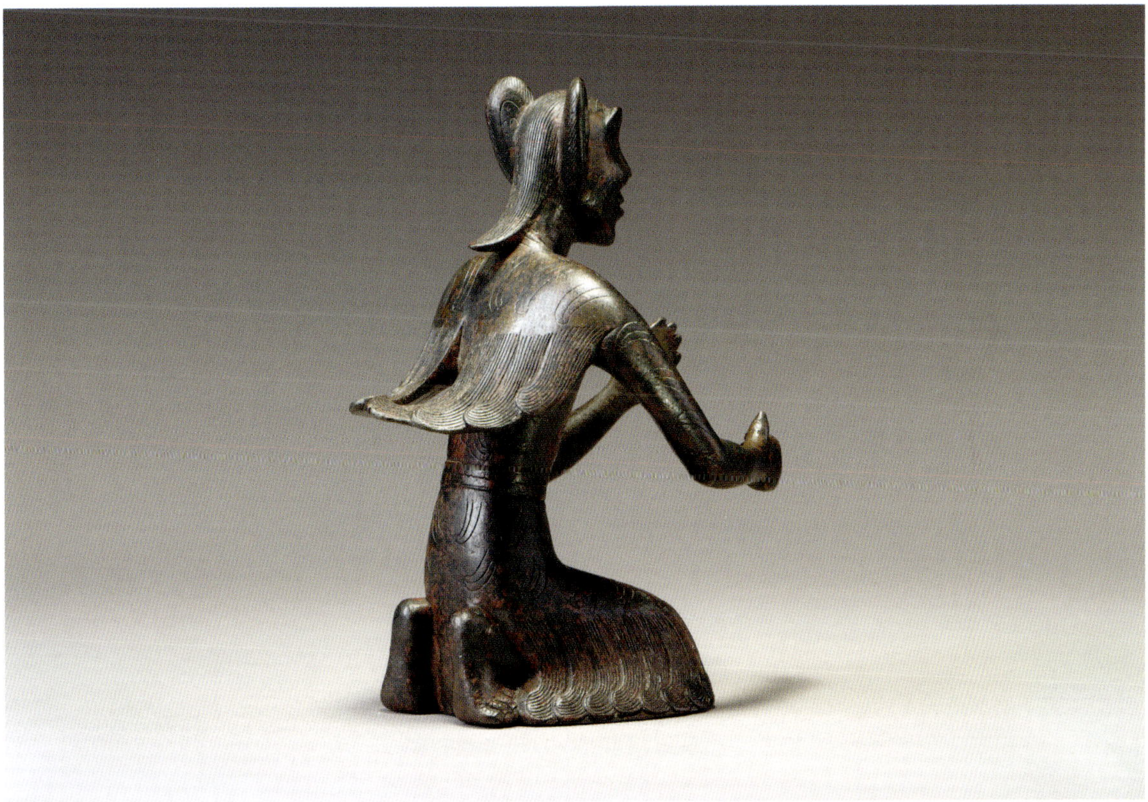

Afterwords

When the Terracotta Army last marched into Wellington in 1986, it was hosted at the National Museum of New Zealand. At that time, Te Papa was not even a twinkle in the establishment's eye. The Shaanxi History Museum was, however, in the process of being built. In 1991, to mark its official opening, Alan Baker, then Director of the National Museum, sourced a large pounamu boulder and had it sliced in two, polished and mounted. He presented one half to the Shaanxi History Museum saying that one half would reside in New Zealand and one in China, a symbol of friendship between the two museums.

This friendship has continued to evolve. In 2014, Te Papa toured *Kura Pounamu: Treasured stone of Aotearoa New Zealand* to Shaanxi History Museum, an exhibition first showcased in Beijing in 2012 to commemorate forty years of diplomatic ties between New Zealand and China. Since then, conversations about further possibilities for collaboration have evolved, culminating in this exhibition *Terracotta Warriors: Guardians of Immortality*.

Terracotta Warriors will be the first international exhibition to be hosted in Toi Art, Te Papa's purpose-built art gallery. It offers an exciting opportunity for visitors to Te Papa to experience first-hand the terracotta warriors, who, for over 2000 years, secretly guarded the First Emperor of China's tomb. The exhibition also includes over 160 exquisite works of ancient Chinese art crafted from gold, jade and bronze, which date from the Western Zhou through to the Qin and Han dynasties (1046 BCE–220 CE). In their very different ways, the Qin and Han eras established a China that has lasted continuously for around two millennia. This exhibition will introduce visitors to these histories, and will consider how they continue to resonate today.

We would like to thank our colleagues at the Shaanxi Provincial Cultural Relics Bureau, Shaanxi History Museum, Shaanxi Cultural Heritage Promotion Center and Emperor Qin Shihuang's Mausoleum Site Museum of the People's Republic of China for their hard work bringing this exhibition to Wellington. We are also grateful to the institutions throughout Shaanxi province who have shared their taonga with us. Thank you to Duncan Campbell, who has lent his scholarship and expertise to the development of the exhibition, and to Nathan Woolley, both of whom have written for the catalogue.

In this 2019 China–New Zealand Year of Tourism, Te Papa is delighted to be hosting this exhibition and we hope that many visitors will take the once-in-a-generation opportunity to visit it.

Geraint Martin
CEO Museum of New Zealand Te Papa Tongarewa

Shaanxi Province is an important birthplace of Chinese civilisation and the Chinese people. Over the course of more than a millennium, between the eleventh century BCE and the tenth century CE, as many as fourteen dynasties established their capital here, including those of the Zhou, Qin, Han, Sui and Tang dynasties. In abbreviated form, the province is referred to as 'Qin', a usage that stems from the resplendent civilisation once founded by the Qin dynasty. In ancient times, Shaanxi's provincial capital of Xi'an, once called Chang'an, the city of 'Everlasting Peace', served as the starting point for the Silk Road, and, more than a thousand years ago, boasted a population of over a million people, the first city in the world to exceed that size.

This long history has bequeathed Shaanxi an immensely rich cultural heritage, with collections that are at once complete, fulsome and of the highest quality, and that are redolent of both distinctive regional characteristics and exquisite cultural status. A particular strength of Shaanxi's historical heritage are the ruins of both capital cities and imperial tombs, including within its provincial boundaries at least eighty known imperial tomb sites. One such site is, of course, the 56.24 kilometres of the Emperor Qin Shihuang's Mausoleum Site Museum (including the Terracotta Warriors and Horses Pit), which was included in the World Heritage List in 1987.

This resplendent ancient civilisation established an early channel for cultural exchange between China and civilisations elsewhere, and nowadays its deep sedimentation of historical heritage continues to offer a rich material embodiment of the manner in which the civilisations of the world can be enhanced through confluence and mutual reflection. Between August 1986 and February 1987, the exhibition entitled *The Buried Army of Qin Shihuang* showed successively in the museums and galleries of Auckland, Christchurch and Wellington, being met with popular acclaim on the part of New Zealand audiences, with the National Museum of New Zealand (Te Papa's forerunner) having been one of the show's venues. It was an exhibition that attracted a viewership of over 270,000 people, close to 10 percent of New Zealand's population at the time. That exhibition played an extremely important role in increasing the understanding among New Zealanders of China's historical culture, but it also served to encourage further levels of cultural exchange between China and New Zealand.

Time has flown since that moment, and, after the passage of thirty years, the Shaanxi Provincial Cultural Relics Bureau is once again working hand in hand with the Museum of New Zealand Te Papa Tongarewa to offer to New Zealanders the exhibition *Terracotta Warriors: Guardians of Immortality*, to show between December 2018 and April 2019. The items that make up this exhibition, including ten terracotta figures, are sourced from twenty museums and collecting organisations in Shaanxi Province. Themed around the First Emperor's Terracotta Army, and with a focus on the culture of the Qin, but including objects dating from both before and after the Qin dynasty and the First Emperor's unification of empire, and the establishment of its succeeding Han dynasty, this exhibition seeks to present a complete picture of Qin dynasty culture in terms of its formation, its flourishing, and its lasting influence.

The word 'China' in all major European languages derives from the name of this dynasty. Although the Qin proved to be the shortest-lived of all major Chinese dynasties, having maintained its rule for only a brief fourteen years, it was nonetheless one of China's most important and influential dynasties. During this period China was unified, as was its written script, and weights and measures. It served to usher in China's first moment of prosperity.

In 2014, in his speech at UNESCO Headquarters, the President of the People's Republic of China, Mr Xi Jinping, stated that: 'Civilisations become more colourful through exchange, civilisations become richer through learning from each other. Exchange and learning from each other provides the impetus for the progress of human civilisation and the peaceful development of the world.' We hope that this present exhibition will provide the opportunity for New Zealanders to better appreciate China's history and culture, and to promote mutual understanding and friendship, thus serving as a platform for the further deepening of the exchange between the peoples of our two nations and their sense of mutual trust.

Finally, may I take this opportunity to thank all those whose assiduous work has served to make this exhibition a reality! I wish the exhibition the greatest of success.

Luo Wenli 罗文利
Director of the Shaanxi Provincial Cultural Relics Bureau

In 2014, the Shaanxi History Museum and the Museum of New Zealand Te Papa Tongarewa established a formal relationship of friendship. The following year, the two museums co-operated to hold the *Kura Pounamu: Treasured Stone of Aotearoa New Zealand* exhibition at the Shaanxi History Museum. At the conclusion of that exhibition, and based on the relationships established over the course of its successful hosting, our two museums began to explore further possibilities for cooperation. After the joint efforts of the museum staff at both our institutions, a Qin terracotta warriors-themed exhibition entitled *Terracotta Warriors: Guardians of Immortality* has now become a reality at Te Papa, marking a further stage in the enhancement of the friendly and cooperative relationships our museums have established.

Shaanxi Province, where the Shaanxi History Museum is located, is one of the most important areas inhabited by the Chinese people, and is where they prospered; it is also a region that fostered the birth and development of Chinese civilisation. Over the course of China's long history, fourteen glorious dynasties have established their capital here, including the Zhou, Qin, Han and Tang dynasties. This rich cultural heritage and profound cultural sedimentation have given rise to Shaanxi's unique historical and cultural features, while also providing a rich collection of resources for the Shaanxi History Museum.

The Shaanxi History Museum is a comprehensive historical museum whose collection of over 380,000 items includes the simple stone tools used in the initial stages of human development down to artefacts derived from various aspects of life up until 1840. As a result of its successful display of the history and culture of Shaanxi Province and ancient China, this museum has been called 'A Pearl of an Ancient Capital, the Treasure House of China'. In 2009, the museum was designated as a national-level key museum project, to be jointly built by the central and provincial governments. In 2016, the museum building was listed in the 20th-Century Chinese Architectural Heritage List. Many exhibitions curated by our museum have won the 'Top Ten Exhibition and Exhibition Excellence Awards'.

We sincerely hope that *Terracotta Warriors: Guardians of Immortality* will serve as a bridge and a window for the New Zealand public to better understand Shaanxi Province and ancient Chinese culture. It is our hope that this exhibition will also help promote and deepen the relationship between our two governments and peoples, and enhance present levels of mutual understanding and cultural exchange.

I wish the exhibition all possible success.

Qiang Yue 强跃
Director of the Shaanxi History Museum

opposite page **Detail of kneeling archer (catalogue number 97).**

'The Terracotta Warriors are a symbol of the spirit of Chinese civilisation.' In their role as cultural envoys promoting the cultural interchange between China and the world, more than ninety exhibitions featuring the First Emperor's terracotta soldiers and horses have already been held, in more than fifty countries and territories since 1982, and in more than one hundred cities. They have attracted foreign audiences of over 20 million viewers. They have served to promote the friendships between the peoples of China and the rest of the world, to enhance levels of cultural exchange and cooperation, and to greatly raise the profile of China on the international stage. As a result, a global 'terracotta warriors fever' can be said to continue to this day.

Between August 1986 and February 1987, *The Buried Army of Qin Shihuang* exhibition showed in Wellington, Auckland and Christchurch, giving a New Zealand audience their first sight of the terracotta warriors, to great acclaim. Between February and July 2003, an exhibition entitled *Two Emperors—China's Ancient Origins*, curated by the Shaanxi Provincial Cultural Relics Bureau and with terracotta warriors as an important component, showed in Auckland, thus giving New Zealand audiences a second occasion on which to view these remarkable artefacts. And now, what brings us even greater pleasure is this present exhibition, entitled *Terracotta Warriors: Guardians of Immortality*, and jointly curated by the Emperor Qin Shihuang's Mausoleum Site Museum and the Shaanxi History Museum, to show at the Museum of New Zealand Te Papa Tongarewa, a museum listed in the world's top twenty museums, between December 2018 and April 2019. More than thirty years after the terracotta warriors were first shown in New Zealand, they have now arrived for a third time. I believe that the successful hosting of this exhibition is both testimony to, and fruit of, the daily-enhanced levels of economic co-operation and cultural engagement that have characterised the relationship between our two nations over the course of the past thirty years.

I well remember welcoming the New Zealand Prime Minister John Key, his wife and accompanying delegation to the Emperor Qin Shihuang's Mausoleum Site Museum on the afternoon of 20 April 2016. During the course of his hour-long visit to the museum, Mr Key showed a deep interest in both the First Emperor's Mausoleum and the terracotta warrior pits, appraising himself fully of the circumstances of the discovery, excavation and repair of the terracotta soldiers and horses, writing in the Visitor's Book as he left the words: 'This was a visit that has left a profound impression, and I deeply appreciate the opportunity afforded us to visit your museum.'

It was at that time that our two nations expressed our desire to cooperate again in the future. 'Civilisations become more colourful through exchange, civilisations become richer through learning from each other. Exchange and learning from each other provide the impetus for the progress of human civilisation and the peaceful development of the world.' I sincerely hope that exchange and cooperation of this kind will continue into the future.

I wish this present exhibition all possible success!

Hou Ningbin 侯宁彬
Director of the Emperor Qin Shihuang's Mausoleum Site Museum

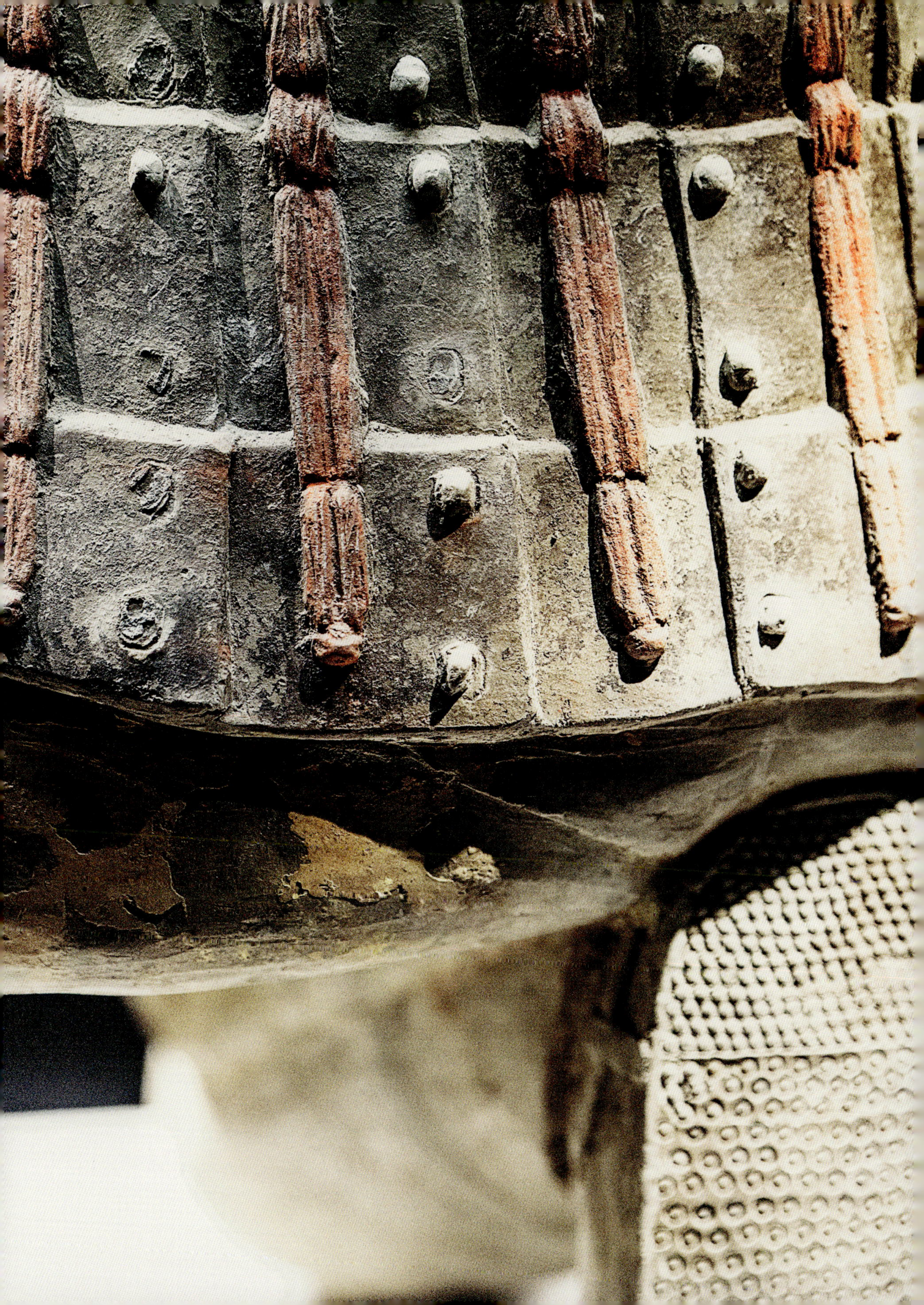

A BRIEF CHRONOLOGY OF CHINESE HISTORY

10,000–*c.*2100 BCE	Neolithic period
***c.*2200– *c.*1700 BCE**	Xia dynasty 夏 (traditionally understood)
***c.*1600– *c.*1046 BCE**	Shang dynasty 商
***c.*1046–256 BCE**	Zhou dynasty 周
	Western Zhou 西周 *c.*1046–771 BCE
	Eastern Zhou 東周 *c.*771–256 BCE
	Spring and Autumn period 春秋 771–475 BCE
	Warring States period 戰國 475–221 BCE
221–206 BCE	Qin dynasty 秦
	First Emperor 221–210 BCE
	Second Emperor 210–207 BCE
	King of Qin 207 BCE
206 BCE–220 CE	Han dynasty 漢
	Western (Former) Han dynasty 西(前)漢 206 BCE–9 CE
	Xin dynasty 新 (Wang Mang interregnum) 9–23 CE
	Eastern (Later) Han dynasty 東(後)漢 25–220 CE
220–265 CE	Three Kingdoms 三國
265–420 CE	Jin dynasty 晉
420–589 CE	Southern dynasties 南朝
	Northern dynasties 北朝
581–618 CE	Sui dynasty 隋
618–907 CE	Tang dynasty 唐
907–960 CE	Five Kingdoms (in the north) 五代
907–979 CE	Ten Kingdoms (in the south) 十國
916–1125 CE	Liao dynasty 遼
960–1279 CE	Song dynasty 宋
1115–1234 CE	Jin dynasty (Jurchen) 金
1279–1368 CE	Yuan dynasty (Mongol) 元
1368–1644 CE	Ming dynasty 明
1644–1911 CE	Qing dynasty (Manchu) 清
1912 CE–	Republic of China 中華民國
1949 CE–	People's Republic of China 中華人民共和國

EMPERORS OF THE QIN AND HAN DYNASTIES

221–206 BCE Qin dynasty

- First Emperor, r. 221–210 BCE
- Second Emperor, r. 210–207 BCE
- Ying, King of Qin, r. 207 BCE

206 BCE–220 CE Han dynasty

- Western (Former) Han dynasty 206 BCE–9 CE
  - Emperor Gaozu, r. 202–195 BCE
  - Emperor Hui, r. 195–188 BCE
  - Emperor Shao Gong (child), r. 187–184 BCE
  - Emperor Shao Hong (child), r. 184–180 BCE
  - Emperor Wen, r. 180–157 BCE
  - Emperor Jing, r. 157–141 BCE
  - Emperor Wu, r. 141–87 BCE
  - Emperor Zhao, r. 87–74 BCE
  - Marquis of Haihun, r. 74 BCE
  - Emperor Xuan, r. 74–49 BCE
  - Emperor Yuan, r. 49–33 BCE
  - Emperor Cheng, r. 33–7 BCE
  - Emperor Ai, r. 7–1 BCE
  - Emperor Ping, r. 1 BCE–6 CE
  - Ying (untitled), r. 6–9 CE
- Xin dynasty 9–23 CE
  - Wang Mang, r. 9–23 CE
- Eastern (Later) Han dynasty 25–220 CE
  - Emperor Guangwu, r. 25–57 CE
  - Emperor Ming, r. 57–75 CE
  - Emperor Zhang, r. 75–88 CE
  - Emperor He, r. 88–106 CE
  - Emperor Shang, r. 106 CE
  - Emperor An, r. 106–125 CE
  - Emperor Shao Yi (child), r. 125 CE
  - Emperor Shun, r. 125–144 CE
  - Emperor Chong, r. 144–145 CE
  - Emperor Zhi, r. 145–146 CE
  - Emperor Huan, r. 146–168 CE
  - Emperor Ling, r. 168–189 CE
  - Emperor Shao Bian (child), r. 189 CE
  - Emperor Xian, r. 189–220 CE

FURTHER READING

Edmund Capon and Liu Yang, *The First Emperor: China's entombed warriors*, Sydney, Art Gallery of New South Wales, 2010.

Patricia Buckley Ebrey, *The Cambridge Illustrated History of China*, Cambridge, Cambridge University Press, 2010.

Lothar Ledderose, *Ten Thousand Things: Module and mass production in Chinese art*, Princeton, Princeton University Press, 2000.

James CS Lin and Xiuzhen Li, *China's First Emperor and the Terracotta Warriors*, Liverpool, National Museums Liverpool, 2018.

Michael Loewe, *Ways to Paradise: The Chinese quest for immortality*, London, George Allen and Unwin, 1979.

Yuri Pines, Lothar von Falkenhausen, Gideon Shelach and Robin DS Yates (eds), *Birth of an Empire: The state of Qin revisited*, Berkeley, University of California Press, 2014.

Jane Portal (ed), *The First Emperor: China's terracotta army*, London, British Museum Press, 2008.

Jessica Rawson, 'Eternal palaces of the Western Han: A new view of the universe', *Artibus Asiae*, vol. 59, no. 1/2, 1999, pp. 5–59.

Sima Qian, *Records of the Grand Historian of China*, 2 vols, translated by Burton Watson, Oxford and New York, Columbia University Press, 1961.

Jason Zhixin Sun, *Age of Empires: Art of the Qin and Han dynasties*, New York, Metropolitan Museum of Art, 2017.

Lillian Lan-Ying Tseng, *Picturing Heaven in Early China*, Cambridge and London, Harvard University Asia Centre, 2011.

Denis Twitchett and Michael Loewe (eds), *The Cambridge History of China: Volume 1: The Ch'in and Han empires, 221 BC–AD 220*, Cambridge, Cambridge University Press, 1986.

ABOUT THE WRITERS

Duncan M Campbell is a graduate of Victoria University of Wellington and spent 1976–78 in China as an exchange student. Since then, he has taught (Chinese language, modern and classical; Chinese literature, modern and classical; and aspects of Chinese history) at the University of Auckland, Victoria University of Wellington and the Australian National University. Between 2015–16 he was the Curator of the Chinese Garden at the Huntington Library in San Marino, USA. The bulk of his research concentrates on the literary and material culture of late imperial China, with particular reference to the late Ming–early Qing period (1550s–1660s).

Nathan Woolley gained his doctorate from the Australian National University in 2011. In the years 2014–16 he worked at the National Library of Australia as curator of the exhibition *Celestial Empire: Life in China, 1644–1911*, held in association with the National Library of China. He currently works at the University of Glasgow. His research primarily concerns religion in medieval China.

Rebecca Rice is Curator Art at Te Papa. She gained her doctorate in Art History from Victoria University of Wellington in 2010. Her research is primarily in the field of New Zealand art, with a particular interest in histories of collecting and display. She has curated major incoming international exhibitions for Te Papa, including *Shi Lu: A revolution in paint*, in association with the National Museum of China, in 2014. She is the curator of *Terracotta Warriors: Guardians of Immortality*.

Zhang Weixing is Curatorial Research Fellow and Director of the Archaeology Department at Emperor Qin Shihuang's Mausoleum Site Museum. He gained his masters in archaeology at Northwest University in 2000 and his doctorate in history and archaeology at Zhengzhou University in 2005. Since 2000, he has devoted himself to the ongoing exploration, investigation and excavation of the great ruins of the Emperor Qin Shihuang's Mausoleum and the terracotta warriors along with associated research into the Qin–Han dynasties. His project highlights to date include excavations of K9901, cemetery ritual architecture and road ruins. He has published eight archaeology reports and monographs as well as over 100 papers.

ORGANISERS AND LENDERS FROM THE PEOPLE'S REPUBLIC OF CHINA

Institution	Individuals
Exhibition organiser 陕西省文物局 Shaanxi Provincial Cultural Relics Bureau	罗文利 Luo Wenli, 钱继奎 Qian Jikui, 张彤 Zhang Tong, 张晓英 Zhang Xiaoying, 张阳 Zhang Yang
Exhibition co-organiser 陕西历史博物馆 Shaanxi History Museum 陕西省文物交流中心 Shaanxi Cultural Heritage Promotion Center	强跃 Qiang Yue, 文军 Wen Jun, 程俊 Cheng Jun, 许晨 Xu Chen, 张正 Zhang Zheng, 王春燕 Wang Chunyan, 郭徽 Guo Hui, 孙强 Sun Qiang, 周永兴 Zhou Yongxing, 刘江英 Liu Jiangying, 王巧英 Wang Qiaoying, 王向农 Wang Xiangnong, 倪元 Ni Yuan, 梁彦民 Liang Yanmin, 贺达炘 He Daxin, 胡薇 Hu Wei, 刘芃 Liu Peng, 赵苗 Zhao Miao, 王涛 Wang Tao, 刘欢 Liu Huan
Exhibition co-organiser 秦始皇帝陵博物院 Emperor Qin Shihuang's Mausoleum Site Museum	侯宁彬 Hou Ningbin, 陈治平 Chen Zhiping, 马生涛 Ma Shengtao, 郑宁 Zheng Ning, 常磊 Chang Lei, 李斌 Li Bin, 夏寅 Xia Yin, 毛小芬 Mao Xiaofen, 何宏 He Hong
陕西省考古研究院 Shaanxi Provincial Institute of Archaeology	孙周勇 SunZhouyong, 李恭 Li Gong, 秦造垣 Qin Zaoyuan, 刘思哲 Liu Sizhe, 赵艺蓬 Zhao Yipeng, 袁明 Yun Ming
西安博物院 Xi'an Museum	余红健 Yu Hongjian, 王锋钧 Wang Fengjun, 伏海翔 Fu Haixiang, 王梓奕 Wang Ziyi, 杨宏毅 Yang Hongyi, 翟荣 Zhai Rong, 张俊 Zhang Jun, 郭金龙 Guo Jinlong, 李超 Li Chao, 王梅 Wang Mei
汉景帝阳陵博物院 Han Yangling Museum	李举刚 Li Jugang, 毕胜 Bi Sheng, 闫华军 Yan Huajun, 陈波 Chen Bo, 张琳 Zhang Lin, 石宁 Shi Ning, 白冬梅 Bai Dongmei, 赵超 Zhao Chao
西安碑林博物馆 Xi'an Beilin Museum	裴建平 Pei Jianping, 张安兴 Zhang Anxing, 傅清音 Fu Qingyin
宝鸡青铜器博物院 Baoji Bronze Museum	陈亮 Chen Liang, 肖琦 Xiao Qi, 王竑 Wang Hong, 付婕 Fu Jie, 王伊宁 Wang Yining, 刘新 Liu Xin, 任雪莉 Ren Xueli
宝鸡市周原博物馆 Zhouyuan Museum, Baoji City	张亚炜 Zhang Yawei, 韩云 Han Yun, 白晓银 Bai Xiaoyin
宝鸡市考古工作队 Baoji City Archaeological Team	辛怡华 Xinyihua, 王颢 Wang Hao, 张程 Zhang Cheng
凤翔县博物馆 Fengxiang County Museum	郁彩铃 Yun Cailing, 曹建宁 Cao Jianning, 王重博 Wang Chongbo
陇县博物馆 Longxian County Museum	王全军 Wang Quanjun, 任怡 Ren Yi, 张智明 Zhang Zhiming
茂陵博物馆 Mao Ling Museum	田晖 Tian Hui, 魏乾涛 Wei Qiantao, 宇文晓妮 Yuwen Xiaoni, 张文玲 Zhang Wenling
咸阳博物院 Xianyang Museum	闫志敏 Yan Zhimin, 王亚庆 Wang Yaqing, 边永峰 Bian Yongfeng, 罗红侠 Luo Hongxia
咸阳市文物考古研究所 Xianyang Institute of Cultural Heritage & Archaeology	申维 Shen Wei, 谢高文 Xie Gaowen
商洛市博物馆 Shangluo City Museum	雷新锋 Lei Xinfeng, 罗元博 Luo Yuanbo, 陈书彤 Chen Shutong
榆林市文物保护研究所 Yulin Institute of Cultural Heritage Conservation	乔建军 Qiao Jianjun, 闫宏东 Yan Hongdong, 秦晓宇 Qin Xiaoyu, 曹丽丽 Cao Lili
米脂县博物馆 Mizhi County Museum	艾剑 Ai Jian, 马林军 Ma Linjun, 马军 Ma Jun, 江波 Jiang Bo, 杜伟 Du Wei
绥德县博物馆 Suide County Museum	王涛 Wang Tao, 雷昱 Lei Yu
甘泉县博物馆 Ganquan County Museum	李延丽 Li Yanli, 庄泽栋 Zhang Zedong, 刘传瑞 Liu Chuanrui, 王晶 Wang Jing
延安市文物研究所 Yan'an City Cultural Relics Research Institute	张华 Zhang Hua, 高洁 Gao Jie, 白小龙 Bai Xiaolong

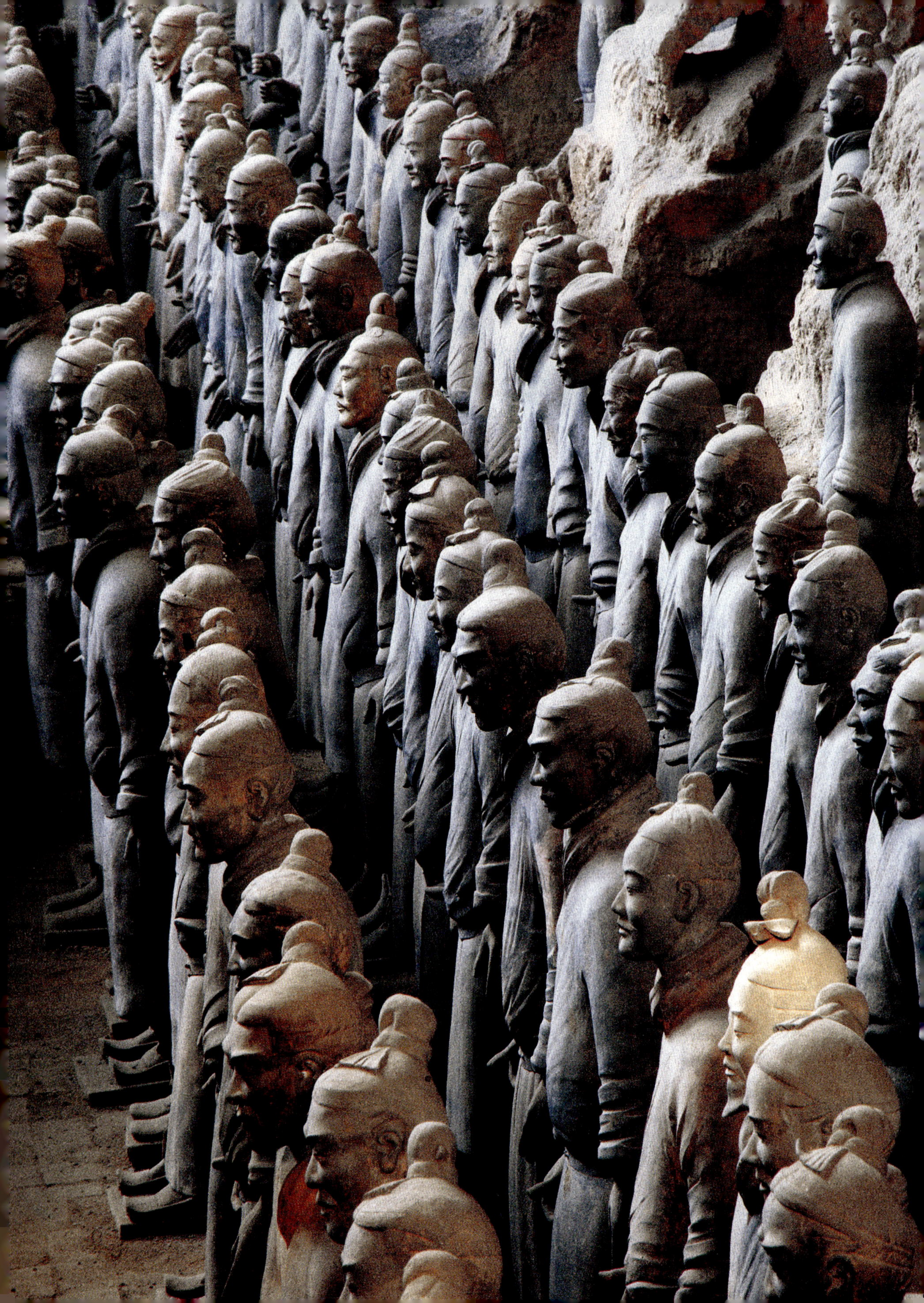

THANKS TO OUR SPONSORS

Exhibition developed by

TOI
.ART

In association with

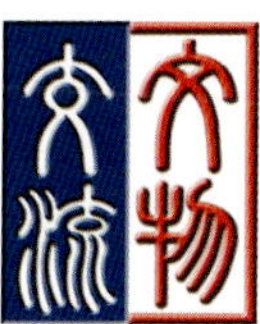

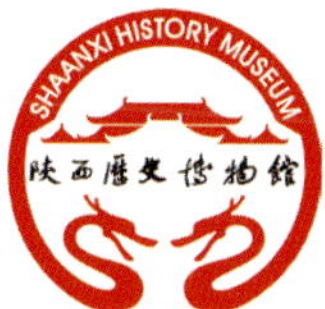

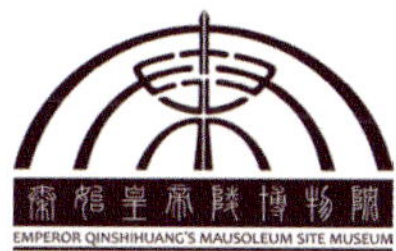

Government Partners

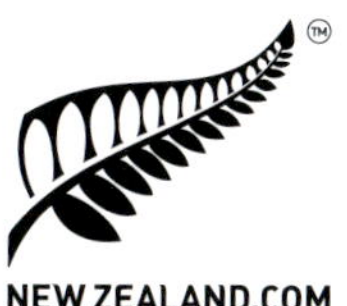

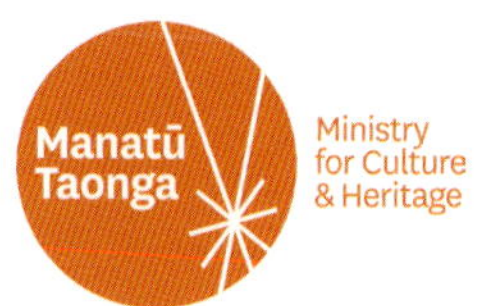

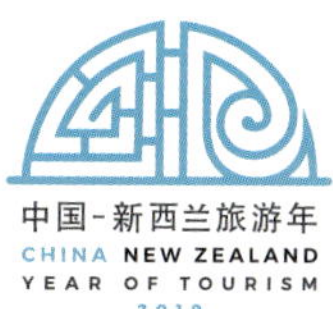

Destination Partner

Absolutely Positively Wellington City Council
Me Heke Ki Pōneke

Airline Partner

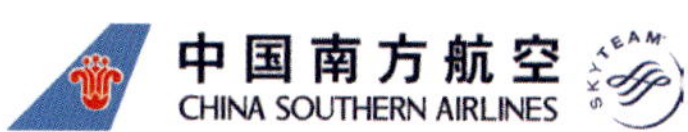

Supporting Partners

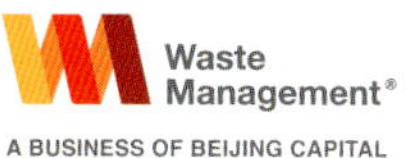

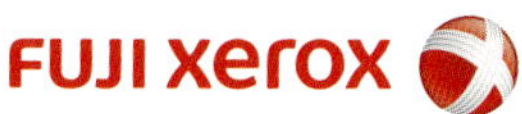

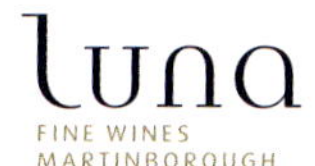

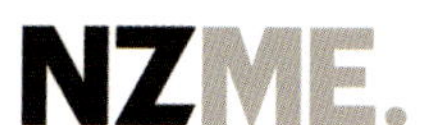

First published in New Zealand in 2018 by Te Papa Press, PO Box 467, Wellington, New Zealand, www.tepapapress.co.nz on the occasion of the Te Papa exhibition *Terracotta Warriors: Guardians of Immortality*. This exhibition was organised by the Museum of New Zealand Te Papa Tongarewa, in partnership with Shaanxi Provincial Cultural Relics Bureau, Shaanxi History Museum, Shaanxi Cultural Heritage Promotion Center, and Emperor Qin Shihuang's Mausoleum Site Museum of the People's Republic of China. Indemnified by the New Zealand Government.

Catalogue photography by Qiu Ziyu, courtesy of Shaanxi History Museum

All other images courtesy of Shaanxi History Museum except as credited below:
pages 4–5 Blue Sky Studio / Shutterstock.com; pages 10–11 © MNAAG, Paris, AP31-8 / RMN-Grand Palais / image musée Guimet; page 15 © British Library Board, B20086-07/ All rights reserved / Bridgeman Images; page 16 map © Museum of New Zealand Te Papa Tongarewa (Te Papa); page 18 Daniel Gilbey Photography / Shutterstock.com; page 21 map © Te Papa; page 23 Te Papa: CT.041284 © Raymond Wai-Man Lau; page 25 Art Gallery of New South Wales / Diana Panuccio, 200.2010.a-b; page 27 ©Bibliothèque Nationale de France, Oe-5-Rfol-Oe-5a-fol; page 36 © The Trustees of the British Museum, 2013,3011.27; page 37 Victor Paul Borg / Alamy Stock Photo; page 130 map © Te Papa; page 166 © Richard Johnson AO MBE

Additional image captions:
pages 2–3 Standing archer (catalogue number 98); page 4–5 Armoured soldiers in Pit 1 of Qin Shihuang's tomb complex; page 6 Detail of kneeling archer (catalogue number 97); page 166 Unarmoured soldiers from Pit 1 of Qin Shihuang's tomb complex; page 168 Burial pit at Han Yangling Mausoleum
Front cover image: Armoured general (catalogue number 93)
Back cover image: Sword blade with inlaid openwork hilt (catalogue number 58)

TE PAPA® is the trademark of the
Museum of New Zealand Te Papa Tongarewa
Te Papa Press is an imprint of the
Museum of New Zealand Te Papa Tongarewa

A catalogue record is available from the
National Library of New Zealand

ISBN 978-0-9951031-1-5

Design by Kate Barraclough
Maps by Janet Hunt
Digital imaging by Jeremy Glyde
Printed by 1010 Printing Asia Ltd

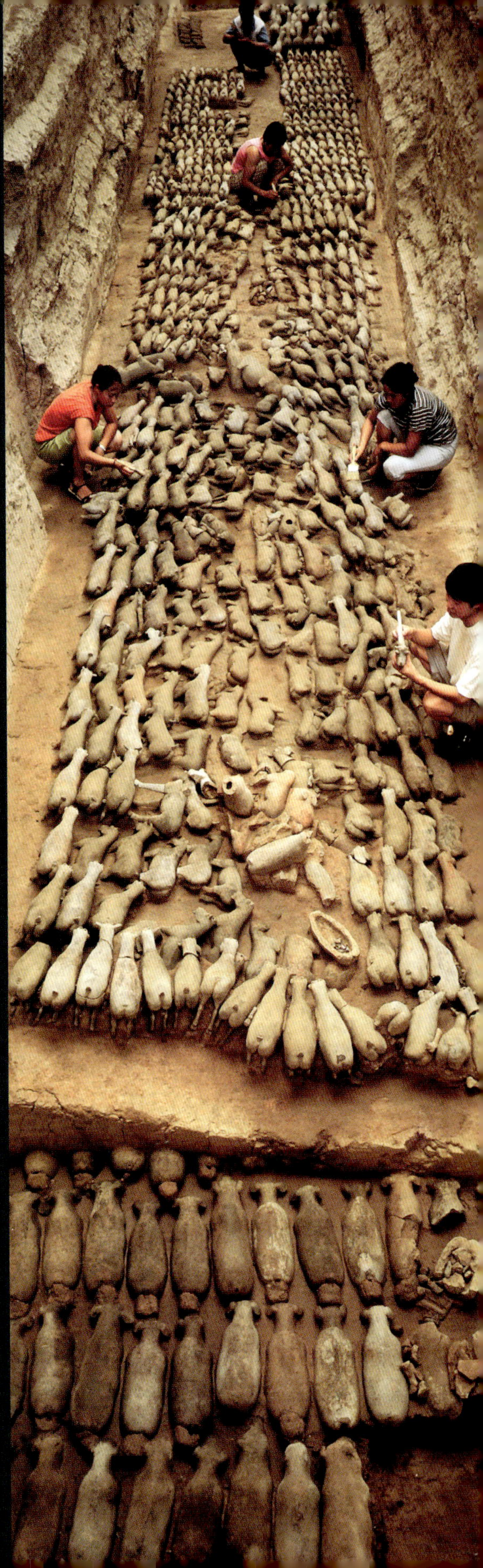